A Conspiracy of Silence

A Conspiracy of Silence

The Health and Death of
Franklin D. Roosevelt

Impact on History

Harry S. Goldsmith, M.D.

iUniverse, Inc.
New York Lincoln Shanghai

A Conspiracy of Silence
The Health and Death of Franklin D. Roosevelt

iUniverse books may be ordered through booksellers or by contacting:

iUniverse
2021 Pine Lake Road, Suite 100
Lincoln, NE 68512
www.iuniverse.com
1-800-Authors (1-800-288-4677)

ISBN-13: 978-0-595-39942-0 (pbk)
ISBN-13: 978-0-595-67762-7 (cloth)
ISBN-13: 978-0-595-84331-2 (ebk)
ISBN-10: 0-595-39942-8 (pbk)
ISBN-10: 0-595-67762-2 (cloth)
ISBN-10: 0-595-84331-X (ebk)

Printed in the United States of America

To my children John, Robert, and Lynne, who have supported my efforts over the years in writing this book. My warmest appreciation goes to my beloved wife Linda who assisted in preparing this book, but more importantly has made my journey through life so pleasant.

Contents

CHAPTER 1

THE BEGINNING

After finishing five years of surgical training in Boston and two years in the United States Army Medical Services, I applied and was accepted for the Senior Surgical Training Program at the Memorial Sloan-Kettering Cancer Center in New York City, which began on July 1, 1963. After I had served at the hospital for several months, a notice was posted stating that Dr. George T. Pack would give a lecture on the "Impact of Illness on World History." Dr. Pack was one of the most respected men at Memorial Hospital, with a worldwide referral practice and the reputation of a renowned surgeon of international fame. It was the belief of many of us in the hospital and throughout the country that Dr. Pack was the world's foremost surgical cancer specialist at the time. He was a master of surgical technique and the author of more than a dozen books, as well as hundreds of papers dealing with the biology and treatment of malignant disease. The surgical residents had the greatest respect for him, since he was truly a surgical genius.

Dr. Pack spoke at the hospital in the Hoffman auditorium in the late afternoon. He discussed the historical impact of the health of various world leaders, citing the epilepsy of Alexander the Great, and Napoleon's excruciatingly painful bladder stone at the Battle of Waterloo, which had an effect on the conflict's outcome.

When Dr. Pack came to the medical problems of President Franklin Delano Roosevelt (FDR), he briefly mentioned the poliomyelitis that FDR contracted as a young man, which we all knew a little about; but then he disclosed an intriguing new aspect of Roosevelt's health. Dr. Pack described a conversation he had had with his friend and surgical colleague, Dr. Frank Lahey, the founder of the Lahey Clinic in Boston. Years earlier, while attending the same surgical conference, the two men arranged to have dinner together, during the course of which they shared stories of the most famous patients they had treated during their professional careers. Dr. Pack recounted his experience with Evita Peron, wife of the Argentinean dictator, Juan Peron. Dr. Lahey discussed FDR. During his lecture,

Dr. Pack gave little information concerning his role as Evita Peron's surgeon, but I was later told that this was not unusual since Dr. Pack rarely discussed the case with anyone, even his associates. Dr. Pack's closest associate, Dr. Irving M. Ariel, who after Dr. Pack's death became the head of the Pack Clinic, later told me the Evita Peron story that he had heard from Dr. Pack..[1]

After the brief mention of Evita Peron, Dr. Pack related to the audience that Dr. Lahey told FDR that he should not run for a fourth term since, even if elected, he would not live to carry out the duties of his last term in office. After the lecture, I asked Dr. Pack if he planned to publish this information; he replied that over the years he had recorded in his diaries medical details of many celebrity patients, but he had no publication plans relating to FDR. Dr. Pack further mentioned, however, that other people knew of FDR's illness. He believed that, in the future, the true medical history of FDR would become public knowledge. However, if this information were not published prior to Dr. Pack's death, he felt his diaries might at some time be useful to someone attempting to write about FDR's medical history.

Over the next few years, I rarely saw Dr. Pack at Memorial Sloan-Kettering, since political problems at the hospital required him to perform most of his surgery at other New York City hospitals. When I did see him on occasion, we would discuss various medical problems, but I don't recall ever discussing FDR

---

1. Dr. Pack operated on Evita Peron, wife of President Juan Peron, in the Royal Palace in Buenos Aires, Argentina. She had cancer of the uterine cervix, but because of her great fear of malignant disease, her doctors hid from her the nature of her illness. When her cervical malignancy began to cause vaginal bleeding, she was told that the bleeding was caused by a dye she had imported from France to color her hair blond—both scalp and pubic hair—the later activity dating back to the time she began dating men. The doctors convinced her that some of the dye, when applied to the pelvic region, inadvertently entered her vagina, which caused irritation that led to vaginal bleeding.

The Argentinean doctors treating Mrs. Peron realized the extreme seriousness of her condition, which prompted the call to Dr. Pack to come to Buenos Aires to perform the necessary surgery. Because Dr. Pack's worldwide reputation as a cancer surgeon had prompted so many wealthy and well-known Argentineans to go to Memorial Sloan-Kettering in New York City to be treated by him for their diseases, it was felt inevitable that if Evita Peron knew of Dr. Pack's involvement in her case, she would have realized her diagnosis. In order to spare her this fear, Dr. Pack was secretly brought into the Royal Palace without Evita Peron's knowledge. She was given general anesthesia, after which Dr. Pack operated. During the next week, Dr. Pack was kept in the Royal Palace without being allowed to make or receive any telephone calls. Evita Peron developed a recurrence of her cervical cancer within a relatively short period following surgery. Dr. Pack was not notified of this. She subsequently received radiation therapy to her pelvis but died shortly thereafter, at the age of 33.

with him. By 1968, I had become chief of the surgical service at Memorial Sloan-Kettering, which Dr. Pack had previously directed so illustriously for twenty-five years. Because of my new clinical position, my relationship with Dr. Pack became somewhat less formal—but only barely.

Dr. Pack suffered, during the last years of his life, from severe brain arteriosclerosis, which eventually caused him to have several strokes. When it became clear that death was approaching, he entered Memorial Sloan-Kettering to die in the hospital he loved and which, because of his surgical skill, had risen to the highest level of prestige as a world-renowned institution.

My family and I lived in an apartment directly across the street from the hospital, which made it possible for me to spend considerable time there at night. Each evening between 8 and 10 PM, I visited patients on whom I planned to operate the following day. During the last weeks of Dr. Pack's life, I saw him in his room for very brief periods during the day, but each evening I spent at least ten or fifteen minutes with him. As death drew near, Dr. Pack began to lose the mental acuity for which he was so respected. What I found remarkable was that regardless of how confused he became during this period prior to his death, his thinking processes remained crystal clear on the subject of surgery. I can remember entering his room where I would find him completely disoriented. After a few preliminary comments, I would begin to discuss with him operations planned for the following day and my rationale for performing some particular surgical procedure. Almost miraculously, his mind would become lucid, and he would either agree or disagree with me concerning the surgery I had planned. He would recall from his enormous personal experience details of the surgical problem being discussed, and even more impressively, he would tell me where in the surgical literature I might find additional information to help me further organize a surgical approach to a particular patient. Once our conversation on surgery ended, however, he would again become disoriented in his farewell as I left his room.

The last thing Dr. Pack ever wrote was his inscription to me in his most widely read book, *Tumors of the Soft Somatic Tissue and Bone*. He inscribed the text several days before he died, and he took almost twenty-four hours to complete the dedication due to his physical weakness. The actual penmanship was disorganized, but the composition was exact and thoughtful, typical Pack traits: "To Dr. Harry Goldsmith— With the compliments of George T. Pack, high approval for the high quality of his cancer research and gratitude for the blessings of his friendship. George T. Pack"

I saw Dr. Pack on the morning he died, January 23, 1969. Those of us who were fortunate enough to have been touched by his personality and surgical skill will never forget him. He was a surgical master who had much to do with setting the standard of excellence in the surgical treatment of malignant disease during the middle decades of the twentieth century.

George T. Pack 1898–1969

CHAPTER 2

DR. PACK'S DIARIES

After Dr. Pack died in 1969, I gave no further thought to FDR. By 1971, however, I had not heard if the doctor's diaries had been published, and I called Mrs. Pack at her home in Engelwood, New Jersey, to inquire about them. She was agreeable to my reading them, but not at that time, and suggested I call her in a month to make an appointment to see them.

Over the next few months, I called Mrs. Pack several times. On each occasion, she told me I could see her husband's diaries—but not at that particular time. The reasons for the delay in being allowed to review the diaries seemed rather vague, but I thought little of it. After telephoning Mrs. Pack several more times, I called her one morning and, after identifying myself, was asked to speak to her lawyer, who was with her at the time. Her attorney immediately asked why I had interest in reviewing Dr. Pack's diaries, and I told him what I had previously told Mrs. Pack: the medical information pertaining to FDR might have significant historical importance. The lawyer informed me that he felt Dr. Pack's diaries were of commercial value and that Mrs. Pack would make the necessary effort to have them published. As I hung up the telephone, I felt assured that Mrs. Pack, perhaps with the help of her lawyer, would choose an established author or editor to work with the diaries and publish them in the near future. The Pack diaries quickly faded from my mind.

Five years had passed, since my last conversation with Mrs. Pack, when I came across a picture of FDR in a newspaper. I suddenly realized that over the years I had heard nothing about Dr. Pack's diaries. Once more, I called Mrs. Pack to learn their status. I was surprised when she told me that *nothing* had been done with her husband's diaries. She did say she had discussed them with two writers; unfortunately, nothing had developed. I again told Mrs. Pack of my interest in reviewing the diaries of her late husband, who had now been

dead for over seven years. She was again agreeable to my reviewing the material, but not at that particular time. She suggested I call her in a month to set
up an appointment. It was *déjà vu,* and after hanging up, I began to wonder
whether I would ever get the opportunity to review Dr. Pack's diaries.

I decided the best thing to do was to take the initiative and visit Mrs. Pack
unannounced, timing my arrival to occur after she had breakfast but before
she might leave her home for the day. On the day of the visit, I drove to Dr.
Pack's home in Engelwood, New Jersey. The house was stone gothic, surrounded by several acres of land, with a large circular driveway in front. I went
to the side door of the house since I hoped this would seem less obtrusive than
making an entrance at the front door. After I rang the bell, a woman came to
the door wearing a housecoat. By way of greeting, she simply said yes through
the screen door, and I asked if I might speak to Mrs. Helen Pack. She then said
she was Mrs. Pack, and I informed her that I was the doctor who had called her
in the past regarding her husband's diaries (I had met Mrs. Pack at Memorial
Sloan-Kettering Hospital during her husband's terminal illness and at his
funeral, but neither she nor I recognized each other.) There was a hiatus of
approximately fifteen seconds, which at the time seemed like twenty minutes.
I was certain Mrs. Pack was considering my rudeness at coming to her home
unannounced at such an early hour. However, at the end of this painful
period, she opened the door and simply said, "Come in. Do you like tomato
juice?" I hoped anyone kind enough to offer me tomato juice was going to be
helpful.

After I entered the house, she quietly led me directly to Dr. Pack's study. I
sat down, and in a few moments Mrs. Pack returned with a glass of tomato
juice. She asked if I liked salt in my tomato juice, and although I rarely drink
tomato juice, much less put salt in it, I quickly said yes. She sprinkled in a
small amount, handed the glass to me, and said she'd be right back. Several
minutes later she returned with two books, one approximately three inches
thick and looking like a stamp album, the other approximately half as large.
She said that these were the only diaries that she could find, that all her husband's diaries and other material had been stored in the basement during the
seven years since his death, and that repairs and renovations during this
period had resulted in the loss and misplacement of many articles. I was
acutely distressed to learn that these apparently were all that remained of Dr.
Pack's diaries, but I said nothing and immediately began to study the material. Mrs. Pack did not return for the next two-and-a-half hours, during
which time I studied the diaries. To my delight, they were fascinating. There
were stories, mementos, souvenirs, and telegrams from well-known people

whom Dr. Pack had treated during the course of his surgical career.[1] But nothing about FDR.

Before leaving, I asked Mrs. Pack if there could possibly be additional material, written by her husband, that might still be present in the house; but she felt that there was nothing to be gained by further searching the basement or attic. I thanked her for her kindness in allowing me to look at what remained of Dr. Pack's writings and said goodbye.

---

[1]. One of Dr. Pack's patients whom I found especially interesting was Admiral William "Bull" Halsey, who had been commander of the third and fifth fleets in the Pacific Theater of Operations during World War II. After the war, Halsey developed colon problems, which were investigated at a naval hospital and diagnosed as being malignant in origin. The admiral was advised to have an operation that would have required the creation of a permanent colostomy. Rather than undergo this operation without further consultation, Halsey saw Dr. Pack in New York for his opinion. Dr. Pack found that Admiral Halsey did not have colon cancer but chronic diverticulitis, an inflammatory condition of the large intestine, which required no operation and was subsequently treated medically at Doctor's Hospital in New York City.

I found in Dr. Pack's diary comments pertaining to Admiral Halsey's great dislike for the Kennedy family. He strongly criticized John F. Kennedy, later president of the United States, for allowing his ship (PT 109) to be rammed and sunk by a Japanese destroyer during the war. Halsey felt that anyone commanding a PT boat, the fastest vessel on the water at the time, who allowed an enemy destroyer to crush his boat, did not deserve a medal but should have been court-martialed. Of interest was a comment by Halsey that he thought the senior Kennedy should be subjected to an orchiectomy (an operation for removal of testicles).

CHAPTER 3

MEMORY CONFIRMATION

I was angry with myself for having allowed so many years to have passed without contacting Mrs. Pack concerning her husband's diaries. The question now was whether I should pursue FDR's health history, realizing that I might have to spend some time searching for information. I thought about it overnight and decided the health and death of FDR might be of such historical importance that it had to be explored further. I thought I could complete the project in perhaps two or three months. If I had known it would last years, I might not have undertaken the study.

Once I made the decision to embark on the FDR health project, my first concern pertained to the accuracy of what I thought I had heard at Memorial Sloan-Kettering Cancer Center more than fourteen years earlier. With the passage of so much time, it is easy to question one's memory. Had I accurately heard Dr. Pack say that Dr. Lahey told him that FDR was unfit to run for the presidency in 1944 and that, if he did run and was elected, he would die while in office? In an attempt to be certain that my recollections were correct, I called surgeons throughout the country with whom I had trained at Memorial Sloan-Kettering and who were likely to have been present with me at Dr. Pack's lecture in 1963. Some of these doctors vaguely remembered the event without specific details; others had forgotten whether they were even at the lecture, let alone details of Dr. Pack's comments. However, a telephone conversation with Dr. Andrew A. Kiely, a practicing surgeon in Long Beach, California, completely assured me that my memory was accurate.

Dr. Kiely stated that, when he was the chief surgical resident at Memorial Sloan-Kettering in 1965, Dr. Pack had developed a particular liking for him and invited him to be his guest at a dinner of the Strollers Club, a social group of New York doctors. Dr. Pack was the speaker, and his talk was entitled "Medicine in World History." Kiely said Dr. Pack's presentation to the Strollers Club was

8

practically identical to the lecture we both heard at Sloan-Kettering. Kiely later confirmed the information he had given me over the phone with the following letter, dated January 25, 1977:

> Following up on our telephone conversation, I recall traveling with Dr. George T. Pack to the Strollers Club on Park Avenue in New York in 1965. The topic of conversation that night was "Medicine in World History," given by George T. Pack. I recall him mentioning that he was told by Dr. Frank Lahey that President Franklin D. Roosevelt went to see him as a patient in the summer prior to his nomination for his fourth term. *Dr. Lahey told him that he had a metastatic carcinoma primary in the prostate, advising him not to run for re-election as he would never complete his term in office.* [Author's emphasis. Here and throughout the manuscript, "author's emphasis" refers to the author of this book.] He told him that he had to run, as no President had ever held office for four terms, he was glad, however, to be told of his condition as he should dump Wallace.
>
> At the democratic convention, Harry S. Truman was put forward by Roosevelt to be the Vice President as he considered him to be the most insignificant candidate, therefore, Roosevelt would be glorified because he would be followed in office by a small insignificant man. This information is factual as the day it took place.

I was now completely reassured that my memory was correct as to what I had heard Dr. Pack say many years earlier about FDR's medical condition. What intrigued me was that this medical information regarding FDR was apparently unknown during the election year of 1944. Rumors of FDR's poor health, which were prevalent after his death, had faded over the years. Why, I asked myself, would such a man as Dr. Pack, who enjoyed an international surgical reputation of the highest rank, have continued to circulate an unfounded rumor almost a quarter of a century after the death of FDR—unless he was convinced it was true? Somewhere there had to be a record of the president's health, official documents that would confirm or disprove the rumor. Where better to find it than at the United States Naval Hospital in Bethesda, Maryland?

CHAPTER 4

THE SEARCH BEGINS

I called the Naval Hospital in Bethesda and was connected to a junior officer, whom I told of my interest in FDR's health. I then asked how I could go about obtaining FDR's medical records. He asked me to wait a few minutes, after which time he returned to the phone to inform me that, regrettably, there was *no record* of a Franklin D. Roosevelt at the Bethesda Naval Hospital. I assured him that there had to be a mistake since I was talking about President Franklin D. Roosevelt who, I was certain, had been a patient at the hospital at some time. In order to keep the naval officer interested in searching further for the chart, I told him that FDR had always loved the navy since being its undersecretary in 1918, and that I had read he was not only personally responsible for obtaining the funds necessary to build the Bethesda Naval Hospital, but he actually sketched his original design of the hospital on the back of an envelope. With this trivial but, I hoped, interesting information, coupled with my confident assurance that FDR had been a patient at the hospital at some time, the young officer once again asked me to wait while he investigated further. After a short period, he returned to tell me he could find no record that FDR had been either an in-patient or an out-patient at the hospital and that anyone who had *ever* been a patient at the facility was listed in their computer. There was simply no record of a Franklin D. Roosevelt. I thanked him for his time and courtesy and hung up.

I was not overly surprised at that time to learn there was no record of FDR at the Bethesda Naval Hospital. With Roosevelt's importance, it was easy to imagine that he was not listed as an ordinary patient on the hospital's computer and that his medical records had been sequestered elsewhere for safekeeping in some secure government facility. Based on this idea, I contacted by telephone the following facilities in Washington: Walter Reed Medical Center, the Armed Forces Institute of Pathology, and the National Archives. I also contacted the National Record Center in St. Louis, Missouri, which maintains records of all former government workers. Each institution said they had no record of FDR in their files. Thinking I might get a different response if I requested information regarding FDR in writing, I sent letters to the same governmental facilities. Rear Admiral Joseph T. Horgan, commanding officer of the National Naval Center in Bethesda, Maryland, promptly replied:

> This is in response to your letter of 5 July 1977, wherein you requested any information pertaining to consultations, hospital admissions, laboratory tests and pathological reports of President Franklin Roosevelt's association with this hospital.
>
> These records are no longer at this institution. I'm sorry that I can not be of assistance to you in this endeavor. My only suggestion would be that you contact a member of the Roosevelt family or someone who may have been designated as responsible for maintaining such records as their consent would be required in obtaining records in any case.

The response to my letter to the Armed Forces Institute of Pathology in Washington came from the director, who simply wrote: "This is in response to your inquiry of 20 June 1977, concerning records pertaining to Franklin D. Roosevelt. Regrettably, there is no such record or materials in the institution files."

The National Archives also stated they had no information relating to FDR's medical records. Of interest was the response I received from the commanding general of the Walter Reed Medical Center: it was not a letter but a standard printed form stating that clinical records were held at the Hospital for a period of five years, after which time they were sent for storage to the National Personnel Record Center in St. Louis, which they suggested I contact. At the bottom of this printed form was an addendum that was a typical governmental Catch-22 suggestion: "It is further suggested that at the time you submit your request, you include the patient's written authorization, name, service number, social security number, dates and place of hospitalization and/or treatment."

I had already written to the National Personnel Record Center in St. Louis, and the letter I received from the chief of the civilian reference branch of this facility stated that they were unable to locate any medical records of President Roosevelt. They suggested that I request a search of the VIP files at the Walter Reed General Hospital. I had now come full circle.

At this point in time, I called the Roosevelt Library in Hyde Park, New York, where I had my first conversation with Dr. William R. Emerson, director of the library. He was delightful to talk to, and he sounded genuinely sorry when he told me there were no medical records of FDR at the library, a situation which he said had always seemed strange to him. He later sent me a letter confirming the absence of FDR's medical records and added this line: "To the best of my knowledge, all clinical and diagnostic reports remain in the custody of the hospitals where they were made."

It was now apparent that FDR's medical records had disappeared. This raised the question as to whether they had been misplaced or, more significantly, destroyed for reasons as yet unknown.

Dr. Emerson sent a list of publications from the Roosevelt Library that he thought might be of help to me in learning more about FDR's health. One of the articles was written by Howard G. Bruenn, M.D., in 1970 and published in the *Annals of Internal Medicine* under the title "Clinical Notes on the Illness and Health of President Franklin D. Roosevelt." The article was purported by Bruenn to be the authentic clinical report on the health of FDR up to and including his death. Bruenn began his article with the following statement[1]:

> Until the past fifteen years the illnesses of a President of the United States had not been exposed in the public press. Indeed, in most instances not only have the details been obscured but the very fact that illness existed has been not infrequently denied. In the case of Franklin D. Roosevelt, rumors about the state of his health began to be bruited about as early as 1936, nine years before his death. These speculations continued throughout the remainder of his life and rose to a crescendo of debate and uncertainty after his death. To my knowledge no factual clinical information regarding his health and illness and the events leading to his death have ever been published. *The original hospital chart in which all clinical progress notes as well as the results of the various tests were incorporated and kept in a safe of the U.S. Naval Hospital, Bethesda, Maryland. After the President's death, this chart could not be found.* [Author's emphasis.]

I was amazed to learn that FDR's medical chart had been missing since 1945. His records were obviously of historical importance, and the fact that they were still missing twenty-five years after his death stimulated my interest in finding out who had access to the safe at the Bethesda Naval Hospital at the time of FDR's death. Three people had access: Captain John Harper, the commanding officer of the National Naval Medical Center; Captain Robert Duncan, the center's executive officer; and Vice Admiral Ross T. McIntire, who was FDR's appointed surgeon general of the navy, personal physician, and close friend. It seems highly unlikely that the more junior administrative officers would have, on their own, removed FDR's medical records. The logical and almost certain choice for this would have been Admiral McIntire.

---

1. H. G. Bruenn, "Clinical Notes on the Illness and Death of President Franklin D. Roosevelt," *Annals of Internal Medicine* 72 (1970): 579–591.

CHAPTER 5

DOCTORS TO
THE PRESIDENT

Medical cover-up is not a novelty in the White House. By the time FDR took office in 1933, the precedent for medical cover-ups stretched back to the late 1800s. Roosevelt and some of his key medical advisors practiced such deception with such skill as to convert FDR's paralytic disability from a liability into a political asset. FDR's manipulation of public perceptions regarding his health throughout the 1930s and early 1940s made it easy for him to hide his physical condition from the media and the public, especially during the last year of his life.

Grover Cleveland exemplified such deception early in his second term as president when he developed a tumor-like growth in his mouth, which appeared to be malignant. In June, 1893, he was examined by Dr. Joseph D. Bryant, a noted surgeon at Bellevue Hospital in New York who earlier had been appointed surgeon general of the New York National Guard by then-Governor Cleveland. Bryant suggested that the mass in the president's mouth be removed. President Cleveland, faced with a national economic crisis and factional feuding within his own Democratic Party, insisted that the operation to remove his intraoral mass be kept strictly secret. Dr. Bryant obliged.

Dr. Bryant quietly brought together a team of doctors, including William W. Keen—the renowned Philadelphia surgeon who later misdiagnosed FDR's polio attack in 1921—and Ferdinand Hasbrouck, an expert dentist whose mission in the case was to extract several teeth necessary for the removal of the president's upper left jaw. A key feature of the cover-up was Bryant's arrangement with a wealthy New York banker, E. Cornelius Benedict, to use his yacht, the *Oneida*, with its combination of motor and sail power. President Cleveland was known to be a friend of Benedict, and his presence as a guest on Benedict's luxury yacht was not expected to excite public concern. The trip took place over the July 4th week-end, 1893, sailing from New York harbor to Gray Gables, Benedict's home at Buzzards Bay on Cape Cod.

The president, attended only by Secretary of War Daniel S. Lamond, his most trusted advisor, left Washington in a private railroad car and boarded the *Oneida* that same evening (Friday, June 30) in New York. The next morning, as the yacht steamed at half speed up the East River and into Long Island Sound, the doctors on board reorganized the salon of the ship into an operating room. At approximately 12:30 PM, the surgical procedure began, with the final stitch of the operation being placed an hour and twenty-five minutes later. A major portion of Grover Cleveland's upper jaw had been removed.

By July 3, the president was out of bed, and when the yacht reached Buzzards Bay two days later, he managed to walk from the dock to Benedict's home on his own. However, this was just the beginning of the story, as the press soon learned of the operation. Dr. Bryant and Secretary Lamond categorically denied a later United Press report, which was in fact an accurate description of the operation. The *New York Times* quoted Dr. Bryant as denying anything untoward had happened beyond the extraction of a "bad tooth." The rumors continued, however, and eventually, on August 29, the *Philadelphia Press* ran an authoritative account with undeniable details, including the names of the doctors involved in the operation (Dr. Bryant blamed the news leak on Dr. Hasbrouck and allegedly never spoke to the dentist again).

President Cleveland served out the remaining years of his term without any recurrence of the supposed cancer, dying 15 years after the operation (in 1908) from a gastrointestinal disorder unrelated to any malignant tumor. The operation was judged a success, but there is an interesting addendum to the story. Dr. Keen had donated remains of Cleveland's jaw to the Mutter Museum of the College of Physicians of Philadelphia, and seventy-five years later, in 1975, pathologic studies were done on the jaw tissue, which have raised serious doubts as to whether the lesion in Cleveland's mouth was in reality a malignant tumor.

The preferred branch of service for the White House doctor in the late 1800s was the U.S. Army. Army surgeon Major Robert M. O'Reilly was assigned to be Cleveland's family doctor in 1885 at the opening of the president's first term of office. The two men discovered they had a mutual love of fishing and soon became fast friends. By 1893, with Cleveland beginning his second term (after a four-year interlude out of power), Major O'Reilly had moved on to other duties; but it was O'Reilly who served as the anesthesiologist during Cleveland's operation in the improvised operating room at sea. Even though the record fails to remember Dr. O'Reilly as a particularly impressive figure in medicine, he was a highly regarded military officer who went on to become surgeon general of the army in 1902.

Following O'Reilly, the next army doctor to become White House physician was a man of action in the best frontier tradition. Before serving as physician during Cleveland's second term and during William McKinley's tenure after the election of 1896, Army Captain Leonard Wood had been awarded the Medal of Honor for bravery as a line officer in the Indian wars of the late nineteenth century. During the McKinley administration, Wood developed a very close relationship with the then-assistant secretary of the navy, Theodore Roosevelt. When war broke out with Spain in 1898, both men left Washington for the excitement of battlefield action. Together they recruited and trained the volunteer Rough Riders—Colonel Wood being in command, Roosevelt his subordinate, but both leading the troops in the field. Wood, having commanded a brigade in the closing battles of the war, stayed on afterwards to be named governor-general of Cuba in 1899. Teddy Roosevelt's career took another direction. When McKinley won re-election in 1900, he was at McKinley's side as his new vice president.

Wood was succeeded as physician to McKinley by another army officer, Colonel George M. Steinberg. During McKinley's second term, selection for this prestigious position shifted to the navy in the person of Presley M. Rixey, a surgeon on the staff of the secretary of the navy. Rixey impressed the president by the manner in which he treated his wife, since Ida McKinley suffered from violent and prolonged epileptic seizures and had virtually become an invalid since the loss of a baby during a difficult childbirth in 1873. Dr. Rixey was a Virginian, whose warmth and concern for Mrs. McKinley was noted and quietly appreciated by the president.

Despite her poor health, Mrs. McKinley insisted on accompanying her husband on his political trips. One such trip was to the West Coast in the summer of 1901, which was to be followed immediately by a presidential visit to Buffalo for the Pan-American Exposition. However, Mrs. McKinley fell seriously ill in California from a dangerous infection in one of her fingers that caused her to postpone her trip to Buffalo. The infection led to acute endocarditis, which is an inflammatory process involving the inner lining of the heart. Because of her condition, the presidential party returned directly to Washington from the West Coast and later moved on to their family home in Canton, Ohio, for Mrs. McKinley's recuperation. The president resumed his postponed schedule and went alone to Buffalo. Once Mrs. McKinley felt well enough, she joined her husband in early September 1901 at the Pan-American Exposition

In the late afternoon of September 6, the president attended a reception at the Buffalo Temple of Music at the same time that his wife was a guest at the home of the president of the exposition, John G. Milburn. Later that day, Dr.

Rixey had the unpleasant duty to inform Mrs. McKinley that her husband had been shot.

McKinley was brought to the Milburn residence where several doctors examined him. However, after eight days, the president succumbed to his devastating abdominal wound.

The new president, Theodore Roosevelt, honored his predecessor's dying wish and appointed Dr. Rixey surgeon general of the navy. The athletic President Roosevelt discovered to his delight that Rixey was also an avid outdoorsman. Although fifty years old (in 1902), eight years the senior of Teddy Roosevelt, Dr. Rixey's physical condition was still equal to that of the robust president, as seen by the brisk horseback ride the two men would take early each morning to the Rixey farm across the Potomac in Arlington, Virginia.

Rixey had a young associate, a navy doctor named Cary T. Grayson, whom he introduced to President Theodore Roosevelt and who later joined the White House medical staff in 1907. Roosevelt grew fond of the young physician who— with charm, manners, and connections—subsequently became a popular figure in Washington. In the next decade, Grayson became the White House doctor to President Woodrow Wilson and his family.

A chance happening helped build this Wilson-Grayson relationship from the outset. As the story goes, Grayson was at the White House on Wilson's Inauguration Day, March 4, 1913, as a thirty-four-year-old naval lieutenant. At the function was the new president's sister, Annie, who was injured in a fall on a marble stairway. Young Grayson quickly moved to help, which involved suturing a laceration on her forehead. Wilson apparently saw this performance and, obviously impressed, made inquiries about the young doctor that led to Grayson's appointment as Wilson's personal physician. Grayson quickly learned he had not simply acquired an honorary position. The job required considerable attendance to the president.

Wilson had chronic abdominal problems, which Grayson tried to alleviate by placing the president on a bland diet. To deal with Wilson's symptomatic arteriosclerosis, the doctor outlined a regular exercise program. Grayson wanted Wilson to take up horseback riding, for the president's benefit and for his own personal love of riding; but the president refused and compromised by taking up golf—which he reportedly played rather poorly. Grayson was resolute in his attempt to force the president to become more active. This resulted in regular golf outings and walks with the president around the White House grounds, as well as into the countryside. Eventually, the two men became inseparable. Grayson, a bachelor, was invited to take his meals at the White House, and in time he was invited to live there. He took up residence in the White House in the latter part of 1913.

Mrs. Wilson's poor health made Grayson's presence in the White House even more important. In the spring of 1914, when she was slowly recovering from a fall in her bedroom, she began to show early signs of Bright's disease, which at that time was a fatal kidney ailment. Dr. Grayson became Mrs. Wilson's doctor and occupied the room next to hers. When she died on August 6, 1914, Dr. Grayson was at her bedside. The president became increasingly dependent on the support of Grayson after her death.

President Wilson's deep melancholy was pervasive after his wife's death. His cousin, Helen Bones, moved into the executive mansion of the White House to act as his hostess at formal functions, the hope being that her presence would improve conditions. Unfortunately, her personal unhappiness only added to the gloom.

Dr. Grayson became engaged to Alice Gertrude Gordon in 1915. Miss Gordon had a close friend, Edith Boiling Galt, a forty-two-year-old widow, who at the request of President Wilson was asked by Grayson to spend some time socially with the lonely Miss Bones. Before long, Miss Bones and Mrs. Galt became close companions. Wilson also became infatuated with Mrs. Galt, whom he courted for a year. With Grayson acting as matchmaker, the president and Mrs. Galt were married on December 18, 1915.

In 1919, Wilson met with leaders of France and Great Britain to lay the groundwork for the treaty with vanquished Germany. During this period, he complained to his wife and Grayson that he felt ill, and in April of that year he was put to bed with a high fever, which Grayson later claimed was an attack of the flu that had developed into a worldwide epidemic causing twenty million deaths.

In June, Wilson signed the Treaty of Versailles, which included permission for establishing the League of Nations, a goal of the utmost importance to Wilson. However, upon his return to Washington, he met with strong opposition in the Senate to both the Treaty of Versailles and the League of Nations, and this led to his decision to go directly to the American people to gain support. Accompanied by his wife, Grayson, aides, and members of the press, President Wilson left Washington on September 3, 1919, for an exhausting campaign-style train trip that eventually covered 10,000 miles. The trip itself would have been punishing even for a younger man, as Wilson gave up to ten speeches a day from the rear of his train. Finally, this strenuous campaign took its toll with the collapse of the president on September 25 in Pueblo, California. Grayson explained to reporters that the president simply suffered from nervous exhaustion and would require seclusion for the rest of the trip.

One week later, on the morning of October 2, 1919, President Wilson was found unconscious on his bathroom floor. He had suffered a massive stroke. Mrs.

Wilson immediately called Dr. Grayson who arrived in twenty minutes. Later that evening, in his first public announcement of the president's condition, Grayson simply said, "The president is a very sick man."

Wilson still had seventeen months remaining in his second presidential term after his stroke, and even at the peak of his recovery during this time, he remained a helpless invalid. Edith Wilson called this period of her husband's infirmity her "stewardship." This meant she took full responsibility for executive decisions that she allegedly made after consulting with her husband. In reality, she sought almost total advice and guidance from Dr. Grayson, who first lied to cabinet members on October 6, 1919, saying that the president had only suffered a nervous breakdown caused by his exhausting cross-country trip. To prevent any first-hand testing of this diagnosis, which would have demonstrated the seriousness of the president's condition, Grayson used his doctor's authority to forbid cabinet members from visiting Wilson. When Secretary of State Robert M. Lansing informed Grayson that the Constitution provided for devolving the powers and duties of an incapacitated president to the vice president, Grayson indignantly responded that he would not be responsible in declaring Woodrow Wilson unfit to fulfill his presidential responsibilities.

Josephus Daniels, the astute and straight-talking North Carolina newspaper editor whom Wilson had named secretary of the navy, and who was FDR's mentor and boss at the time, was one of only two cabinet members told of Wilson's actual condition. The other was Secretary of the Treasury William G. McAdoo, the president's son-in-law. The reason Grayson confided in Daniels was to show his appreciation to Daniels for supporting Wilson against Senator Henry Cabot Lodge (Republican-Massachusetts) and other Republicans who tried to block Grayson's appointment to be medical director of the navy with the rank of rear admiral. It was this political battle that solidified the relationship between Grayson and Daniels.

On October 20, Wilson received the Belgium King and Queen, who were his first official visitors since his stroke. A week later, he met with Gilbert Hitchcock of Nebraska, the Democratic leader in the Senate who informed him of the almost impossible difficulties he faced in trying to get the League of Nations treaty through the Senate since a two-thirds vote was required to approve the treaty, and not even a majority could be counted on to vote for it.

By mid-November, the president was well enough to assert his strong support for the League of Nations, but by then the situation in the Senate was lost. Senator Lodge, chairman of the Foreign Relations Committee, backed by the Republican majority, reported a ratification resolution that contained so many reservations it would cripple any United States participation in the League of Nations. On November 19, Wilson's hope for a League of Nations was defeated in the Senate. His dream of the League of Nations as his monument to history was lost. He left office a sick and broken man. Grayson had been Wilson's support during these trying times, and a decade later it was Grayson who became the direct medical link to Franklin D. Roosevelt by way of another naval doctor, Ross T. McIntire, the physician who was later responsible for the medical cover-up of FDR's failing health.

Admiral McIntire was a graduate of Willamette Medical School, now part of the University of Oregon Medical School. His post-graduate training was in otolaryngology (ear, nose, and throat) and ophthalmology (eye). After spending a brief period in private practice in Oregon, McIntire went to Washington in 1917 to become an assistant surgeon in the Medical Corps of the United States Navy. His rank was that of a lieutenant junior grade at the time he first met Admiral Cary Grayson, the private White House physician to President Woodrow Wilson.

McIntire first served in the United States naval dispensary in Washington before being sent on sea duty for three years. He was reassigned to the U.S. Naval Hospital in Washington in 1931, where Admiral Grayson was commanding officer. During the following year, FDR was elected president, and he asked Grayson whom he would recommend to be the new presidential personal physician. Grayson recommended McIntire, who held this position until FDR's death.

Grayson's suggestion to FDR to appoint McIntire his personal physician made the recommendation almost a certainty. Grayson and FDR had become extremely good friends from the time they began working together in 1918 in the Wilson administration. FDR's respect for Grayson can be seen in FDR's appointing the admiral to be chairman of the presidential Inauguration committee in both 1932 and 1936. The president also appointed Grayson to head the American Red Cross shortly after FDR took office for his first term.

When Grayson died at the age of sixty in 1938, he knew it was he who was responsible for McIntire's position as personal physician to President Roosevelt. The continuity of Grayson's cover-up of President Wilson's health would subsequently be established in the manner in which McIntire would cover up the true physical status of President Roosevelt.

CHAPTER 6

LOOKING FOR LEADS

By the end of the summer of 1977, I was still without any medical information to substantiate Dr. Lahey's comments that FDR was a dying man in 1944. It was apparent that if such information were to be gained, it would be through people who had direct contact with FDR, Dr. Lahey, or those who were privy to private information regarding the president. Since it might mention at least some of his close friends, with whom he might have discussed FDR's health, I decided to learn how I might obtain Dr. Lahey's last will and testament. I contacted one of my closest friends, Arthur Tiernan, an assistant district attorney for Suffolk County in Boston. He told me that a probated will is a public document that is available for anyone's review. Since Mr. Tiernan worked in the Boston courthouse in which Dr. Lahey's will was probated, he offered to locate it for me. The will consisted of eleven pages, signed by Dr. Lahey on January 28, 1943. He made bequests to many of his associates at the Lahey Clinic. Sixteen doctors were so honored, all individuals with national and international reputations in their respective fields of medicine. I contacted the doctors who were alive—their families if they were deceased—asking for any information they might have regarding Dr. Lahey's relationship with FDR. Everyone tried to be helpful, but no one could give me any direct information. All that was known was that Dr. Lahey had seen FDR in consultation and that Dr. Lahey was a private person who rarely, if ever, discussed such matters with his colleagues.

I visited the Lahey Clinic, which at that time was located in Boston, attempting to find any information, including notes relating to FDR, which Dr.Lahey might have left. I was unsuccessful, as I learned others before me had been, in locating such information.

Dr. Lahey had no children and left his estate to his wife, Alice C. Lahey. He stated in his will that if his wife were deceased at the time of his death, his assets were to be bequeathed to the Lahey Foundation with the Old Colony Trust

Frank H. Lahey M.D. (1880–1953)

Frank H. Lahey (1880–1953)

Company of Boston to act as his trustee. This stipulation by Dr. Lahey raised the possibility that his personal papers might still be in the custody of the Old Colony Trust Company. Working at the Old Colony at that time was Chester Dalrymple, a trust officer at the bank. He was also the president of the Surgical Research Foundation of Boston, a charitable organization that had contributed funds to my research laboratory over a number of years. Mr. Dalrymple and I had become close friends during this time. I telephoned him to ask if he would investigate to see if Dr. Lahey's papers might be in the vaults at the Old Colony Trust. He later informed me that no documents could be found.

Significantly, Dr. Lahey's will did reveal the existence of Linda M. Strand of Sudbury, Massachusetts, whom he had appointed to be the executrix of his estate. Mrs. Strand had been Dr. Lahey's business manager for more than twenty-five years, during which time he had obviously developed tremendous respect for her as a person and for her administrative skills. The statement in his will pertaining to Mrs. Strand specified: "My Executrix shall have full power of sale both of personal property and real estate without the necessity of obtaining leave or license of any court."

In effect, Dr. Lahey had left the Lahey Clinic in the hands of Mrs. Strand. Based on this information, it seemed that if anyone had any knowledge regarding Dr. Lahey's relationship with FDR, it would have been Mrs. Strand. I tried to locate her in the town of Sudbury, which Dr. Lahey's will listed as her place of residence, but was unsuccessful. I made telephone calls to people whose last name was "Strand" who lived in or around the town of Sudbury, again with no success.

During the period when I was trying to locate Mrs. Strand, doctors who had been affiliated with the Lahey Clinic when Mrs. Strand was an employee told me of a bitter lawsuit between Mrs. Strand and the Lahey Clinic for control of the clinic after Dr. Lahey's death. One can easily imagine the difficulty the professional staff at the clinic must have had in accepting Dr. Lahey's previous business manager as president of the institution. The case lasted in the courts from 1958 to 1962 with a settlement eventually being made to Mrs. Strand by the Lahey Clinic.

While trying to locate Mrs. Strand, I was aware she would have had to be at least in her eighties, having worked for Dr. Lahey in the 1920s. I reasoned that, if she were still alive, the legal settlement she made with the Lahey Clinic in 1962 might still require their sending her money. I called the personnel office of the Lahey Clinic and asked the young secretary who answered the phone if she would please give me the address of a Linda M. Strand who had previously worked at the clinic and was receiving a retirement pension from the institution. I was fortunate that I was connected to an inexperienced secretary because one more experienced might have asked for details as to why I was trying to locate Mrs. Strand, a confession on my part that could well have led to difficulties. The cordial secretary excused herself momentarily; upon returning to the phone, she informed me that the Lahey Clinic was sending checks to Mrs. Strand at Box 195, Mount Dora, Florida.

I immediately tried to call Mrs. Strand in Mount Dora, but the operator said the telephone was no longer in use. I then wrote Mrs. Strand the following letter:

> I am a surgeon who has interested himself during the past year in reviewing the health of Franklin D. Roosevelt while he was in Washington. As you are well aware, President Roosevelt's consultant, Dr. McIntire, of the Naval Medical Center, Bethesda, Maryland asked Dr. Lahey to be consultant to the President in 1943. I have been trying to get any original records of this consultation by Dr. Lahey. There is nothing in the Archives that either Ropes and Gray (Lahey Clinic law firm) or the Old Colony Trust in Boston have that might shed some light on the subject. However, the Trust people at Old Colony have suggested that perhaps you might have some material of what I consider an important historical situation.
>
> I tried to call you at home but was informed that the line is no longer in use. I should greatly appreciate it if you would contact me either by letter or by calling collect at 215-829-6923. If for any reasons you wish to talk personally to me about this matter, I would be happy to come to Mount Dora to discuss it with you.

I did not receive a response from Mrs. Strand regarding this letter; I wrote a second, once again to no avail. It seemed that Mrs. Strand was going to be difficult, if not impossible, to locate. There was a strong possibility that she was deceased.

A longtime acquaintance, Dr. Malcom C. Veidenheimer, chairman of the Department of Surgery at the Lahey Clinic at that time, told me that he had been a resident at the Lahey Clinic in the early 1950s while Dr. Lahey was active. Even though he had no firsthand information regarding any relationship between FDR and Dr. Lahey, he suggested two people who might be helpful: Louise Poe, Dr. Lahey's personal secretary, and Blanche Wallace, Dr. Lahey's operating room scrub nurse.

I first located Miss Wallace who was a patient at the Waban Nursing Home in Massachusetts. At the time of our conversation, she was eighty-five years old but had a mind that was crystal clear and a delightful sense of humor. Other than a recent bilateral hip operation, she considered herself to be quite well. When I asked if she had any knowledge of a medical relationship between FDR and Dr. Lahey, she replied that her association with Dr. Lahey had always been very formal, and it would have been highly unlikely for him to discuss such a topic with her. However, she did recall him returning to the Lahey Clinic from Washington after having seen the president in consultation. Dr. Lahey told her that when he was first introduced to the president, he told FDR that he wanted him to know that he was not a member of the president's "political persuasion"; but as a doctor, he would offer FDR the best of medical advice. The president laughed and stated that he would be pleased to have such an individual as his surgical consultant.

Miss Wallace had no further information to offer but felt that, if anyone had any knowledge pertaining to FDR and Dr. Lahey, it would be Mrs. Louise M. Poe who had been Dr. Lahey's private secretary for many years.

I obtained Mrs. Poe's telephone number through the Boston telephone directory and called her. I told her I was trying to gather historical information for a possible medical paper on FDR. I also told her of my admiration for Dr. Lahey and assured her that I would never write anything that would hurt the reputation of Dr. Lahey since I considered him to have been one of America's leading surgeons. Mrs. Poe immediately informed me that any information she had pertaining to Dr. Lahey and FDR was confidential and that she didn't wish to discuss the matter further; end of conversation.

As I hung up the telephone, I felt Mrs. Poe questioned my motives for calling her. It therefore seemed important to find a way to meet her so that she would have a better idea as to why I was seeking information about Dr. Lahey. Mrs. Poe lived in Auburndale, Massachusetts, a town located several miles out of Boston. A week or so later, I drove to Boston with the hope that I would meet Mrs. Poe. I decided not to call her directly since I felt almost certain that she would tell me not to come to her home, a request that I would have had to honor. As I had done with Mrs. Pack, I considered the best option was to visit Mrs. Poe unannounced. Even though it was a very warm summer day, I wore a suit and tie since I wanted to look respectable. I thought my appearance might make a difference in her decision as to whether she would talk to me. It didn't.

I rang the front doorbell. Because of the heat, Mrs. Poe's front door was open with the outer screen door closed. As she came to answer the bell, she asked who I was and I told her. She didn't open the screen door. She quickly stated that her mind hadn't changed since our recent phone conversation regarding the confidential nature of the relationship between Dr. Lahey and FDR, and she would not discuss the issue with me. There was nothing further I could say, and she closed her front door without another word. It was several years before Mrs. Poe proved helpful.

CHAPTER 7

MEDICAL IMPRESSIONS

I began seeking information on FDR's health, trivia that would be of interest to a doctor. In studying pictures taken of FDR during his lifetime, I became curious about a pigmented lesion (mole) over Roosevelt's left eye. Photos taken during FDR's early life at Groton, Harvard, and during his early days in politics did not show a pigmented spot over the left eye, but over the following years this pigmented area developed in association with the robust health of the president. However, after FDR's wartime conference in Tehran in November 1943, the mole disappeared and was replaced by a scar. (see pages 27–30)

This pigmented mole intrigued me since I was at one time chief of the surgical service at the Memorial Sloan-Kettering Cancer Center that treated large numbers of patients with melanoma, a malignant skin tumor. Could FDR's failing health in the latter years of his life have been caused by a melanoma over his left eye? In order to make such a diagnosis, it would be necessary to review the pathological description of the excised tissue taken from FDR's eyebrow, which would have been recorded in his medical chart. Unfortunately, FDR had no medical chart to study.

In order to gain more information about the pigmented spot over FDR's left eye, I tried to locate James Roosevelt, the eldest of FDR's four sons. Since James had been with his father during Roosevelt's last political campaign in 1944, I hoped he might be well informed regarding his father's overall health and, especially, the lesion over his left eye. I had no idea where James Roosevelt lived, but I had heard that he had been mayor of a city in California and had been a congressman from that state. I called an administrative office at the United States House of Representatives in Washington and asked if they would give me Mr. Roosevelt's telephone number. I was told it was against Congressional policy to give out information on former members, so the search for James Roosevelt temporarily stopped.

Sometime in the spring of 1978, I was late for a meeting at the First National Bank building in Boston. Upon entering the building I realized I had forgotten the number of the particular office where the meeting was to take place. In the

FDR in 1920. No lesion noted over left eyebrow.
From: The Glorious Burden, The American Presidency,
By Stefan Lorant Authors Edition Inc. Lenox, MA

FDR in 1932, Lesion over left eyebrow is clearly evident.
From The Glorious Burden; The American Presidency By Stefen Lorrent.
Authors Edition, Inc. Lenox, MA

FDR in 1936, pigmentation over left eyebrow has begun to show linear extensions toward eyebrows. From The Glorious Burden; The American Presidency. By Stefan Lorant, Authors Edition, Inc. Lenox, MA

"FDR taken on 18 August, 1944 after his nomination for a fourth term.
Note apparent scar over left lateral eyebrow with disappearance of
pigmented area and sparse lateral eyebrow."
From The Glorious Burden, The American Presidency,
By Stefan Lorant, Authors edition, inc. Lenox, MA.

lobby under an elongated glass case were the office numbers and floor location of individuals and corporations listed in the building. As I looked down at the directory, the name that drew my immediate attention was James Roosevelt III. I wrote down his location and, after attending my scheduled meeting, went to Roosevelt's office in the large law firm of Herrick, Smith, Donald, Farley, and Ketchum, of which Roosevelt was a member. I asked the receptionist if it might be possible to see Mr. Roosevelt, and shortly thereafter, I was ushered into his office. His pleasant manner made it easy for me to begin our conversation by simply asking if he was FDR's grandson. After his affirmative answer, I told him of my interests in his grandfather's health and that I had been trying to locate his father, James Roosevelt. He gave me his father's address and telephone number in Newport Beach, California. I called James Roosevelt, who was very courteous and showed interest in the hypothesis that perhaps his father had had a melanoma over his left eye. He asked for pictures that were the basis for my melanoma hypothesis. He seemed incredulous that I had been unable to locate any of his father's medical records.

Shortly after the phone call, I wrote James Roosevelt on May 1, 1978, enclosing the pictures he requested. My letter contained the following:

> I certainly enjoyed talking with you last week. As my conversation probably indicated, I have given a great deal of time and thought over the years to Dr. Pack's comments to me concerning your father's health from 1943 until his death in 1945. My efforts in trying to uncover more about his medical history have been a labor of love since I have always felt that it was your father, almost single-handedly, who kept England from going down in 1940.
>
> My personal theory as to the cause of your father's deteriorating health during the last 12 to 24 months of his life is that he probably had some form of malignancy which very well might have originated from a pigmented area (melanoma).
>
> Enclosed you will find some pictures which I believe well demonstrate the possibility that his disease might have originated from the area over his left eye. I have placed numbers on the backs of the pictures with numbers 1 to 5 showing the involved area and pictures 6 to 11 showing that this pigmented area has been removed. Close scrutiny of picture 2 shows that the pigmentation was increasing extensively in comparison to picture 1 and in fact, it even now appears to be streaming into his left eyebrow. Picture 6, which was taken during the summer of 1944, shows what appears to be a healing scar over the left eyebrow. I personally tried to get the pathology report of the excised tissue at the Bethesda Naval Hospital

but this proved impossible since all medical information pertaining to your father, even data which had been kept in the safe at the Bethesda Naval Hospital, has disappeared.

I think your father knew the extent of his illness all along which could explain why he never asked questions regarding his condition. His life might have been extended if he had begun to slow down in 1944 but he probably became fatalistic concerning his health.

There is a very large amount of medical information that I have accumulated concerning your father's health over the years and I hope that I might have the opportunity to discuss this with you some time in the future. Any help you can give me in my project would be tremendously appreciated since I would like to set history straight, if my theory is correct, by showing what an extraordinarily courageous man your father had to be in order to continue in office knowing his medical condition.

On May 8, 1978, I received a reply from James Roosevelt:

Thank you so very much for your most interesting letter of May 1st and the photographs of my father. Your theory is a most intriguing one but unfortunately I am not competent medically to make comments. There must be someone who is able to make observation. I do hope that you are able to run down Lieutenant Commander Fox. If I can help, if there is any trouble doing so, let me know.

I do think you ought to authenticate when the pictures were taken to make sure they are chronologically correct. I think it would be interesting historically to make an appeal to anyone who may have been present. I also feel a much more definitive effort should be made to locate the medical information which "had been kept in the safe at Bethesda Naval Hospital, has disappeared." There must have been more than one copy.

It is certainly a fascinating theory and if I can be of any help, please let me know.

James Roosevelt's suggestion regarding the importance of locating Lieutenant Commander Fox seemed worthwhile since he had been Roosevelt's personal aide and masseur and would have been aware of any deterioration in the president's health. I subsequently learned that Commander Fox had died and was unsuccessful in locating his family. Several months later, I again wrote James Roosevelt in California explaining this difficulty, and he replied, "Jim mentioned you were having trouble finding information on Lieutenant Commander Fox. I wish I could help you on that but have drawn a blank."

Search for any information regarding the health of FDR continued. There were scattered reports that his health was failing even before he ran for a third term in 1940. Jim Farley, who until 1940 was chairman of the Democratic National Committee, visited the president in late 1937 and said he was shocked by his appearance: "His color was bad; his face was lined and he appeared to be worn out. His jaw was swollen as a result of a tooth infection ... And I learned there was worry over strain on Roosevelt's heart."[1]

This account was dismissed by some who said Farley was compelled by his own personal political ambition to view FDR as being unfit to run for a third term, but Farley's successor, Democratic National Chairman Edward J. Flynn, also felt the president wasn't up to running in 1940. William C. Bullitt, the ambassador to France, told of a White House dinner in February 1940 at which FDR collapsed. Admiral McIntire was summoned and said Roosevelt had only suffered "a very slight heart attack."[2]

These unconfirmed comments aside, the general feeling among FDR's associates was that the president was in fairly good physical condition until the end of 1943, after which time he went into physical decline following his meeting with Stalin and Churchill in Teheran in November. Samuel I. Rosenman had been FDR's personal lawyer and speechwriter since the 1928 campaign for governor of New York. He continued as a consultant to Roosevelt while serving as a New York Supreme Court justice and was sensitive to FDR's declining health near the end of 1943:

> The President developed some sort of bronchial affliction in Teheran, which gave him a racking cough. It took him a long time to shake it off. While Teheran was a high point in the President's career as Commander-in-Chief of our armed forces and as our leader in foreign affairs, it seemed to me to be also the turning point of his physical career. I think that his physical decline can be dated from Tehran, although at that time we did not see it.

Roosevelt recovered from the "Teheran flu," but in January 1944 he began to complain of headaches. It got to a point that those who saw him most often—his daughter Anna, who was residing at the White House, and his secretary, Grace Tully—became alarmed. Tully discussed it in her book:[3]

[1.] James A. Farley, *James Farley Story* (New York: Mc-Graw Hill, 1948), pp. 108–109.

[2.] Will Brownell and Richard N. Billings, *So Close to Greatness: A Biography of William C. Bullitt* (New York: Macmillan, 1988).

It was in the last year that I found the Boss occasionally nodding over his mail or dozing a moment during dictation. At first I was surprised but considered it merely a fatigue of the moment. He would grin in slight embarrassment as he caught himself ... But as it began to occur with increasing frequency I became seriously alarmed. It was evident that the grind was becoming too severe for him; the next step might be a real breakdown in his health ... After some troubled thought over the matter I finally decided to talk to Anna.

Anna Boettiger went to McIntire and demanded action on behalf of her father. Roosevelt was then scheduled for a physical examination at the Bethesda Naval Hospital at 11 AM on March 27, 1944, by Lieutenant Commander Howard Bruenn, a thirty-eight-year-old cardiologist who was the consultant in cardiology to the National Naval Medical Center in Washington and to the Third Naval District. Bruenn received orders to report his medical findings only to McIntire without any discussion with FDR or his family. Admiral McIntire also ordered the Bethesda Naval Hospital commanding officer, Captain John Harper, to make certain all of FDR's medical results be kept secret.

Bruenn's clinical findings on March 27, 1944, were summarized in his 1970 article in the *Annals of Internal Medicine*[4]: "patient breathless and slightly cyanotic (blue color of lips due to poor oxygenation); enlarged left ventricle (the main chamber of the heart); blood pressure 186/108 (high). These physical signs and symptoms exhibited by FDR justified the diagnosis of hypertension, hypertensive cardiac disease, cardiac failure and acute bronchitis."[5]

Bruenn made several recommendations that he believed should be carried out immediately: complete bed rest for at least a week with nursing care, a light diet, and, most important, digitalis for FDR's failing *heart;* but the suggestions were unacceptable to Admiral McIntire, due to "exigencies and demands on the president." Instead, FDR was placed on modified bed rest and given cough syrup. When Bruenn saw him the next day (March 28) at the White House, FDR's deteriorating cardiac function had allowed fluid to back up in his lungs, particularly at the base of his right lung; a sign of congestive heart failure. At a press and radio conference (#945) that afternoon at 4:00 PM, the president was asked about his condition, and he simply replied, "I got bronchitis."

3. G. Tully, *Franklin Delano Roosevelt, My Boss* (Chicago: People's Book Club, 1949), p. 274.
4. Bruenn, "Clinical Notes on the Illness and Death of President Franklin D. Roosevelt": *Annals of Internal Medicine* 72: 579-591, 1970.
5. *Ibid.*

When Bruenn saw the president on March 30, "he appeared to be somewhat better." But when the details of <u>Bruenn's</u> follow-up examination are studied, it appears that the president was not better; in fact, he seemed worse. There was now fluid at the base of both lungs, and his heart was becoming grossly enlarged to the left, with markedly palpable impulses at the apex. Bruenn's summary of the clinical situation was as follows: "[I]t seemed apparent that some degree of congestive heart failure was present, and digitalization was again suggested to the surgeon general and urged as an essential form of therapy."

In spite of this request and the presence of obvious cardiac deterioration, McIntire continued to disregard the strong request by Bruenn that FDR be given digitalis, the drug required for a heart in failure.

Bruenn was in a difficult position. FDR was in heart failure and was receiving inadequate treatment because a medically unsophisticated superior officer, who was basically an administrator, was in charge of the case. Fortunately, Bruenn was finally able to convince McIntire that the situation warranted the convening, on March 31, 1944, of a group of medical consultants to help weigh decisions as to how FDR should be treated. The military doctors in the group included McIntire, Bruenn, Captains Harper and Duncan (the commanding and executive officers at the Naval Hospital), and Captain Charles Behrens, chief radiologist at the facility.

The two civilian doctors called in consultation were Frank H. Lahey of Boston and James A. Paullin of Atlanta, the president of the American Medical Association. Lahey and Paullin saw the president that afternoon, and the group met on the following morning, April 1, 1944.

The main issue discussed was whether the president should be put on digitalis, the cardiac drug made from leaves of the foxglove plant. Siding with McIntire, Paullin did not believe the medication was indicated. Bruenn countered with a list of FDR's symptoms that included cyanosis, diminished myocardial reserve, and orthopnea (difficulty breathing when lying flat)—symptoms that indicated the presence of congestive heart failure. Bruenn threatened to withdraw from FDR's case if his recommendation for digitalis treatment was rejected.

The decision was made to proceed with the proposed digitalization, as Bruenn noted in his report, and the effect of the medication became evident by April 3. Roosevelt could now lie flat without becoming short of breath, his color had improved, and the fluid in both lungs had disappeared. His blood pressure remained very high, however, at 210/110. An electrocardiogram further demonstrated the beneficial effects of the digitalis that Bruenn had so strongly requested. FDR continued to take this medicine until his death thirteen months later.

Over the next few days, Roosevelt's condition remained stable except for blood pressure readings that at times went as high as 210/120. With the digitalis having had its desired effect in improving FDR's cardiac status, it was decided that he had to have a vacation. In early April, FDR left for a month at Hobcaw Barony, the 23,000-acre South Carolina retreat of the financier and his personal friend, Bernard Baruch, who had been an economics adviser to presidents, starting with Woodrow Wilson. At Baruch's estate, FDR said all he wanted to do was "Sleep and sleep. Twelve hours a night, and let the world go hang."

While FDR was in South Carolina, visitors were kept to a minimum—only family and close friends. Eleanor came for a day with Anna, and when she returned to Washington, Mrs. Roosevelt wrote in her diary, "F. looks well but said he still has no 'pep.' Dr. McIntire says they will do final tests when he gets home."

There was no phone at Hobcaw Barony, but Roosevelt had two army field phones in his bedroom, one connected to the White House switchboard and one for personal calls. FDR called Lucy Mercer Rutherford (FDR's early love who nearly cost him his marriage) almost daily in Aiken, South Carolina, 140 miles across the state, and Bruenn noted in his published medical paper that Mrs. Rutherford was among FDR's visitors at Baruch's estate (Lucy Mercer Rutherford had been recently widowed with the death of her husband Winthrop on March 20, 1944, at their home in Aiken.)

McIntire and Bruenn accompanied Roosevelt while he was in South Carolina, and Bruenn said FDR felt well at first, slept soundly, and ate well "He was asymptomatic until April 28, when late in the afternoon he began to complain of abdominal pain and tenderness associated with slight nausea."

FDR was diagnosed as having acute cholecystitis, a condition caused by inflammation of the gallbladder. Bruenn treated it with a half-grain of codeine by hypodermic injection, for the pain; by May 1, FDR was free of all abdominal distress. The pain returned on the following day, however, with the attack lasting for an additional forty-eight hours. Bruenn reported that FDR was acutely uncomfortable during this time and was treated with heat to his abdomen and codeine administered hypodermically during the night. After two days of such treatment, FDR was pain-free.

It is astonishing that FDR was allowed to suffer the acute abdominal pain of cholecystitis for six days while under the care of a cardiologist, Bruenn. The only other medical advice that might have been received by the president would have come from Admiral McIntire, a high-ranking naval administrator whose medical background was in eye, ear, nose, and throat diseases (at that time otolaryngology and ophthalmology were a combined specialty).

Acute cholecystitis is a serious inflammatory condition of the gallbladder that can potentially progress to peritonitis and death. It seems totally inappropriate that FDR's abdominal condition was only treated by a cardiologist and the surgeon general of the United States Navy, neither of whom would have had experience with acute abdominal surgical conditions. It seems difficult to believe that the acute abdominal pain suffered by FDR for a week was not addressed by at least one consulting surgeon as warranted by the potentially catastrophic progression that this serious abdominal condition can pose. FDR received medical care that apparently was unsatisfactory for any patient, let alone the president of the United States.

Dr. Lahey had examined FDR in Washington shortly before his gallbladder attack, and it seems logical if a surgical consultant was needed in South Carolina, it would almost certainly have been Dr. Lahey. (David Preston Boyd, a noted Lahey Clinic surgeon, later wrote that it was "beyond the outposts of reason for Lahey not to almost certainly have been consulted when Roosevelt suffered an acute abdomen."[6]

After reading the reports on FDR's gallbladder attacks, I detected several major discrepancies concerning the incident, both from the Secret Service and FDR's doctors, discrepancies that are difficult to explain. Bruenn stated that FDR had severe abdominal pain that began on 28 April 1944 and, except for two days in which FDR was pain-free, the president was otherwise "acutely" uncomfortable and from May 2 to 4 was "kept in bed." In contrast to this medical report by Bruenn is a report in the Roosevelt Library written by the Secret Service entitled "Brief Diary of Vacation," referring to FDR's time at South Carolina from April 9th until May 6th, after which time he left for Washington by special train. During the days that Bruenn reported FDR was acutely ill, the abbreviated report by the Secret Service indicated no physical problems:

April 28—Held informal press conference at Hobcaw, speaking almost entirely of the death of the Secretary of the Navy Knox.

April 29—Cruised up Black River fishing on the way as far as Beneventum Plantation.

April 30—A quiet Sunday at Hobcaw.

May 1—Fish Black River again off Inman Plantation. Poor luck.

May 2—Trolled unsuccessfully in the ocean just outside Winyah Bay Jetties.

---

6. From a chapter in a book written by Dr. Boyd on the history of the Lahey Clinic. Dr. Boyd died in 1989 before his book was completed.

May 3—A routine day at the mansion working on papers. Major General E. M. Watson, Secretary and Military Aid, returned from attending Secretary Knox's funeral in Washington.

May 4—Miss Margaret Suckley, a cousin from New York, arrived for a brief visit.

May 5—An afternoon in the sun on the beach at Arcadia Plantation.

It seems apparent that the Secret Service was party to Roosevelt's gall bladder deception, and the press corps is implicated as well. Merriman Smith of United Press, who covered the White House in the Roosevelt years, wrote a book in which he described FDR's Baruch trip in detail. Smith made no mention of FDR's illness when he was in South Carolina. On April 28, the day Bruenn said Roosevelt began to complain of abdominal pains, Smith noted that McIntire had returned from Washington to tell the president of the death of Navy Secretary Frank Knox. "That actually was the first time during the trip we had seen the President to talk to," Smith wrote, "and he called for us about eight in the evening."[7] According to Bruenn, FDR was in acute pain at the time, but Smith reported him roaring with delight in the company of reporters.

When Roosevelt returned to Washington on May 6, Bruenn wrote that he "looked well," and his lungs were "entirely clear." However, his heart was still reported as being enlarged, and his blood pressure remained very high, averaging 196/112. Soon after his return to Washington from Baruch's estate, FDR underwent a cholecystogram (gallbladder X-ray) in which dye, given by mouth, concentrates in the gallbladder so that an X-ray can be taken of the organ. A surprising discrepancy occurred in a direct disagreement between Dr. Bruenn and Admiral McIntire concerning the X-ray interpretation of FDR's gallbladder. McIntire reported that the president had a normal cholecystogram; i.e., a normal gallbladder. However, Bruenn's report of the X-ray findings gave a completely different interpretation of FDR's gallbladder findings. Bruenn claimed: "[T]he x-rays showed a good functional response but there were indications of a group of cholesterol stones."

The presence of stones in the gallbladder is unequivocal evidence of a diseased gallbladder. Bruenn's knowledge that FDR had a gallbladder condition caused

---

7. A. M. Smith, *Thank You, Mr. President: A White House Notebook* (New York: Harper, 1946), p. 141.

him to place the president on a low-fat diet in the hope it would prevent future gallbladder attacks.

It is impossible to resolve the discrepancy in the X-ray interpretation between Bruenn and McIntire concerning FDR's gallbladder. It is a good example, however, of how McIntire always presented FDR as being completely healthy and disease free, especially preceding the presidential election in 1944. In fact, McIntire never admitted, either before or after Roosevelt's death, that FDR suffered anything other than occasional bouts of flu or bronchitis.

Three months after his gallbladder attack, on July 20, 1944, FDR accepted the Democratic Party nomination for a fourth term as president of the United States. Throughout that summer the president continued to lose weight, which Bruenn claimed was due to the low-fat diet he had ordered for the president following his gallbladder episode. In early August, FDR gave his first major 1944 campaign speech at the Puget Sound Naval Base in Bremmerton, Washington. During the previous year, Roosevelt gave his speeches in a sitting position, but because of the political overtones of having what might appear to be a presidential candidate in a condition of failing health, FDR decided to speak at Bremmerton while standing up. Rosenman observed[8]:

> During the year since he had last stood on his braces, FDR had lost considerable weight; as a result, his braces no longer fitted him.

The loose braces gave FDR little support while standing at the speaker's podium, and this situation required tremendous arm effort to support his body. By the time he had finished speaking, FDR had developed severe substernal (chest) pain, which radiated to both shoulders. It was feared that FDR had sustained a myocardial infarction (heart attack), but subsequent examinations showed that the pain was not cardiac in origin. This event strongly indicated that FDR's weight loss had become generalized and extensive since even his legs (which had atrophied over the years following his attack of poliomyelitis in 1921) had lost additional muscle mass. Roseman's statement that the president's weight loss had caused his leg braces to no longer fit him corroborates this impression.

FDR's condition continued to fail throughout the summer of 1944. In June of that year, Bruenn said that the president weighed 188 pounds, the president's normal weight. By September, Robert Sherwood, one of FDR's speechwriters who had not seen the president for several months, commented:[9]

---

8. Samuel I. Rosenman, *Working with Roosevelt* (New York: Harper Brothers, 1952), p. 461.

I was shocked by his appearance. I had heard that he had lost a lot of weight, but I was unprepared for the almost ravaged appearance of his face. He had his coat off and his shirt collar seemed several sizes too large for his emaciated neck.

Weight loss and anorexia (loss of appetite) had now become a continuing problem for the president. Roosevelt, probably with McIntire's approval, made the decision by early 1944 to run for a fourth term in spite of the fact that he was obviously ill. By election time in November, 1944, FDR was clearly in poor health, but McIntire stated, "The President's health is excellent. I can say that unqualifyingly."

FDR remained on digitalis, his blood pressure readings went as high as 240/130, and his weight loss continued. Because of his weight loss, all restrictions were removed from his diet and eggnog supplements were begun.

FDR had to have known he was ill. Even before the presidential election in November 1944, some of his actions suggested that he was thinking of his death. He gave specific information regarding his burial plans, suggesting where he wished his memorial in Washington to be located; he also began giving personal mementos to close friends and secretaries.

FDR defeated Thomas E. Dewey of New York in 1944 for an unprecedented fourth term as president of the United States. Shortly after the election, FDR went to Warm Springs, Georgia, for rest and recuperation. Loss of appetite was then his major health problem, with Bruenn stating that Roosevelt now weighed only 165 pounds. FDR was unable to eat the food set before him; even when he tried, he said he could not taste it. Bruenn stated that the president lost further weight at Warm Springs, which would have now brought his weight to around 160 pounds or less, FDR's normal weight being between 188 to 190 as recorded by McIntire.

Roosevelt's weight problem became so acute that in spite of electrocardiographic tracings that showed no digitalis toxicity (a reaction from the drug can cause loss of appetite), the heart medication was stopped temporarily to see if the president's appetite would improve. There was no apparent change, and the cardiac drug was therefore resumed.

Concern for FDR's loss of appetite had been ongoing for months; by the early summer of 1944, Eleanor Roosevelt showed her increasing concern about FDR's continuing indigestion and weight loss by restricting visitors when FDR had his

9. Robert E.Sherwood, *Roosevelt and Hopkins: An Intimate History* (New York: Harper Brothers, 1948), p. 821.

meals. FDR's weight loss must also have been of concern to his doctors since a cardinal feature of a malignant tumor is loss of appetite and unexplained weight loss.

Following his presidential victory in November 1944, FDR went to Warm Springs, Georgia, where he routinely went over the years in the hope of recuperating from his poliomyelitis. He returned to Washington on December 19, to prepare for his inauguration. His son James had returned from wartime duty to be with his father, and he said that when he saw him, "I realized with awful irrevocable certainty that we were going to lose him."[10] James Roosevelt further stated that his father "looked sick, his color was bad, he looked terribly tired and I noted that he was short of breath." When he questioned his father about his apparent poor health, FDR told him that he was fine and "a few days in Warms Springs will fix me right up." James became so concerned about his father's failing health that he went to Admiral McIntire, who assured him that everything was fine. Referring to the responses received from his father and McIntire, James Roosevelt said that "it was as though together they'd written the dialogue."

Immediately after delivering his fourth Inaugural Day address on January 20, 1945, FDR had an intimate meeting with his son James, during which he informed him that he had made James trustee of his estate and the executor of his will. The president also gave him funeral instructions and the Roosevelt family ring that he requested he wear. James Roosevelt in retrospect said,

> "[T]his meeting with my father clearly indicated that he was thinking of death, but I took it to mean that he was thinking of a death which had to come. Now that I look back, I realize why he insisted Mother go to the trouble of having all 13 of his grandchildren at the inauguration but I did not see that then."

Shortly after the inauguration, FDR left Washington for Yalta where many of the postwar problems began between the East and West. Signs of the physical decline of Roosevelt were now clearly obvious, and there were people at the Yalta meeting who believed that FDR's mental deterioration was now evident. Pictures taken of Roosevelt at Yalta were clearly those of a dying man, and yet these pictures were carefully selected before distribution as being the most favorable of those taken of the president.

Following the Yalta meeting (February 3–10, 1945), Roosevelt returned to the United States by sea, which was physically beneficial to him. William D. Hassett, his private secretary, stated that "the President hadn't looked this well in a

---

10. James Roosevelt and Bill Libby, *My Parents: A Differing View* (Chicago: Playboy Press, 1976), p. 281.

year...." This statement had significance since in Hassett's personal diary there is an entry on December 24, 1944, concerning FDR's health: "I fear for his health despite assurances from the doctors that he is OK."[11]

Through March, 1945, Roosevelt's health continued to fail. His weight loss persisted. Digitalis was again stopped in the hope of increasing his appetite and food intake, but when this proved again to be ineffective, digitalis was resumed. By the end of the month, FDR's condition warranted a period of total rest. He left Washington for Warm Springs on March 29, 1945, and after a week or so, the president allegedly had improved slightly; Bruenn called McIntire in Washington on the morning of April 12 to convey this impression. However, at 1:15 PM that day, the president developed a crushing headache, lost consciousness, and despite attempts at resuscitation, was declared dead at 3:35 PM. The cause of the president's death was apparently a massive cerebral hemorrhage. There has never been an official report of the cause of FDR's death.

---

11. William D. Hassett, *Off the Record with F.D.R: 1942–1945* (New Brunswick, New Brunswick, N.J.: Rutgers University Press, 1958), p. 307.

CHAPTER 8

WHY DID FDR RUN?

Dr. Lahey told President Roosevelt that he would not survive a fourth term as president. The question this raises is why FDR would run for a fourth term if he knew he was so gravely ill? Most likely he did it for two reasons: to continue as president until the final victory of World War II, and to establish the United Nations, which he felt would be his monument to history. Just prior to his inauguration in 1944, FDR told his son, "I don't dare shake the faith of the people, that's why I ran again, Jimmy. The People elected me their leader and I can't quit in the middle of the war."[1]

As for the second reason, FDR was well aware during the time he served under Woodrow Wilson after World War I of the serious political problems that confronted Wilson in his quest to gain membership of the United States in the League of Nations. A quarter of a century later in his own quest to establish the United Nations, FDR faced the same situation, and he realized he stood a greater chance of gaining United States Senate approval of the United Nations from the strength of the presidential office as opposed to the role of ex-president.

When FDR finally made the decision to seek his last term in office, he undoubtedly had the approval of Admiral McIntire, as was stated in *Life* magazine in 1944:[2]

> [W]hen President Roosevelt announced that he would run for a fourth term, it was not a wholly personal decision. The person who presumably made up the president's mind, therefore, was not Harry Hopkins, Robert Hannegan, or even Mrs. Roosevelt, but Vice Admiral Ross T. McIntire, surgeon general of the United States Navy, official White House physician and vigilant watchdog over the chief executive's health.

---

1. Roosevelt and Libby, *My Parents*, p. 283.
2. J. Perkins, "The Presidents Doctor," *Life* 17 (July 31, 1944): p. 4.

The close relationship between McIntire and Roosevelt makes it almost certain that FDR was aware of his physical state. McIntire stated, "[A]s far as President Roosevelt himself was concerned, he had a clear understanding of his physical condition at all times."

This statement made by McIntire after Roosevelt's death can also explain Bruenn's expressed puzzlement as to why, during the thirteen months he saw FDR on a regular basis as a consultant:

> [A]t no time did the President ever comment on the frequency of his visits or question the reason for electrocardiograms or other laboratory tests that were performed from time to time, nor did he ever ask any questions as to the type and variety of the medications we used.

One might conclude that Roosevelt never asked Bruenn for information about his physical condition because he already had a "clear understanding" of his declining medical condition, as supplied by Admiral McIntire.

Roosevelt probably made the decision by late 1943 or early 1944 to run for a fourth term, which would have made it necessary to disguise any indication of his deteriorating health from the public. The control of this disinformation was apparently successful since James A. Farley, Roosevelt's former associate and cabinet member, stated after FDR's death, in a letter to the *New York Times* on February 20, 1951: "In 1944 it was widely known among leaders that FDR was a dying man." Farley's statement appeared in an editorial in the *Washington Post* (March 1, 1951), prompting an immediate rebuttal by McIntire. The *Washington Post* (March 10, 1951) quickly responded to McIntire's rebuttal: "Citing Admiral McIntire's 1944 statement about the President's good health ... if Mr. Farley is right, this was calculated deception."

Farley's comment regarding FDR's health led me to wonder if Farley had discussed the subject with members of his family. As a result, a search for Farley's relatives was initiated. Both Farley and his wife were deceased, but I found their son was living in New York and had an unlisted phone number. I also learned that Farley's son had been a former New York state boxing commissioner. I contacted the then-current New York boxing commissioner and, after explaining my reason for trying to reach Farley, was given his phone number. I found him to be extremely cordial. He was unable, however, to recall his father's discussing FDR's health in any greater detail than the comments published by the *Washington Post* years earlier.

If one accepts the hypothesis that political expediency resulted in Roosevelt and McIntire concealing the true extent of FDR's health from the public prior to the election in 1944, any unfounded rumors regarding the president's health were probably minor and could have been left unanswered. However, prior to the time of the presidential election, reliable information concerning the president's actual condition would have had to have been contained when possible.

The Roosevelt Library in Hyde Park has preserved an example of this containment in a letter (November 1, 1944) from J. Edgar Hoover, chief of the Federal Bureau of Investigation (FBI) to Stephen Early, secretary to President Roosevelt, under the heading "Personal and Confidential by Special Messenger." Attached to this letter is a four-page memorandum entitled "Re: Circulation of Story Alleging the President has a Serious Heart Affliction." Information had surfaced regarding the serious cardiac condition of the president, which Mayo Clinic doctors, who had been temporarily assigned to the United States Naval Hospital at Bethesda, Maryland, leaked. Secretary Early requested the FBI to trace the source of the leak. The memorandum from Hoover to Early is too long to quote in its entirety, but the flavor of the letter may be appreciated by the following single paragraph. (Identifying names have been censored by the FBI.)

> It seems that Dr. ***** is a Lieutenant in the Navy, assigned to the Bethesda Medical Center and residing in *****. When interviewed on the evening of October 27 relative to any statement which had been made concerning the state of President's health, Dr. ***** denied making any statements of this kind, but stated that the President's health had been the subject of a general discussion at a luncheon recently held at the Naval Hospital in Bethesda. When asked to name specifically the person who had attended the luncheon, Dr. ***** declined to do so and stated the discussions were only general in nature and no specific statements were made concerning the President's health. Dr. ***** stated that the reasons the President's health had been discussed at the hospital was because members of the hospital staff recognized the picture of one of the Navy hospital doctors, Dr. H.G. Bruenn, on the President's train at the time he was making the acceptance speech. Dr. ***** stated that he had not discussed the subject of the President's health with Dr. Bruenn. Dr. ***** was obviously disturbed and uneasy during the interview.

The FBI again interrogated Dr. ***** but no additional information was gathered. A leading specialist at the Mayo Clinic, who had recently returned from a temporary assignment at the Bethesda Naval Hospital, was also interviewed in Rochester, Minnesota, simply because he had made the statement at a luncheon in Washington "that the President had a serious heart ailment." Hoover summarized his four-page memorandum to Early by stating:

"[A] lot of loose conversation and talk [took place], all predicated upon the supposition that the President was suffering from some heart ailment by reason of the fact that Bruenn's picture appeared in the group with the President."

Hoover's letter is an intriguing look into the FBI's interrogation of a group of physicians for merely speculating on the poor health of FDR. Of interest in this investigation, and attempt at containment by the FBI, is that the rumor of cardiac decompensation [heart failure] of the president was more than just a rumor; it was an accurate assessment of the president's medical condition. FDR may not have initiated the investigation by the FBI concerning his health, but it is reasonable to believe that he may have been aware of inquiries.

While the FBI was investigating leaks from sources outside the White House regarding Roosevelt's health, McIntire was containing rumors coming from inside the White House by people who knew FDR's true condition. Evidence of this is found in a letter preserved at the Roosevelt Museum at Hyde Park. The letter was written by Dr. Lahey to Admiral McIntire, dated September 12, 1944, approximately five months after Lahey saw Roosevelt, allegedly for the first time and just weeks before the presidential election.

A newspaper reporter had been sent by the editor of the *St. Louis Dispatch* to question Dr. Lahey regarding FDR's health, which had become the major issue in the forthcoming election. The central question at that pre-election time was whether FDR was well enough to run for a fourth term. In his letter to McIntire, Lahey explained:

> I told him that I did not see how an editor could send an assistant editor on such a foolish mission. He asked me if I had seen the President professionally and I told him that I thought that was something that he had no right to ask and that the only answer I could make was *what you had told me and it was my opinion that he was in excellent health.* [Author's emphasis.] If all of the above seems foolish, it is merely to state the facts lest there be any distortion at this time. I suppose we must expect more and more of this business as we get close to election time.

Lahey's letter to McIntire is awkward, since Lahey could have simply told the reporter that FDR was in good health. But Lahey knew that FDR was in poor health.

Dr. Lahey was medically and professionally powerful. He was head of the Lahey Clinic and chairman of the board of the War Manpower Commission, which was responsible for procuring and assigning all physicians, dentists, and veterinarians during World War II. In addition to his many medical and administrative responsibilities, Lahey was a prolific writer and a scholarly individual who was well aware of the historical importance of being a surgical consultant to a president of the United States. It would have been inconsistent with Lahey's character to have left no notes or records pertaining to the health of President Roosevelt. It was not until many years after Lahey's death, and after a bitter legal fight, that a valuable document written by him, confirming FDR's poor health in 1944, was finally uncovered: the so-called "Lahey Memorandum."

CHAPTER 9

THE FDR PUBLICATION

I had gathered a sizable amount of data in 1977 and 1978 regarding the health of FDR, and the time had come to organize the accumulated material as an article for publication. The purpose of the article was to present the data and to make a plea for information from anyone who might have knowledge regarding FDR's health. The last paragraph in the article exemplified the purpose of the paper:[1]

> [I]t is hoped a recollection will be rekindled in the minds of people who have direct or indirect knowledge of the health of President Roosevelt during the last year of his life. Even though many of his close associates have passed with the years, there still remain individuals who might shed some light regarding the health of Roosevelt. Perhaps even the United States government will assume some responsibilities in an attempt to locate the President's records to allow an accurate and final decision to be made regarding his death. Rumors as to its cause, will persist until there is historic truth, and only then will the continuing questions with regard to the last year of the life of Franklin D. Roosevelt finally be silenced.

The FDR paper was published in the surgical journal *Surgery, Gynecology and Obstetrics* (*SGO*), which after ninety years was renamed, in 1994, the *Journal of the American College of Surgeons*. In this publication, I raised the idea that perhaps FDR had a malignant skin cancer (melanoma) located over his left eye, which could have been the underlying cause for his physical decline. I implied this hypothesis by titling the paper, "The Death of Franklin D. Roosevelt: Was it Melanoma?"

---

[1] H. S. Goldsmith, "Unanswered Mysteries in the Death of Franklin D. Roosevelt," *Surgery, Gynecology and Obstetrics* 149 (1979): 899–908.

Several weeks after I submitted the paper, a letter arrived from Dr. Loyal Davis, editor of *SGO*, accepting the paper with the request that I change the title to something definitive. I changed it to "Unanswered Mysteries in the Death of Franklin D. Roosevelt."

SGO published the article in its December 1979 issue which caused immediate interest as evidenced by the publication being reported on the evening ABC, CBS, and NBC television networks. Many articles were subsequently published in newspapers throughout the country in response to the *SGO* paper. Kevin McKean of the Associated Press sent out an extensive press release that further generated a great deal of national interest. Lawrence K. Altman, M.D., of the *New York Times* wrote an article (December 17, 1979) in support of the SGO paper "with the aim of bringing into sharper focus the medical events that occurred in the last years of Roosevelt's life."

An issue of *Time* magazine (December 17, 1979) summed up the article: "[N]ow a doctor has raised anew the suggestion that Roosevelt had terminal cancer, knew it, but chose to run for re-election in 1944 anyway."

I received letters from people who claimed to have had direct or indirect knowledge about FDR. Many were simply rumors, and several claimed (without any supporting evidence) that FDR had committed suicide. The following is an example of this:

> If you would like to check what I have written above (FDR had shot himself) please feel free to contact the doctor as I am sure he will be willing to confirm the story. I feel strong enough that the public has the right to know about the health of the person that represents the United States, and his ability to carry out his duties. I will remain anonymous for reasons of my own, but you may contact the doctor if you wish and I list his name below.

The doctor alluded to in the above letter allegedly lived in Paradise Valley, Arizona; but when I tried to locate him, he was unknown in that community. It was of interest, however, that the author of this letter wished to remain anonymous even though more than forty years had passed since FDR's death.

Most of the letters concerning FDR's health were uninformative, but some were significant. One such letter came on January 9, 1980, from Dr. Thomas Throckmorton of Des Moines, Iowa, who had trained at the Mayo Clinic:

> I greatly enjoyed your article in the recent <u>SGO</u> as regards the final health problems of Franklin D. Roosevelt. As a matter of fact, I enjoyed it

enough to share with you a bit of apocryphal information which may or not be of continuing interest to you.

I was a Fellow and first assistant at Mayo from 1939 to 1943 and then left to take up surgical practice in Des Moines. I have continued close relationships with Mayo and especially the surgical staff. Not long before I arrived at Mayo, James Roosevelt, the son of the President, had gastric surgery performed by the late Dr. Howard Fray. Also, Roosevelt's alter ego, Harry Hopkins had gastric surgery performed at about the same time by Dr. Waltman Walters who is still hale and hearty in his 80's. To the best of my knowledge, Roosevelt himself was never a patient at Mayo.

Shortly after his death, I was in Rochester and talking over the rather obvious disabilities Roosevelt had before he died. This was during the period of marked criticism and cries of "cover-up" directed towards Admiral McIntyre [*sic*]. I cannot remember at this date which of my acquaintances related the following material to me. When the hue and cry arose following Roosevelt's death, McIntire offered to send the entire protocol of Roosevelt's health history on to Mayo for their judgment. The obvious reason was to use the Mayo name to strengthen his decision as regards the President's ability to "run" for a fourth term. Mayo, in my opinion, very wisely refused to accept this material and to act on the basis of data supplied by other sources. I suspect this story was related to me by the late John Waugh because we were close friends during this period of time and just preceding Dr. Waugh's death.

If one thinks this anecdote through, it is obvious that the *material for which you have been so laboriously searching regarding Roosevelt's health was indeed in McIntire's hands for a period of time following the death. His offer to share such material with Mayo would make it obvious that he was in control of the necessary data* [Author's emphasis.] I must leave it to you or your imagination to decide what course he subsequently took with the data.

At the end of his letter, Dr. Throckmorton mentioned several other doctors at the Mayo Clinic who might give me further information on FDR's medical record. I contacted them but, unfortunately, they had nothing to contribute.

One letter received after publication of my FDR paper proved both informative and great fun to read. I had already received two other letters referring to the same subject, one from West Virginia and the other from California. Both suggested that I contact a Dr. George Webster of Pasadena, California, if I wished to learn more about a certain skin lesion that had been excised from FDR's scalp.

Even before I had the opportunity to track Dr. Webster down, I received the following letter from him on December 4, 1979:

> I enclosed a Xerox article from the *Los Angeles Times* which I read with considerable interest. I personally operated on FDR in February, 1944. Admiral McIntire's statement that "the only surgery that Roosevelt had during his White House years was a tooth extraction" is false.
>
> The circumstances were these: I was Chief of Plastic Surgery at the National Naval Medical Center in Bethesda, Maryland from July 1943 to April 1946. On a Monday, early in February, 1944, I was called to the Office of Captain William Harper, Commanding Officer at the Naval Medical Center and told that the President would be brought out on Wednesday morning for the removal of an epidermoid cyst of his posterior scalp. This had been present for some years but had increased in size and was irritated by the President's hat band. It gave him some trouble when he was wearing his hat for any length of time. Accordingly, on Tuesday afternoon, the Secret Service came out, and surveyed the entire operating suite at the Naval Medical Center, going over with the head nurse all the sterile packs to make sure that she knew what was in each one. The Secret Service also reviewed the status of the windows which commanded the view of the outside of the operating room.
>
> The Chief of Neurosurgery was Winchell M. Craig, M.D. (former Chief of Neurosurgery at the Mayo Clinic and a Captain, Medical Corp, U.S.N.R.). We did not have a chance to examine the President before his arrival but were told by Admiral McIntire that the lesion was "about the size of a hen's egg and almost exactly in the midline where the hat band would hit the head". The description proved to be accurate.
>
> Captain Craig and I discussed ahead of time how we would position the President for our excision since it was in an awkward place in the back of the head and the President could not very well lie down for this procedure. Together we decided to use the cerebellar headrest, reversed, so that his wheelchair could be wheeled up to the end of the operating table. The metal frame was padded for his face.
>
> The President came up a one story rear elevator and surrounded by Secret Service men, came down the main hall of the operating suite. He was then wheeled into operating room 1. At the time of the surgery, the following persons were present: the President, Admiral McIntire, Captain Harper, Captain Duncan (Executive Officer), Captain Winchell Craig, Captain Gilje (Chief of General Surgery at the Medical Center), Helen Vlacik, Registered Nurse, the head operating room nurse whose nickname

was "Minnie" but whose name I have forgotten, Dr. John Pender (an anesthesiologist from the Mayo Clinic who was on duty at the center). He injected the local for the excision (Dr. Pender now lives in Palo Alto, California).

The lesion itself was a typical benign epidermoid cyst in the midline posterior cranial region, just above the nuchal line. Its excision occasioned no difficulty. The specimen was sent to the laboratory at Bethesda. I presume that Dr. Charles Geshickter, who was Chief of Pathology, at the time, would have a record of the pathological diagnosis which was "benign epidermoid cyst."

After incision, the wound was closed, using a plastic suture material which was probably 3–0 Dermalon, although names of sutures have changed and it is impossible to remember exactly what sutures were used. The dressing was held in place by a single layer of coarse mesh gauze over a dressing of finer mesh gauze and secured to the scalp with collodion (much as we used to do in the dog laboratory to hold the animal dressings on experimental animals).

The President said that he had already concocted a story for the press being somewhat like the Spirit of 76 with a big bandage around his head, as he had anticipated such a bandage. He was surprised to find that we would use only a light local dressing.

He was brought back to the center on the following Sunday for removal of sutures. The Secret Service routine was repeated. Removing the collodion adherent dressing was a bit painful as it pulled on the hair, but he did not complain. His much publicized charm and charisma were certainly apparent and as Admiral McIntire said "He is a good patient."

There is an interesting side light about the surgery itself in that the surgery like all scalp wounds was necessarily rather bloody. The President had taken off his shirt and his polka dot bow tie, which to my amazement was a clip-on bow tie and not a hand tied one. He removed his t-shirt during the procedure. His shoulders were massive from his long years of using crutches. His wheelchair was simply a flat seat without arms but with handles for those pushing him and maneuvering the wheelchair. The t-shirt which he wore became soiled with some blood. It was taken off and replaced by a fresh t-shirt from the Ship's Store in the enlisted men's quarters. One of the hospital corpsmen supplied this. The bloody t-shirt, however, disappeared much to the consternation of the head nurse "Minnie" and the Captain and the Executive Officer of the hospital. The entire operating crew were restricted to base for a considerable length of time and yet the bloody t-shirt never appeared. Where it is or whatever happened to it we will never know.

In regard to your comment as to a possible melanoma, I most seriously doubt this because he had multiple rather than large plaque like keratoses on his face and in his scalp. These were the typical brown ones that might have been present in previous photographs, although I do not recall seeing them specifically. I think the chance of these being a "mole" which underwent malignant degeneration is extremely remote. *As to the President's general health, the removal of the epidermoid cyst was an incidental part of the hospital visit for which he came out from the White House for chest x-rays to see about his "cigarette cough". On x-ray, he was found to have some pulmonary edema and was, in effect, in early mild cardiac failure.* [Author's emphasis.] This was recognized and he was immediately digitalized. Admiral McIntire had called Dr. Howard Bruenn, a Naval Reserve Officer and Cardiologist who was a good friend of mine from my days at Columbia-Presbyterian Medical Center in New York City where he was an Attending Cardiologist. From the time of the President's visit to Bethesda, Dr. Bruenn traveled with the President at all times, including Yalta, Tehran and other junkets. From one of these trips, Howard, as a member of the Presidential party bought home a lavish chest of caviar and Russian cigarettes which he generously shared with us at his home out near Rockville, Maryland.

Dr. Breunn was an extremely thorough internist and cardiologist of high repute. I am sure he knows as much as it is possible to know about the President's health.

I hope this account is of some value to you in your life long study of Roosevelt's health. Best wishes.

Commenting on the president's general health, Dr. Webster said the removal of the cyst was only an incidental reason for FDR's visit to Bethesda. He indicated that Roosevelt had come to the hospital mainly to have chest X-rays as his "cigarette cough" had become a cause for concern and that the X-rays indicated pulmonary edema with mild cardiac failure. This letter by Webster would indicate that Roosevelt was in cardiac failure as early as February 1944 (if Dr. Webster's date was correct) as opposed to McIntire and Bruenn's statements that Roosevelt's serious heart condition wasn't diagnosed until March 28, 1944.

Dr. Webster's letter was of great interest because of its humor, thoroughness, and particularly because of its possible importance. Historians have repeatedly reported, based on information from Bruenn, that FDR was first seen by Bruenn on March 28, 1944, who diagnosed the president as exhibiting evidence of congestive heart failure. And yet, Dr. Webster said in his letter that FDR demonstrated evidence of heart failure in early February 1944, which resulted in Dr. Bruenn being called into the case and the immediate administration of digitalis. If Dr. Webster were accurate in his dates, which seemed reasonable because of the specificity of events in his letter, it would mean that Bruenn's dates, as to the beginning of FDR's heart failure diagnosis, were inaccurate and that FDR was in heart failure for a much longer time than has been previously reported by Bruenn and historians.

My first thoughts were that Dr. Webster had somehow gotten his dates confused regarding when FDR visited the Bethesda Naval Hospital for the excision of his sebaceous cyst (wen) and the findings of FDR's heart failure. However, the matter became clear following the publication of a book in 1995 by Geoffrey C. Ward. The book was the diary of Margaret Suckley, FDR's cousin, which was found under her bed following her death in 1991.

From Miss Suckley's diary:[2]

> *Feb 1, 1944 There is some jokes about P's [President]having his wen removed from the back of his head at the Naval Hospital tomorrow* [Author's emphasis]—who should go with him?
>
> *Feb 2, 1944 Anna and I are going out to the hospital with him and he will return straight to the W.H. (White House) after the operation* [Author's emphasis.].... Four doctors are to be there—even a wen, if on the P of U.S. is an important matter. At the door of the operating unit, Dr. McIntire told us we could go in if we wanted to, I think we both felt they didn't really want us, so we remained outside. It took altogether about 50 minutes and when P came out, he looked quite cheerful and normal and had nothing but a local bandage on the back of his head.

The above information convinced me that Dr. Webster's dates of FDR's visit to Bethesda were accurate, as Miss Suckley's diary confirmed, thus indicating that FDR was in heart failure before March 28, 1944, and the basis for his reported "cigarette cough" could well have been his failing heart.

The letters I received following publication of the FDR paper in *SGO* were cordial, informative, and of interest regardless of their comments. However, one was upsetting. On January 16, 1980, Dr. Howard G. Breunn, the naval doctor

---

2. Geoffrey. C. Ward, *Closest Companion: The Unknown Story of the Intimate Friendship between Franklin Roosevelt and Margaret Suckley* (Boston: Houghton Mifflin, 1995), p. 275.

whom McIntyre assigned to care for FDR during the last year of his life, wrote a letter to Dr. Loyal Davis, editor òf *SGO*:

Dear Sir,

First, allow me to identify myself. I was graduated from the Johns Hopkins School of Medicine in 1929 and furthered my training in Boston with a medical internship on the Harvard Medical Service of the Boston City Hospital. I then went through the residencies in internal medicine at the Presbyterian Hospital of the Columbia Medical Center in New York becoming Chief Resident in Medicine in 1935. Subsequently, I became Clinical Professor of Medicine and Attending Physician of the Presbyterian Hospital. I am now a Consultant in medicine to the Columbia Medical Center.

The article "Unanswered Mysteries in The Death of Franklin D. Roosevelt" by Dr. Harry S. Goldsmith and published in your Journal (SG&O) on December, 1979 has just come to my attention. The content of this article is so charged with innuendoes, assumptions, inaccuracies, and pure guesses, that it would be futile for me to answer these in detail. However, there are several points among the many which demand to be clarified.

Dr. Frank Lahey was one of the Honorary Medical Consultants to the Navy and he did see President Roosevelt on one occasion—some two weeks after I had first examined the President [Author's emphasis]. James A. Paullin (not Dr. Pullin) was the other Honorary Consultant. After presenting to these gentlemen the clinical and laboratory data which I had assembled, Dr. Lahey's remark was "there was no problem here for the surgeon." If Dr. Lahey had suspected a malignancy, it seems to me that he certainly would have informed me, inasmuch as I was literally and practically in charge of the case. He made no such remark. At no time was the question of presence of a malignancy suggested to me or to the President.

Secondly, the medical chart of the President was of the unit type in that the complete medical history of the President was inscribed in chronological order. I wrote progress notes and incorporated it repeatedly for the event and clinical findings for the previous twelve years. Categorically, he never had an operation on his face. He did have a sebaceous cyst removed from the top of his head largely because it had become infected and it was associated with discomfort when he combed his hair.

It was my intention when I wrote my paper in 1970 and which was published in the *Annals of Internal Medicine,* i.e., "Clinical Notes on the

Illness and Death of President Roosevelt", to set at rest, finally and clearly, all rumors and suspicions about the medical history of President Roosevelt. Apparently, I failed.

It is with more than resentment that I view Dr. Goldsmith's remark that "an article by Bruenn written in 1970 was purported to be the authentic clinical report...." It is ironic that despite Dr. Goldsmith's somewhat frantic search for evidence in this case and his final plea for recollection on the part of individuals who had direct or indirect knowledge of the health of President Roosevelt during his last illness, he never bothered to get in touch with me. I only happened to be the physician in charge.

Dr. Bruenn's letter to Dr. Davis was obviously sent to be published as a letter to the editor in *SG&O*. Dr. Davis realized that if he published Dr. Bruenn's letter, I would have to be given the opportunity to respond in print to Dr. Bruenn's criticisms. Dr. Davis handled the situation skillfully by sending me a note on February 28, 1980, which simply stated: "We have Dr. Bruenn's permission to forward his letter to the editor to you. Perhaps you and Dr. Bruenn would like to correspond farther."

Saddened that Dr. Bruenn had misinterpreted my motives for writing about FDR's health, I wrote him on March 7, 1980, explaining the actions I had taken:

Dear Dr. Bruenn:

I recently received a letter from Dr. Loyal Davis that he received from you concerning my article "Unanswered Mysteries in the Death of Franklin D. Roosevelt." I was sorry that you felt so upset about my paper, but I wrote it with no purpose other than to try to get definitive information regarding the death of the President. In your letter you said that you wrote your paper in 1970 "to set at rest finally and clearly all the rumors and suspicions about the medical history of President Roosevelt." You must admit that there still remains unresolved discrepancies regarding this matter even between you and Admiral McIntire.

You mention in your letter that I had never bothered to get in touch with you. You may not recall, but I spoke to you on two occasions at great length. In my notes that I took of one of our telephone conversations, I wrote the statement "he was delightful to talk to and gave me a great deal of his time". I think our telephone conversation itself can give you some idea of how information can be inaccurate no matter how well intentioned. I expressly asked you during one of our telephone conversations about the lesion over the President's left eye. Your answer to me, which I recorded, was as follows: "I asked about the lesion over Roosevelt's eye. Dr. B said it was a small lesion removed by Dr. Winchell Craig of the Mayo Clinic under local. Stated it was only a sebaceous cyst. Path slide should be at Bethesda."

After you had given me this lead regarding the lesion over the President's eye, I looked through every dermatology textbook I could find and in no instance was I ever able to find a recording of a pigmented sebaceous cyst. I then further learned, after reading a press conference of President Roosevelt, that the sebaceous cyst you alluded to was on the back of his neck and not, as your letter to Dr. Davis mentioned, from the *top* of his head (underlining of "top" was in your letter). [Dr. Bruenn was talking about the president's scalp lesion and not the lesion over the president's left eye.]

I have subsequently spent a great deal of time tracking down further information regarding this sebaceous cyst and I find that the lesion was not removed by Dr. Winchell Craig as you had believed but by Dr. George Webster, Chief of Plastic Surgery at the National Naval Medical Center in Bethesda from July 1943 to April 1946. [Dr. Bruenn was not in the operating room at the time FDR's scalp lesion was removed.] The lesion removed was reported to me to have been a benign epidermoid cyst, but again, unfortunately, there are no slides available of this lesion at Bethesda.

The example I have just mentioned regarding the President's sebaceous cyst gives you some idea of how there remains uncertainty regarding many aspects of FDR's health. It was and continues to be my desire to get accurate and objective documentation so that history will not have continuing rumors, but rather, concrete historical information.

I have spoken to many people who knew you both while you were in the service, and subsequently, during your tenure at Columbia Medical School. I have heard nothing but fine remarks concerning your integrity and medical ability and I want you to know that you have my highest respect.

Unfortunately, Dr. Bruenn never responded to my letter; if he had, he might have settled questions that still remain unanswered. His comment that, if Dr. Lahey had suspected FDR had malignancy, "he certainly would have informed me" was troubling. I wasn't so sure, and in due course learned that Bruenn was kept in the dark on certain aspects of the case even though he felt he was "literally and practically in charge of the case."

I will always remain grateful to Dr. Loyal Davis for defusing a possible dispute that could have arisen in print between Dr. Bruenn and me. Dr. Davis was an exceptional man having achieved worldwide respect as a neurosurgeon prior to becoming the Editor of *Surgery, Gynecology and Obstetrics* in 1945, a position he held until 1980.

Dr. Davis had a sensitive awareness of political issues and human responses. It should be noted that he was the stepfather to Nancy Reagan and supposedly was one of, if not the instrumental figure in changing the political persuasion of President Ronald Reagan from that of Democrat to Republican. Dr. Davis remained close to his daughter and President Reagan until his death in 1982 at the age of 85.

CHAPTER 10

THE SEARCH CONTINUES

I continued to explore for additional avenues of information related to FDR's health. Leads arose from various letters I received and telephone calls I made, but most proved unrewarding. An idea occurred that perhaps the campaign manager for Thomas E. Dewey, FDR's Republican opponent for the presidency in 1944, could still be alive and, if he were, might have information concerning the deteriorating health of FDR that he had learned during the presidential campaign of 1944. I contacted the Republican Committee in New York and was informed that Dewey's campaign manager in 1944 was Herbert Brownell, who was then practicing law in New York City.

Brownell was a highly respected person, having served in the cabinet of President Dwight D. Eisenhower as secretary of Commerce from 1953 to 1958. I located Mr. Brownell and when asked if he had any information pertaining to FDR's health, especially during Dewey's campaign, he replied that everyone was aware that Roosevelt was ill at that time; but neither he nor people he knew had direct information regarding FDR's condition.

Although it had nothing to do with Roosevelt's health, Mr. Brownell mentioned one particular episode concerning FDR and Dewey that I found of extreme interest. Mr. Brownell said a letter arrived directly from the White House to Governor Dewey and on the envelope was written, "For the eyes only of Thomas E. Dewey." Mr. Brownell said he didn't ask Governor Dewey the contents of the letter, but after Roosevelt died and the Second World War had ended, Dewey told him what was in the letter. The message from Roosevelt stated that the United States was winning the war, which would probably end in Europe by early 1945. Following this victory over Germany, the major concern of the United States military command involved the tremendous losses that were considered inevitable when the United States invaded Japan. It was estimated that one million American casualties would result from the invasion. As has now been well documented, the United States Intelligence Service had access to the Japanese military codes during the war and was continuously intercepting Japanese military information during this time. Rumors had been circulating in Washington that the United States had broken the Japanese codes prior to the attack on Pearl Harbor and therefore should have been aware of the Japanese military plans for the assault. The political implications of this rumor during the presidential campaign in 1944, that FDR was aware of the impending attack on Pearl Harbor prior to the attack, were obvious.

In this letter, FDR told Dewey that under no condition could there be any discussion during the presidential campaign of the possibility that the U.S. Intelligence Service was aware of an impending attack on Pearl Harbor. This would have alerted the Japanese to the fact that we had broken their military codes, which had remained unchanged throughout the war. Roosevelt stressed to Dewey that if there were even a hint that the Japanese military codes had been breached, the Japanese would rectify the situation immediately and change the codes. The result would be a marked increase in the number of American casualties during the impending invasion of the Japanese homelands. Because of FDR's admonition, Dewey never raised the issue during the presidential campaign as to whether the United States had prior knowledge of the Pearl Harbor attack. (As will be shown later, FDR very likely had such knowledge.)

The search for additional information concerning FDR's health continued to evolve slowly. I received an interesting letter on December 14, 1979, from Edward E. Martin of Wellesley, Massachusetts, who was the brother of Congressman Joseph Martin of Massachusetts, the powerful Democrat who was the Speaker of the United States House of Representatives from 1940 to 1956:

> In the spring of 1953 (the day Stalin died), I was sitting at the head table at a physician and surgeon's dinner. My brother, speaker Joe Martin, was the main speaker. Next to me was Dr. Lahey and we talked at length during the dinner because the man on the other side of the doctor was continually smoking and you know the doctor's view on smoking.
>
> He told me about being on a team of doctors who examined President Roosevelt before he announced for a fourth term. He told me he told the President that he could not live through another term. Dr. Lahey said the President replied that he fooled the doctors before and would again. Mrs. Roosevelt wrote that no one ever told the President he would not live. It's very likely the President never told her of what he had been told.
>
> Incidentally, Dr. Lahey said he wrote up his findings and put them in a safe in the event he died before the President. He said he destroyed the papers after the President died.

This was my first indication that Dr. Lahey had documented his findings regarding Roosevelt's physical condition. Additional corroboration of such documentation came in a letter on June 26, 1986, from Dr. Irving Ariel of New York City, who was Dr. Pack's closest associate and the head of the Pack Medical Group following Pack's death in 1969. In describing FDR's condition, Dr. Ariel said:

> Pack and Lahey both swore to secrecy but Lahey told Pack that he had described the entire incident which was placed in a safe at the Lahey clinic to be opened only after both Roosevelt and he were already dead, I understand that the account was never found.

It now seemed evident that Dr. Lahey had made a record of Roosevelt's medical condition and had made plans to safeguard the report.

Next, I tried to learn if Roosevelt had ever been in Boston for medical evaluation or treatment, a rumor which was prevalent in Washington in 1944. I received a letter from a Mrs. Jan Gilbert Stern who claimed that FDR came to Boston during 1944, allegedly for medical reasons. She based this on information she received from a nurse from one of the major Boston hospitals who told her that after the presidential election in 1944, Roosevelt was brought to Boston at night in a railroad car that was put off in an out-of-the-way place, after which FDR was driven to a local hospital. The nurse said FDR had a malignant tumor. Mrs. Stern's letter further stated:

> [T]he fact that the railroad car was where the nurse said it had been was verified to me by some friends who were employed by the railroad company where they were in a position to know the whereabouts and presence of equipment.

I contacted Mrs. Stern, who told me whom I might contact for further information regarding FDR's travels to and from Boston. She did not know if the people to whom she was referring me were still alive, but I was fortunate to locate several. I had hoped to interview the assistant stationmaster at Boston's South Station during World War II, but after locating his family, I learned he had died. I was more fortunate, however, in locating a Mr. John Fine who had been the night agent for the Pullman Sleeping Company at the South Station in Boston from 1942 to 1948. He was very helpful. He said that sometime between 1942 and 1944, carpenters came to the South Station to erect wooden ramps to allow for FDR's wheelchair to move from his Pullman car to the railroad platform. He vividly recalled an incident where secret arrangements had been made to bring a certain Pullman car into South Station, and that sometime on the day of its arrival, all employees and passengers were cleared for a period of time from the station. This activity struck Mr. Fine as being quite unusual at that time since the war was in progress and there was constant activity at South Station. On the day following the arrival of this particular Pullman car, Fine said he had been told that FDR had come in the previous evening under strict security conditions. He was unaware of the reason for FDR's journey to Boston.

Based on Fine's information, I visited South Station to see if I could locate the records of private Pullman cars that had come in and out of South Station from 1942 to 1944, but Boston's South Station has been bought, sold, and renovated many times over the years following the war, and records of the station no longer exist.

I later located Mr. Mark Gorham who had been a baggage handler at the South Station in Boston in 1943 and was still working in that capacity. He claimed FDR had used the station during 1943 and 1944, but he didn't know the reason for the president's visits. Mr. Gorham then gave me the name of a Mr. George E. Slattery who had been the stationmaster at the South Station in Boston during World War II. Mr. Slattery was retired and living in Brockton, Massachusetts. I called him and he was very specific about FDR using the South Station during the war. He stated that the president's private railroad car, on entering the station, was placed at the end of a string of cars which were always routed to tracks 14, 15, or 16, at which location the president's car was uncoupled and brought to the platform adjacent to the wooden ramps that had been constructed to accommodate his wheelchair. Mr. Slattery tried to locate the carpenter for me, who had built the wooden ramps, but without success. Like Mr. Gorham, Slattery didn't know the reason for FDR's travels to Boston.

It now seemed certain that FDR had come to Boston in 1944; if his purpose in coming were for medical reasons, Dr. Lahey would have almost certainly been involved.

During this period of trying to establish FDR's presence in Boston, I received the following letter from W. W. Jeckell of Cincinnati, Ohio:

> I read the article in the *Time* issue (regarding my FDR paper) of December 17, 1979 and the details seemed to fit into information I learned in December of 1964. I wrote to the magazine on December 26, 1964 and told them I had an article I might write for them on President Roosevelt that might be of national interest. After some delay they wrote back rejecting it.
>
> I had attended a banquet with Oregon Governor Mark Hatfield as the main speaker. At our table of seven persons was a reputable Cincinnati

surgeon who told us about a contact he had with Roosevelt under secrecy in the operating room of a Boston hospital in December of 1944 and he mentioned Dr. Lahey as one of four other surgeons and himself who were present. The operation disclosed an inoperable case of cancer of the liver. He said they just sewed him back up.

He went on to say that an official, confidential report was at that time given by the doctors to the President's closest advisors warning that the cancer was creeping to the brain. You may recall Roosevelt prior to this date as having trouble coordinating his thoughts and he was stumbling over words with delay when he spoke. Truman in his book "Decision" wrote that FDR was "a spent man and that he knew Roosevelt was going to die."

The Cincinnati surgeon is still alive and has moved some place in Arizona. I believe I can get his address as his son here is a fraternity brother of mine. I do not know at this point whether it would be best for you to contact him directly after I got his address or for me to let him know that you want to talk to him? This surgeon firmly believes that Roosevelt's death was a suicide but that is another matter altogether.

I called Mr. Jeckell, who gave the name of the surgeon's son, who in turn gave me the telephone number of his father, Dr. George McClure, who was living in Sun City, Arizona. I immediately called Dr. McClure in Arizona and told him how I obtained his name. My notes of our conversation stated that he was cordial over the phone and seemed to be extremely alert. He said that in 1944, while a fellow in surgery at the Lahey Clinic, he knew that President Roosevelt was operated upon and had been found to have an abdominal malignancy. He was not sure whether the tumor originated in the liver or gallbladder. I asked him in which hospital FDR's surgery took place. He said he could not answer this because he was sworn to secrecy. When I asked who had asked for this secrecy, he mentioned Dr. Lahey and Dr. Richard Cattell, the surgeon who succeeded Dr. Lahey as the head of the Lahey Clinic. I asked who was in the operating room at the time FDR was allegedly operated upon, and he mentioned Drs. Lahey and Cattell; but he also thought Dr. Samuel Marshall, another internationally known Lahey Clinic surgeon, was present. Dr. McClure wasn't certain, but he thought the operation took place during the first or second week in December of 1944. He claimed that FDR apparently had been brought to Boston in great secrecy.

Dr. McClure stated he could not continue to talk to me over the telephone because he had to maintain "secrecy." However, he claimed that this secrecy regarding FDR had been broken in the early part of the 1950s when Dr. James Poppen, a former chief of Neurosurgery at the Lahey Clinic, allegedly gave an interview to the *Cincinnati Inquirer* with the details I had just heard from Dr. McClure. Dr. McClure further stated that many years earlier, Westbrook Pegler, the well-known news columnist, came to his office with Dr. Poppen's story that he had read in the *Cincinnati Inquirer*, asking if it were true. Dr. McClure said he confirmed the story but refused to sign a paper to this effect when requested to do so by Pegler. Because of the important implications of what I had just heard, I asked Dr. McClure if I might fly to Arizona to discuss the FDR matter with him, to which he agreed.

Before flying to Sun City, I tried to track down the story regarding Dr. Poppen and the *Cincinnati Inquirer* but was unsuccessful. I therefore called Dr. Poppen's home and had a delightful conversation with Mrs. Poppen, at which time I mentioned to her that I was aware of the loss of her highly respected husband approximately a year earlier. I told her of my conversation with Dr. McClure regarding the possibility that Dr. Poppen had given an interview to a reporter regarding Dr. Lahey's medical relationship with FDR. Mrs. Poppen said she was unaware of such an interview. She did mention, however, that her husband and Dr. Lahey were very close, both professionally and socially, and there were many occasions when the Poppens and the Laheys would have a quiet dinner together at one or the other's home.

Mrs. Poppen recalled that Dr. Lahey had a dislike for Dr. McIntire because Dr. Lahey felt that McIntire had not informed FDR as to what was medically in his best interest. I told Mrs. Poppen that I had received a letter from Edward Martin stating that Dr. Lahey had kept a record of Roosevelt's health in his safe but had eventually destroyed the papers. Mrs. Poppen felt this was unlike Dr. Lahey who, she believed, would only destroy such a document if he had guilt feelings or because of a previous commitment. She said, however, that during a dinner at her home one evening, she vividly recalled Dr. Lahey stating that he was asked to see FDR in consultation with several other doctors; they were asked to write their opinions concerning the president's health and his chances of surviving a fourth term. They placed these opinions in a sealed envelope. Mrs. Poppen was not sure to whom this sealed envelope was given or if a copy of this report was kept in Dr. Lahey's safe.

Shortly after my conversation with Mrs. Poppen, I flew to Arizona to interview Dr. McClure. My plane landed in Phoenix and I took a bus to Sun City. When I arrived at the bus terminal, Dr. McClure was waiting for me in his automobile. He was very pleasant and immediately drove me to his home. After I met his wife, we picked up where we had left off in our previous telephone conversation. He repeated his story that FDR had a malignancy, was in Boston for it, and received treatment at the Lahey Clinic. However, when I questioned him for specific details, it quickly became apparent that he was not present in the operating room when FDR was allegedly operated upon, and his information was not first-hand. When it became apparent that I could not use Dr. McClure as a primary source regarding Roosevelt's medical condition, the conversation easily and pleasantly ended. I flew home—disappointed, to say the least.

I continued to try to establish that FDR had been at the Lahey Clinic in Boston for medical treatment or at least for medical advice. Even though I had failed to do this with Dr. McClure, letters continued to arrive that suggested such an event or events had occurred. One such letter arrived from an old acquaintance, Dr. William H. Remine, an internationally known surgeon at the Mayo Clinic. In this letter, Dr. Remine said:

> A number of years ago I had heard through a friend of mine who might be of help to you if you wish to pursue this further. His name is Dr. Tom Alm, a surgeon whom I worked with while I was in the service in World War II. I don't know where he is at the present time but he did practice at the Lahey Clinic when Roosevelt was a patient there and he on several occasions alluded to the fact that Roosevelt had a malignant process but never came forth with any details.

I tracked down Dr. Aim's family in Sand Point, Idaho, and learned Dr. Alm had died several years earlier. Mrs. Alm said she had never heard her husband mention the health of Franklin D. Roosevelt.

One of the most interesting leads I received, which further increased my belief that Roosevelt had visited Boston for medical reasons, was based on information supplied by Dr. Rutledge W. Howard of Evanston, Illinois. Dr. Howard had been a young resident surgeon in Boston at the Peter Bent Brigham Hospital during the latter part of World War II. He contacted me and offered information over the telephone regarding FDR, which he confirmed with the following undated letter:

> My recollection of FDR's visit to the Deaconess Hospital (a Harvard teaching hospital which is close to the Peter Bent Brigham Hospital) is as follows: In the winter of 43–44, the weather was cold but it was a clear night with no snow on the ground. I lived at 306 Riverway in a rear apartment facing Deaconess Road. My apartment was on the third floor and was directly next to the rear entrance of the Boston Deaconess Hospital. I was employed as a House Officer at the Peter Bent Brigham Hospital (assistant resident and Harvey Cushing Fellow) at the time. Having returned late in the evening from the Peter Bent Brigham to my apartment, I heard the sound of automobiles on Deaconess Road and looked

out to see three long black sedans (they looked like Cadillacs) stopping at the rear entrance of the Deaconess Hospital. Several men got out of the first and third cars and a driver got out of the middle car to open the curb-side rear door of the car. Then quickly with no awkwardness, two men brought out a wheelchair, spread it open and helped a gray-haired man in a sitting position into the wheelchair. The man in the wheelchair put his fedora on and put a cigarette holder in his mouth. The lighted rear entrance to the Deaconess Hospital gave good light to the scene. The man in the wheelchair looked like FDR or a double. The next move was to enter the Deaconess. The next morning at the Peter Bent Brigham Hospital, several of the house staff talked of FDR at the Deaconess but none of us knew who was attending him. We simply knew the Deaconess for two principal medical qualities; it had one of the best cancer patholo-gists (Shields Warren) and what we believed to be the best diabetic clinic (Elliot P. Joslin) and one economic quality (it never needed help from the United Fund).

A dear friend of mine at the Brigham (Robert F. Myers) had a relative on the city desk at the (Boston *Herald Traveler*) newspaper who told him a few days later that they had a story on the city desk which they could not use: FDR had a malignancy.

Because we were still at war and because we as house staff, felt our knowledge of FDR's visit to the Deaconess might hurt domestic morale and possibly help our active and potential adversaries, none of us gossiped or spoke publicly on the matter. I do know that I saw a person, who looked exactly like Franklin D. Roosevelt on that cold clear night on Deaconess Road, enter the rear door of the place in a wheelchair. I do not know the exact date in the winter of '43–'44.

In a follow-up conversation with Dr. Howard, he said that the incident reported in his letter took place between 11:00 to 12:00 o'clock at night, that the three limousines he observed came from a left to right direction and that he was impressed that large floodlights over the rear entrance of the hospital were on since this was war time, and night lighting was highly irregular during that period. He also said that only 100 to 150 feet separated the window of his apart-ment from the rear entrance of the hospital.

From Dr. Howard's letter, there appeared a possibility that information regarding FDR might exist in the files of the New England Deaconess Hospital. I called an old friend, William V. McDermott, M.D., who at that time was chief of Surgery at the hospital and the Cheever Professor of Surgery at Harvard Medical School. I discussed with him my interest in FDR and read him Dr. Howard's letter. He told me he would look into the matter and requested that I send him my published paper on FDR. Within a short period of time I received the following letter from Dr. McDermott:

> Just a brief note to acknowledge the receipt of the fascinating material on Roosevelt. I am not sure what I can turn up for you but I am in the process of investigating this admission of Roosevelt to the Deaconess Hospital some time in the winter of 1943 to 1944. I will certainly communicate with you anything of interest which I turn up. It was good to hear from you and particularly interesting to read your fascinating article.

Several weeks later Dr. McDermott called to inform me that he had been unable to locate any information from the files of the Deaconess Hospital relating to FDR. This was not totally unexpected since FDR's medical report most likely would have been recorded under a fictitious name.

Although I had drawn a blank from the Deaconess Hospital files, there was something in Dr. Howard's letter on FDR that deserved further follow-up. In the letter he claimed a relative working at the City Desk of the Boston Herald Traveler newspaper had told a friend of his at the Peter Bent Brigham Hospital, that FDR had a malignancy. I thought this might prove to be an important lead.

The *Boston Herald Traveler* newspaper purchased the *Record-American* after World War II, and the name of the paper has changed over the years; presently it is called the *Boston Herald.* I visited their office and asked if there were any employees presently working at the paper who had been employed there from 1943 to 1945. There were none, but I was told that the former assistant city editor of the newspaper at that time, John Brooks, was retired and living in Wilmington, Massachusetts. I called Mr. Brooks and read Dr. Howard's letter to him pertaining to Roosevelt's alleged malignancy that had been mentioned by someone at his newspaper in 1943–1944. Brooks said he had never heard the story and could give me no information on the matter. He said there were many stories about Roosevelt at that time, many with which he was unfamiliar or had long forgotten. He added, however, that there were many reports on FDR that had passed over his desk but were never published for a variety of reasons. He also said that his newspaper almost broke the press corps's unwritten rule of silence concerning FDR's paralysis. According to Brooks, when FDR visited Boston during the presidential campaign in 1944, he occasionally used his son James's apartment on Commonwealth Avenue. It was on the first floor, street level, with a back entrance that faced toward the Charles River on a lower level. This arrangement allowed the president to be brought to the back entrance of the apartment, unseen from the street, and carried up to his son's first-floor apartment. Someone at the *Record-American* newspaper had a friend who lived in the building in an apartment that had a window directly above the back entrance of the building. The newspaper sent a reporter, John Riley, and a cameraman, Donald Robinson, to go to this apartment and wait for Roosevelt to be carried in with the hope that a good picture might be obtained of the president. In the mid-1940s, a modified strobe light for a camera had been developed at the Massachusetts Institute of Technology, which generated an extremely strong light. Mr. Robinson, the cameraman, had one of these early strobe units that allowed pictures to be taken without much lighting. While he and Riley waited, FDR arrived at the back entrance of the building at dusk. He was lifted from the back seat of his car by Secret Service agents who then carried him to the rear entrance of the building. Robinson, sitting above in an apartment window, took a picture of FDR in this paralytic condition. The strobe light from his camera lit up the area, blinding the Secret Service agents. Within seconds, several of them raced up the stairs to the apartment, broke open the door with guns drawn, roughed up Riley and Robinson, and then took the film out of Robinson's camera. The agents were extremely agitated because it was obvious that if someone could take a picture of the president in this manner, they could just as easily have shot him.

After Mr. Brooks told me this story, he mentioned that Edward C. Holland, who had been the editor of the *Record American* during the war, was retired and living in Belmont, Massachusetts; he might have information on FDR's health. I called Mr. Holland, who remembered little about FDR's health. However, he also recalled vividly the story I had just been told by Mr. Brooks. Holland said there was more to the story than was known by Brooks. Holland said that when Robinson, the cameraman, realized that Secret Service agents were rushing up the stairs, he pulled the wooden frame from his camera in which the film was held and placed it underneath the living room couch and then put another frame back into the camera. When the Secret Service agents broke into the apartment, they pulled out the film holder from Robinson's camera and exposed the film that they believed held the picture of the president. After the agents left, Riley and Robinson want back to their newspaper offices with the film that had been hidden under the couch. It was immediately developed and the print given to Holland, who studied it with several associates. He said the picture was overexposed because of the strobe light and they couldn't use it.

Since FDR's physical condition was a major issue in the forthcoming 1944 election, and no picture of FDR in this helpless condition had ever been published, Holland and his associates felt that such a photograph could have had a direct effect on the election's outcome. He said if the picture had been technically better, he might have considered publishing it. But Robinson and Riley believed that the picture was not printed because of political pressure. Perhaps if the strobe unit on Robinson's camera had worked better that evening, the only known picture of the president being carried by aides might have been published.

I subsequently called James Roosevelt to tell him the story. He was fascinated by it and amazed that I knew of his apartment in Boston that his father had used on occasion.

CHAPTER 11

A MEDICAL HISTORIAN

One of the benefits of pursuing FDR's medical history was my introduction to Dr. Hugh L. L'Etang, the noted British medical historian.

After reading my FDR paper in *SG&O*, Dr. L'Etang, whom I had never met, wrote to tell of his longstanding fascination with FDR's health. More letters were exchanged as we explored our mutual interests in medical history. I was amazed one morning to receive a true gift of friendship—Dr. L'Etang's file on the health of FDR. Much of the material that he had accumulated over the years was known to me. However, the file contained several letters of interest. One was written by Dr. Teresa McGovern to Dr. L'Etang on June 29, 1973:

> I have your communication of June 11 at hand. I wish to state that I know the whole story of President Roosevelt's illnesses going back to 1941. I haven't had an opportunity of contacting the doctor who examined him, and incidentally, he is still alive, to ask whether I can divulge the information that I have.

I called Dr. McGovern, who practiced family medicine in California, and she gave me the name of the doctor she believed knew undisclosed facts of FDR's health: Dr. Harry Ungerleider, who was retired and living in Long Beach, California. Dr. Ungerleider had an unlisted phone number so I sent him a telegram that simply said, "Please call Dr. Harry Goldsmith collect at 603-643-5815."

My cryptic telegram quickly resulted in a telephone call from Dr. Ungerleider, at which time I explained my interest in Roosevelt and also how I had learned of him through Dr. McGovern. He became agitated as he talked about the personal difficulties he had encountered following his contact with FDR. As the medical director of the ETNA Life insurance company in the mid-1930s, he had examined FDR for an insurance policy. During the examination some medical problems (which he would not reveal to me) were uncovered and recorded in Roosevelt's medical chart. Ungerleider claimed that because he would not release FDR's medical records to government agents who requested them, the Federal Bureau of Investigation (FBI) began to harass him, and the Internal Revenue Service (IRS) instituted an investigation of his personal tax records. The pressure on him became so unbearable that he told me he personally burned Roosevelt's medical file. When I asked Dr. Ungerleider to send me written corroboration of these incidents, he refused. He was convinced that if his name became connected to any publication related to FDR's health, he might again attract the attention of the FBI and the IRS. He was certain that, inevitably, I too would be pressured by these governmental agencies, and he prevailed upon me to give up my study of FDR.

As our talk ended, I said I would send him my FDR paper, hoping that after reading it he might reconsider his decision to remain silent and make available to me the information he had on FDR's medical history. A few weeks later, on January 21, 1981, the following letter arrived from Dr. Ungerleider:

> Since your phone call, I have read and re-read your excellent article concerning the death of Franklin D. Roosevelt and I have been greatly impressed with the careful research you have pursued in this matter.
>
> However, since my involvement took place in 1935 and all materials relating to the incident are non-existent, I find it difficult to marshal any facts that would be accurate. Also, that your interest appears to be with the latter years of FDR's life, so any contribution of mine would have little relevance.
>
> Consequently, with great regret I cannot be of any help to you in your endeavors.

I thought it sad that an American citizen, a doctor in his eighties, was still fearful of intimidation by the United States Government.

Another pertinent letter I received from Dr. L'Etang was one that he had received on February 5, 1970, from Dr. Samuel M. Day, a general surgeon in Jacksonville, Florida:

> Recently I have read two reviews of your book, *The Pathology of Leadership* which must be a most interesting volume. The review by William B. Ober from "Medical Opinions and Review" commented on your evaluation of President Roosevelt's final illness and said "the evident weight loss, anorexia and cachexia could be equally consistent with

metastatic malignancy." This statement seemed to show deep perception in view of the story I will relate to you. I presume that President Roosevelt did die of a carcinoma. Apparently, the primary was in the stomach.

Many years ago the late Dr. George Pack of New York spent a night in my home after delivering a talk to a medical group. We had a long and interesting discussion about many things during the evening in the course of which he related the following story. Dr. Frank Lahey told Dr. Pack that in the summer before the election for Roosevelt's fourth term the President came to Boston by special train to be examined by Dr. Lahey at the Lahey Clinic. On completion of the examinations it was Dr. Lahey's opinion that President Roosevelt had an advanced cancer of the stomach, apparently too far advanced for a surgical cure to be considered. Dr. Lahey told the President of his diagnosis, told him he was gravely ill and should not run for a fourth term. The President replied that he was going to run for a fourth term so Dr. Lahey made the statement, "I suggest if you insist on running that you select a strong Vice Presidential candidate to run with you." With that Mr. Roosevelt returned to Washington and as far as I know nothing more was heard of the cancer. Dr. Pack wondered why Dr. Lahey had never revealed it and stated that later he asked the doctor why he had not made this information public. He stated that it was never to be revealed as long as any of the involved figures were still alive. Dr. Pack indicated that he even argued a little with Dr. Lahey about the fact that this was a public figure, and since he was dead there would be no harm in revealing these facts. Dr. Lahey would not hear of it.

Several years later after the death of Dr. Lahey, I again asked Dr. Pack about this story. He stated that he had discussed it with Dr. Catell [*sic*] who had succeeded Dr. Lahey in charge of the Clinic and he had asked Dr. Catell why they did not make this revelation. He stated that Dr. Catell was quite irritated with him for even bringing it up saying that it would never be told as long as any of them were alive. Apparently, Dr. Pack brought out that President Roosevelt, Mrs. Roosevelt and Dr. Lahey were dead and there was a certain obligation on the part of the Clinic to reveal this for history but Dr. Catell was adamant and would not hear of any further persuasion.

I realize this is a third party story and that I have absolutely no factual data to support it; however, it might give you the impetus to inquire further. Possibly, now that Dr. Catell is also dead, this information could be revealed. It does seem a pity that for an historic figure as famous as President Roosevelt, significant facts such as these are kept hidden.

It has been so many years since our discussion that I could not swear it was a cancer of the stomach. It may have been of some other organ, such as the lung, but I do not think so.

I hope to have the opportunity to read your book before too long. Congratulations on its success and, apparently, on its excellence.

Dr. L'Etang replied to Dr. Day, who then wrote another letter to Dr. L'Etang dated January 13, 1972:

Your interesting letter of January 9, 1972 has been received.

Apparently, the story about the visit to the Lahey Clinic and the conversation that followed was accurate but I'm not sure of the diagnosis of cancer. I mentioned this to Ken Warren who is now the Head Surgeon at Lahey, about a year ago, and he said that it was not cancer but he did not clarify what it was. I see no reason why you could not use the information that I gave you.

You might even write to Ken Warren (Kenneth Warren, M.D., Lahey Clinic, Boston, MA) and tell him of your interest and give him a brief resume of what you heard, stating that you would be factual and would appreciate it if he would clarify the diagnosis since there seems to be some confusion at that point. I wish I could be present and hear your presentation, I'm sure it will be interesting.

Dr. L'Etang must have contacted Dr. Kenneth Warren because Dr. Warren sent a letter to Dr. L'Etang on February 6, 1972:

I was intrigued by your letter regarding the late President Roosevelt. I'm sure that you are a sincere student of medical history and for this you should be congratulated.

I would suggest that you pursue the history of the late President Roosevelt's illness, but I would suggest that you do it through his family.

Realizing what a strong lead Dr. Day might prove to be, I contacted him in Jacksonville, Florida, and told him of my interest in FDR. I asked if he would send me any information he might have accumulated since his initial contact with Dr. L'Etang in the early 1970s. On May 8, 1981, I received the following letter from Dr. Day:

A few days ago I discovered a letter from George Pack dated, November 10, 1956, which was written following his participation in the Southern States Cancer Seminar here. I believe that this must have been the time that he first told me about President Roosevelt's visit to the Lahey Clinic and subsequent events regarding his last race for the presidency. Dr. Pack was here in 1949 and was my guest speaker at the annual meeting of the Florida Medical Association in Miami in 1965 during my term as president. I do not recall the exact dates of our discussions regarding FDR. I doubt that it was as early as '49 since he was not my guest then. In 1965 he told me of trying to get Lahey's successors to publish the information, and of the refusal of Dick Cattell in an almost insulting way when he was approached by Pack.

I think I told you, too, that I mentioned it to Ken Warren at dinner at a Southern Surgical Association meeting a few years later and received a negative reaction. I had thought I would find a copy of my letter to Lynn De Tang [*sic*] telling him the details of our conversation but thus far I have not found it. If I find it, I shall send it to you.

After reading Dr. Day's letter, I called Dr. Kenneth Warren, who was an internationally known American surgeon and emeritus chief of Surgery at the Lahey Clinic. In 1974 we spent several days together in Tehran as surgical consultants to an Iranian patient and it was, therefore, easy for me to call him to discuss Dr. Samuel Day's letter. Dr. Warren tried to be helpful but stated that he had no direct knowledge of Dr. Lahey's relationship with FDR. He did say that he had heard the rumor that Dr. Lahey told FDR he was a dying man and should not run for a fourth term because, even if elected, he would not survive his term in office.

CHAPTER 12

GOVERNMENT AGENCIES

Sometime during the latter part of 1978, I contacted the FBI in Washington, D.C., to request their help in obtaining information concerning FDR, which I told them could have important historical significance. Several such contacts were unproductive, and I felt forced to either give up the search or ask for other assistance.

William V. Roth, the former senior United States senator from Delaware, was a personal friend and supporter of my research work for many years. With his powerful senatorial position in Washington, he seemed the logical person to ask for assistance in trying to contact the FBI. I called him and asked if he might be able to arrange a contact for me at the FBI who might help in the Roosevelt search. Senator Roth, chairman of the Senate Investigating Committee at that time, explained that the FBI, in order to maintain Congressional goodwill for annual funding, assigns one of its agents to the "Hill" to assist members of Congress needing services provided by the FBI. He arranged a contact and shortly afterward an FBI agent called and said, "We heard from Senator Roth's office and how can we be of help to you?" I told him what I wanted and within a reasonable period of time received a package of non-classified FBI material regarding Roosevelt's health. The information was sparse; more information from the FBI was necessary to continue the FDR search. On May 25, 1979, I decided to write directly to William Webster, director of the FBI:

> I am presently doing research on the health of Franklin D. Roosevelt during the last year of his life. I would appreciate it if you would gather information for me concerning any health matters in your records regarding President Roosevelt between November, 1943 and the death of the President in April, 1945.

I have spoken to Mr. Emil Moschella of the Federal Bureau of Investigation and he has informed me that you will assist me in this matter.

Although I did not expect Mr. Webster to become directly involved, I did assume he would assign my request to a subordinate. On June 11, 1979, I received a printed form from David G. Flanders, the FBI chief of the Freedom of Information-Privacy Act Branch and Record Management Division. The form simply acknowledged receipt of my Freedom of Information-Privacy Act (FOIPA) request; it stated that the FBI would search their records and I would hear from them at the earliest possible date. Two months later (August 13, 1979), I received another letter from Mr. Flanders:

> This is in further response to your Freedom of Information-Privacy Acts (FOIPA) request concerning the health of Franklin D. Roosevelt during the years 1943–1945.
>
> A preliminary review of the index throughout our central records system discloses references pertaining to President Roosevelt during the time period you have requested. These references consist of approximately 28,600 pages. *In order for us to locate the specific documents pertaining to the health of President Roosevelt, should they exist, the entire 28,600 pages have to be reviewed.* [Author's emphasis.] There's a clerical search fee of $8.00 an hour for searching the material you seek.

I telephoned the FBI to begin the search and on January 10, 1980, received a third letter from Mr. Flanders:

> This is to refer to my letter to you dated August 13, 1979 and telephone conversation between yourself and supervisor David M. Cook of this Branch on January 9, 1980.
>
> On January 9, 1980 you were advised that our records concerning the late President Franklin D. Roosevelt between the period November 1943 and April 1945, reflect approximately 28,600 pages of documents. *It is unknown to us at this time, without a search of those records, if there are any medical records of the President or any investigation pertaining to his health contained within those documents.* [Author's emphasis.] Since you have telephonically agreed to pay reasonable search fees at $8 per hour to locate the specific documents, we will begin a review of those documents forthwith.

On January 25, 1980, I answered Mr. Flander's latest letter:

I am responding to your recent letter in which you inform me that the FBI has begun a search for me on the health of Franklin D. Roosevelt during the years 1943 through 1945.

I am enclosing an article that I wrote pertaining to Roosevelt's death. I would appreciate it if you could forward this to Mr. Cook in your department, who told me over the phone that he would give my paper to the analyst who is working on the material in which I have interest. *I also would like to request, if it is permissible, the name of the analyst who is looking at this information so that I might have the opportunity to talk to him so that he has a better understanding of the material which I seek.* [Author's emphasis.]

I was pleased that the FBI had so much information about FDR, but was disturbed that the agency planned to have these records reviewed by a non-medical person with little or no knowledge of what I was searching for and no awareness of FDR's medical condition. I called the FBI to discuss the matter. I never mentioned the eight dollars per hour they were asking to review 28,600 pages, which could have been prohibitively expensive. I felt that if I brought this matter up, the FBI might have used it as an excuse to further delay the search of FDR's file. I also believed that once the record search began, the FBI would not review the entire 28,600 pages prior to billing me, thereby giving me the chance to stop their search any time I felt no progress was being made.

I heard nothing from the FBI for almost a year, other than a few telephone calls that I initiated. Over this period I began to conclude the FBI was not going to come up with the kind of information I sought. I knew they handled many requests for Freedom of Information searches, and my request was probably of very low priority. There was also the probability that a lay person, searching a large amount of medical data, would not know what to look for and, even more important, would fail to appreciate the significance of information that might be missing in a physical examination or a medical report. These concerns no longer were relevant after receiving a letter on January 9, 1981, from Thomas H. Bresson, the newly appointed chief of the Freedom of Information-Privacy Acts Branch and Records Management Division at the FBI.

Mr. Bresson confirmed a telephone conversation I had had with Special Agent David H. Cook concerning the FDR search. Of major importance was the statement, "The search for medical records pertaining to President Franklin D. Roosevelt was completed." He added:

As advised no documents were located relating to the specific information you requested. The searching time involved was 32 hours with a total cost of $127.00 representing a cost of $4.00 an hour after the first quarter hour, which is free.

You may submit your check or money order in the amount of $ 127.00 payable to the Federal Bureau of Investigation to pay clerical search fees.

It appeared from the tone of this letter that the FBI believed they had completed my request with an extremely limited amount of search time. I was not satisfied; no details were produced to assure me that the request was even carried out, let alone conducted by someone with the necessary medical skills to investigate the material. I contacted Peter J. DesMeules, a friend and lawyer in Norwich, Vermont, who suggested that legal pressure through the Freedom of Information Act (FOIA) might cause the FBI to take my request more seriously. On August 3, 1981, Mr. DesMeules contacted the FBI for the first time:

Dear Mr. Bresson;

The law firm of Brownell, Hoyt and Brooks, of Norwich, Vermont, has been retained by Harry S. Goldsmith, M.D., of Hanover, New Hampshire, to represent him in his efforts to obtain from the Federal Government copies of certain documents under the Freedom of information-Privacy Act (FOIPA).

This letter is a formal request on behalf of my client that you produce certain documents for inspection and copying viz; any and all documents in your agency's custody, including but not limited to all medical records, where ever located, pertaining to or in connection with President Franklin Delano Roosevelt.

Access to such documents is required by Dr. Goldsmith to enable him to further his research and to complete his writings.

By your letter to Dr. Goldsmith of January 9, 1981 and in prior telephone conversations with my client, your agency has acknowledged the existence in your files of documents pertaining to President Roosevelt. [Author's emphasis.]

As you well know, my client is entitled, pursuant to 5, U.S.C., Section 522(a), to access to the requested documents to allow him to inspect and copy the same.

I will look forward to hearing from you within the statutory time limit provided for your response so that a suitable time and place might be arranged for my client to inspect and copy the requested documents.

On August 17, 1981, Mr. DesMeules received a letter from James K. Hall, the new chief of the Freedom of Information-Privacy Act Section and Records Management Division of the FBI:

> We shall continue our efforts to locate documents which are pertinent to Dr. Goldsmith's request. As was discussed with you by Agent Smith, any information which Dr. Goldsmith could furnish, such as names of the late President's physicians, could possibly assist us in locating material which your client desires, but which might not surface in the search off our central index system under the late President's name.

Two days later (August 19, 1981) Mr. DesMeules wrote a letter to Mr. Hall of the FBI with attention to Donald L. Smith, the special FBI agent who had been assigned to my Roosevelt project:

> This letter is a formal request on behalf of my client for copies of all documents in File #62–6894 titled "Rumors Regarding the Health of the President (1944)."
>
> As we discussed, it appears that all documents in this file, with the exception of Hoover's Memorandum to Early titled "Re: Circulation of Story Alleging the President has a Serious Affliction", would be of interest to the doctor in the furtherance of his ongoing research into the circumstances leading to the death of President Franklin Delano Roosevelt.
>
> This letter also represents a formal request for any and all information in your files regarding Dr. Frank H. Lahey, Chairman of War Procurement during World War II, Dr. James A. Paullin, Vice-Admiral Ross T. McIntyre [*sic*], White House Physician, and Dr. Howard G. Bruenn, relating in any way to the health or medical condition of President Roosevelt in the 1940's.

After waiting a month, Mr. DesMeules received the following letter on September 21, 1981, from James K. Hall, chief of the FOIA section:

> This is in response to your Freedom of Information-Privacy Act (FOIPA) request regarding medical records concerning the late President, Franklin Delano Roosevelt.
>
> *Documents which appear responsive to your request have been located and will be assigned for processing in the near future.* [Author's emphasis.]
>
> For your information, as a result of the large number of FOIPA requests received by the FBI, some delay may be encountered in processing

your request. You may be assured that the FBI has allocated substantial resources, including manpower, to insure that delays in responding to FOIPA requests are minimized. We solicit your patience and understanding and assure you that your request will be processed as soon as possible.

After waiting another month without hearing from the FBI, Mr. DesMeules again wrote the Agency (October 20, 1981):

This letter is in response to yours of September 21, 1981 in connection with the above-captioned matter.

Although I can appreciate your backlog of Freedom of Information-Privacy Acts requests, I feel, in fairness to my client, that I must be provided with a realistic timetable from you. *I am sure you can appreciate my unwillingness to sit and wait for a substantive response from your department indefinitely, especially insofar as Dr. Goldsmith, when dealing directly with your department, was waiting for as long as a year, only to be told that no documents were available pursuant to his request.* [Author's emphasis.]

Hopefully, your prompt response will be forthcoming and no further action will be necessary from this office.

Your assistance in this matter is greatly appreciated.

On December 21, 1981, Mr. DesMeules again wrote Donald L. Smith, the special agent for the FBI in their Records Management Division and James Hall, the chief of that section:

Dear Messrs Hall and Smith:

By my cover letter of August 19, 1981, I formally requested on behalf of my client, Dr. Harry S. Goldsmith, all information in your files regarding Dr. Frank H. Lahey, Chairman of War Procurement during World War II, Dr. James A. Paullin, Vice-Admiral Ross T. McIntire, White House Physician, and Dr. Howard G. Bruenn relating in any way to the health and medical condition of President Roosevelt in the 1940's.

On November 25, 1981, we received copies of documents in file #62–76894, titled "Rumors Regarding the Health of the President" (1944). We did not however, receive the information in your files regarding the individuals whose names are listed above, relating in any way to the health and medical condition of President Roosevelt.

This information is particularly important to us, and I would request you forward the same as soon as possible.

Your prompt response to this request would be greatly appreciated.

Nothing further was heard from the FBI until February 12, 1982, at which time Mr. DesMeules received the following letter from Mr. Hall:

Reference is made to your letter dated December 21, 1981, wherein you requested information regarding Dr. Frank H. Lahey, Dr. James Paullin, Vice Admiral Ross T. McIntyre, and Dr. Howard G. Bruenn, relating in any way to the health and medical condition of President Roosevelt in the 1940's.

A search of the indices to our central records system at FBI Headquarters reveals no information other than what was processed for release in file #62–76894, titled "Rumors Regarding the Health of the President," and sent to you by our letter dated November 25, 1981.

This letter from the FBI prompted Mr. DesMeules to write me the following letter on February 16, 1982:

Enclosed is a copy of the FBI's no-response to our many requests in connection with the above-captioned matter.

Obviously, the FBI is unwilling, without further prodding, to afford us any help whatsoever.

Please advise if you wish me to pursue this matter. Perhaps Senator Roth could now be apprised of our progress and his influence brought to bear.

I tried one last time to get information from the United States Secret Service and the FBI. Each of these governmental agencies has a periodic newsletter that is distributed to all agents, including those who are retired. I requested editors of these newsletters to place items in each of their publications asking any former Secret Service or FBI agent for any personal experience or information regarding FDR's health. No response was received from the Secret Service newsletter, but on June 27, 1983, I received the following letter from a former member of the FBI:

Dear Dr. Goldsmith:

This letter responds to a news item entitled "Dartmouth Surgeon Seeking FDR Health Data" which appeared in the May, 1983 issue of the Grapevine, the official organ of the Society of Former Special Agents of the FBI. No doubt you are aware of the existence and content of that item.

A friend and I have some information which may be of use to you. As Special Agents of the FBI in 1944 we participated directly, as ordered officially, in what proved to be an attempt to prevent the information on FDR's circulatory disease from becoming public knowledge. We will readily divulge this information to you but only on certain conditions. First, we would like the information used in such a way that neither of us can plausibly be accused of seeking personal publicity. We already have had all the personal publicity that we ever shall need except, of course, for a couple of nice, long obituaries. My friend reached the executive level in the FBI, retired under honorable conditions and then served until his second retirement in an executive position connected with an automobile company that is a household name. I served longer in the FBI, became Assistant Director and Legal Counsel and served in that capacity under Hoover and for some eight months or so under Pat Gray, Hoover's successor, until I retired.

We also do not wish to participate in any form of political scandal mongering. Regardless of any differences or similarities in our personal politics, we are in agreement that FDR now belongs "to the Ages" and that he should be left there beyond partisan political bickering. Yet, we know that the knowledge that we have could be viewed by competent historians, medical and otherwise, as a fascinating bit of American history, and we would like to deliver it up for such use if we can do so without becoming embroiled in a "dogfight" of any kind.

Would you kindly give us your views on the positions that I have staked out here? If you wish to so respond, send your reply to Mr. Andrew M. Dinsmore, 302 Draw Park Drive, Lake Charles, LA 70601 and to me at the address shown above. After receipt of your reply we shall give consideration to sending you an account of what happened in this case, to the limit of the facts that we know.

Dwight J. Dalbey

I immediately replied:

Just a short note to thank you for writing to me regarding Franklin Delano Roosevelt.

I am enclosing an article I have written about FDR which I hope you will find of interest since a portion of the material pertains to FBI investigations.

I attempted to telephone Mr. Dinsmore today but I could not reach him so I shall try again tomorrow. I hope that both of you will see by this paper that my interest in Roosevelt is that of a medical historian rather than somebody who is attempting to cause political unrest and/or speculation.

As I mentioned over the phone, any information pertaining to FDR is of great interest to me. Your comments would eventually be incorporated into my next paper on Roosevelt and all this material will one day be of historical importance long after we are gone. Again, thank you so such for your kindness.

I finally reached Mr. Dinsmore by phone and on July 14, 1983, wrote him the following letter:

I certainly enjoyed talking with you this morning. It was a pleasure to receive Mr. Dalbey's letter yesterday and to make contact with both of you.

Enclosed you will find my paper on Roosevelt. I trust it will be of interest to you. I have also sent a copy of this paper to Mr. Dalbey. I hope that after both of you have reviewed it, your memories on issues pertaining to FDR will be rejuvenated.

After Mr. Dalbey and Mr. Dinsmore received my letters and the FDR paper that I had written, they spoke to each other over the phone and apparently felt that my interest in President Roosevelt was sincere. On August 19, 1983, I received the following letter from Mr. Dalbey:

Thank you for sending me a copy of your article entitled "Unanswered Mysteries in the Death of Franklin D. Roosevelt."

I read it with uncommon interest because of my own minor participation in one of those mysteries.

Your article convinces me that a long report on the part that I played in suppressing the information concerning President Roosevelt's cardiovascular condition in 1944 is unnecessary. The basic facts already are in your possession. The quoted part in your article of Director Hoover's FBI memorandum to Stephen Early leaves no doubt in my mind that the preceding and unquoted part of the FBI memorandum gives a fair summary of the interview conducted in the Mayo Brothers Hospitals at Rochester, Minnesota. Mr. Dinsmore and I did nothing in the case other than conduct that interview, concerning which I shall here add a few details which may be pertinent or of interest to you for other reasons.

At the time of this interview Andrew M. Dinsmore and I were special Agents in the St. Paul, Minn. office of the FBI which was responsible for FBI work in Minnesota, North Dakota and South Dakota. The top authority of that office was exercised at that moment by veteran Special Agent Ed Notesteen (now deceased) in the absence of the official Special Agent in Charge, one "Dusty" Rhodes (deceased) and his Assistant Special Agent in Charge, both absent on other business.

The time was a morning late in *October, 1944*. Mr. Dinsmore and I were summoned to Notesteen's office. Notesteen said he had just had an urgent telephone call from Mr. Clyde Tolson (deceased), Associate Director of the FBI and second in command, in which Mr. Tolson said a false rumor is being spread to the effect that President Roosevelt has "heart trouble". Further, that a Dr. Barnes, a heart specialist at Mayo Brothers Hospital had been circulating the rumor, and that "The White House" wants these rumors tracked down and stopped. Tolson instructed Notesteen to send two "mature and experienced" Special Agents to interview Dr. Barnes immediately. Notesteen designated Dinsmore as the lead Agent, and Dinsmore chose me to assist him.

Interviewed later that day at the Mayo Brothers Hospitals, Dr Barnes soon stated that he recently had heard that President Roosevelt had cardiovascular trouble. He believed the report to be true, he said, because a certain heart specialist, whom he named but whose name I do not remember, recently had been seen as a member of the entourage during the President's public appearances. That doctor, Dr. Barnes said, had no known reason to be present other than to use his skills should they be needed.

Dr. Barnes denied circulating the rumor about the President's illness. Moreover, he was reluctant to name his sources claiming that he was ethically bound to silence. After much persuasion he relented, yielding to the argument that should this rumor be widely spread at home and abroad the result might be a detrimental effect on the morale of our own people and an encouragement to the enemy which might prolong the war at the cost of much human life and treasure. He named as his source a young doctor or surgeon then a member of the staff at the National Naval Medical Hospital in Bethesda, Maryland. I do not remember his name but later that evening my wife, who only a few years earlier had graduated from the Kahler School of Nursing in Rochester, said her memory was that the young man was a protégé of Dr. Barnes.

On our return to St. Paul that afternoon we officially reported the details and the results of our interview to FBI headquarters in Washington, D.C. Someone there dispatched two more "mature and experienced Agents" whose names I never learned, to interview the doctor at the National Naval Medical Center. I heard that those Agents came up with what the petroleum people call a "dry hole". St. Paul took no other investigative action.

May I here emphasize certain points? First, we did believe the rumor to be false. Those who speak from the certainty of hindsight may believe our belief to have been naive. Not at all. President Roosevelt, having been highly controversial in many ways, had long been the subject of rumors, some of them almost vicious in nature. It was logical enough to believe, also, that when Mr. Tolson characterized the rumor as "false" that it was false indeed. We were not privy, of course, to such contrary information if any, that Director Hoover and a few others in the top echelon of the FBI may have had.

Second, in the single telephone conversation that Mr. Dinsmore and I have had to refresh our memories we have had some slight disagreements over names. Mr. Dinsmore remembers the name of a Dr. Dixon as having come up in this episode. I do not. It is not necessary to dispute the matter. I am sure that the name of the doctor whom we interviewed is shown in your copy of the Hoover to Early memorandum. If it was Dr. Barnes, then who was Dr. Dixon? Was he the doctor seen in President Roosevelt's personal appearances? Hoping to clear this point up I called Dr. Clifton Skinner, head of the Skinner Clinic in San Antonio, Texas whom I have long known. Dr. Skinner was a Fellow or whatever it is that you call such folks at Mayo for a time prior to establishing his own practice in 1940. He remembers Dr. Barnes as an internist specializing in cardiovascular disease and also remembers a Mayo doctor named Dr. Dixon who was a rather large, bluff and red haired man who was a specialist in surgery of the colon. Incidentally, or otherwise, Dr. Skinner also remembers if I have my facts straight, that President Roosevelt spent a bit of time at Mayo in 1938 when his son Elliot, I think, was being treated there and that at that time President Roosevelt suffered a stroke. You may wish to discuss this matter with Dr. Skinner; if you do so you may use my name to introduce the matter.

Third, I take friendly issue with the statement in your article that "Incredibly, Doctor *CENSORED* was again interrogated without any additional information being gathered." Assuming the usual weaknesses of human resolve, it is the opposite result that would have been incredible. The doctor was in the Navy under Navy discipline, and a Navy strongly dominated by the President. Need I say more? Perhaps discretion suggested that his patron saint should be Hippocrates, not commonly made by all manner of man (and women).

A copy of this letter is being sent to Mr. Dinsmore who will, I trust, advise you of his disagreement, if any. If I have left any pertinent question unanswered, please advise. And thanks again for answering a question of our own; I had never seen a written report of the results of the FBI inquiry in Bethesda.

Dwight J. Dalbey

With this final piece of information from an FBI agent, I felt there was little to be gained in pressing the FBI further for information regarding FDR other than through litigation under the Freedom of Information Act, an action I did not wish to pursue. The prohibitive expenses and loss of time required for such an undertaking would in no way ensure that the FBI would release further information other than what I had already obtained. Additionally, I had never been involved in any lawsuit and the thought of doing so was not appealing. My long effort to gain medical information from the FBI concerning FDR's health had come to an end.

CHAPTER 13

PROSTATE CANCER

I raised the question in my medical publication in *SG&O* in 1979 that the pigmented lesion over FDR's left eye might have been a malignant melanoma, which could have accounted for the physical deterioration that occurred during his final year. Sequential pictures in Stephen Laurant's book, *The Glorious Burden*, were the seed for this idea. (see page 26) However, with no medical records of FDR to examine and little information to further suggest that he had a melanoma, the melanoma idea became unsupportable.[1] However, what became increasingly possible, from continuing research, was that FDR suffered from a slow-growing prostatic malignancy.

The first suggestion that FDR had prostate cancer came from Dr. Kiely of Long Beach, California, who recalled in his earlier letter to me that Dr. Lahey told FDR he had "metastatic carcinoma primary in the prostate." This statement was later reinforced by information from the FBI. I received a copy of a letter from them that was sent on November 10, 1944 to the city editor of the *Chicago World American*. Several days later, on November 14, 1944, this letter was referred to a Mr. S. J. Drayton, head of the FBI in Chicago. Drayton then sent the letter to Director J. Edgar Hoover of the FBI who in turn sent the letter on November 29th to Mr. Frank J. Wilson, chief of the U.S. Secret Service Division. The letter originated in Chicago and was signed only with the initials A.A.C.:

Dear Sir:

Were we greatly deceived or is this not true?

---

1. It is of interest that I have been quoted as saying FDR had a melanoma. I never said and do not believe that FDR had melanoma. I have also been quoted as saying FDR had gastric cancer. This is another statement that has been wrongly attributed to me and is not factual.

It is reliably told to us that the President will be operated on for *cancer of the prostate gland* on the 15 of November 1944.

Perhaps he was not told of his serious condition?

Perhaps the political bosses, his intimates and close ones did not advise him?

Perhaps he was used by certain people to put over the ticket, knowing they could not win without his selecting a man to run with him that they can handle?

If the above information is true, it should be made public before the meeting of the electors, and a careful eye should be placed on the secretary of the state job.

Perhaps God blessed Dewey, he is lucky or else.

The Times, The Sun, and the other newspapers of the inner circle are a party to this greatest of all deceit, dishonesty if that is true, and if true, Churchill with his talk of a meeting in Paris done so with the intention of deceiving the American people that the President was needed there for war, for peace, and that he was very able to make such a trip.

Perhaps without the President knowing the facts, the American people have been deceived dishonestly and led down the river?

Please check on these matters at once and advise the country promptly. America is BIG enough to take anything, if these reports are true tell the American people the truth and tell it to them now. That is the only fair way. The reaction to any covering up of this matter, if true, will be worse than not having the facts now.

A.A.C"

The above letter was discussed in letters between the FBI and the Secret Service indicating that they knew the identity of A.A.C., but in the copies of the letters that I received from the FBI, the identity of A.A.C. was censored.

Another letter that alluded to the possibility that FDR had a malignant tumor of the prostate was sent on June 2, 1945 from W.G. Bannister, chief of the Secret Service office in Butte, Montana, to J. Edgar Hoover of the FBI. The letter was underlined "Personal and Confidential." The copy I received from the FBI was censored:

Information has been received by the writer to the effect that *CENSORED* received a telephone call from someone in New York some time prior to the last Presidential election, requesting that he make a news release or publish an item to the effect that Pres. Roosevelt would not be a candidate for a fourth term. The person calling, apparently connected with the publishing industry and well acquainted with *CENSORED* advised that the basis for this was a physical examination given President Roosevelt by his physicians, at which time it was discovered that *he was suffering from a cancer of the prostate gland* and that if he continued in office, he probably would not live more than one year.

The person calling said that it was desired to have this item released from some small place far away from the East rather than have it come out of New York City or any of the large centers of population.

CENSORED made a release or published the item and was, as described, "left out on the limb." *CENSORED* recently returned from New York and the rumors are now circulating that President Roosevelt's mind was affected and he made so many commitments at Yalta that neither President Truman nor anyone else knows exactly what commitments were made and that this is the reason so much trouble is being encountered with the Russians at the present time.

The writer noticed recently a newspaper columnist's report to the effect that Premier Stalin assigned a young physician to President Roosevelt as an attendant in some minor capacity. President Roosevelt was observed during the Yalta Conference and this physician reported to Stalin that President Roosevelt was a sick man and probably would not live out the next term of office.

This letter to J. Edgar Hoover, from FBI agent Bannister, was written six weeks after the death of FDR. Prior to this event, there is an article in the March 3, 1945, issue of *Colliers* magazine, which claimed Roosevelt was suffering from prostatic cancer. During my research on FDR, I remember hearing or reading, but do not recall the source, that Mrs. Roosevelt allegedly had told actresses Gypsy Rose Lee and Veronica Lake that FDR was suffering from cancer of the prostate. Although unsuccessful in finding evidence of such a conversation between Gypsy Rose Lee and Mrs. Roosevelt regarding FDR and prostate cancer, I was successful in establishing such a conversation between Veronica Lake and Mrs. Roosevelt.

Veronica Lake was a popular movie star during World War II and was well known for the way her long blond hair swept across the left side of her face, a hairstyle that became known as the "Veronica Lake Look." Miss Lake attended a birthday party for FDR held in the White House in January, 1945, during which several movie stars were present. The party included Veronica Lake, Joe E. Brown, Gene Kelly, Jane Wyman, Danny Kaye, Alan Ladd, and Victor Borge. The president, although unable to attend this White House party, had arranged it to show his appreciation to the celebrities who had raised a great deal of money for his favorite charity, the Infantile Paralysis Foundation.

In the book *Veronica*, by Veronica Lake with Donald Bain (London: W. H. Allen, 1969, page 132), Miss Lake alludes to this party where at the time she saw a particular spoon she liked. She asked Mrs. Roosevelt if she might have it as a souvenir. The following is an excerpt regarding the occasion:

> Mrs. Roosevelt said to me, "I want you to know Miss Lake, that I was very happy to give you that spoon. I was happy because you asked me for it. Most people wouldn't bother asking. They would take them and walk out." I wish my mother could have heard that. And then the nation's First Lady turned very solemn and gazed through the window onto the green. I didn't dare interrupt her thoughts although I started to wonder if that wouldn't be what she was expecting me to do. She finally broke the silence by getting up and walking across the room. She stopped in front of a lovely cabinet and slowly perused the items behind the glass. Then she turned to me.
>
> "The President is ill, you know." She said it so flatly, so without emotion or tone to draw emotion from me. I said nothing.
>
> "The President has cancer of the prostate gland. He'll be operated on when he returns."
>
> I sat there wishing desperately she hadn't told me that. It would have been bad enough if she'd been the wife of a dear friend. But she was talking about the President, a man as familiar to everyone as their closest friend.
>
> "I don't know what to say," I said, "I'm sorry, I mean ..."
>
> "And I don't know why I've told you this," Mrs. Roosevelt said with a smile. "I'm the one to be sorry. I suppose we all need to tell these things to someone. I chose you for no reason. No one knows of this except his physician and a few close advisers, please respect my confidence."
>
> "Yes, of course, Mrs. Roosevelt. Of course."
>
> The President returned from Yalta and I waited day by day to read of him entering the hospital for the surgery. I suppose he wanted to but never got around to it in the press of his schedule. It all became meaningless, on April 12 when he died of the cerebral hemorrhage in Warm Springs, Georgia. His death brought to me a strange and childish sense of importance. I never repeated what Mrs. Roosevelt told me. Never. I don't know why.

One of the most interesting bits of information provided me by the FBI, regarding the possibility that FDR had a urologic problem, was reported in a memorandum from J. Edgar Hoover to Stephen Early, the personal secretary to

President Roosevelt. It was dated December 14, 1944, was headed and underlined "Personal and Strictly Confidential—By Special Messenger," and contained the following:

MEMORANDUM

Recurrent rumors concerning the President's health are surging and echoing through Washington. The present "inside" story currently being discussed by most people, but mostly newspapermen, is alleged to emanate from "informed White House circles." The story is as follows:

Dr. William Calhoun "Pete" Sterling has established a good reputation for his surgery specializing in prostate, kidney and similar ailments. The story states that "Pete" Sterling was recently called for an extensive examination of the President and although an operation was necessary, Dr. Sterling refused to operate because of the very bad condition of the President's health. "Pete" Sterling is alleged to have declined to operate on the grounds that the President's condition was so bad that he would probably die from the operation and Dr. Sterling did not want to jeopardize his entire future in the medical practice by being known as the man who killed the President. Accordingly, the "White House" called into the case Dr. Frank Lahey of Boston. Dr. Lahey allegedly concluded that an operation was absolutely necessary and the "White House" decided that the operation would be performed after the presidential election.

The story continues that the President is suffering from "paroxysmal tachycardia (phonetic)," which is described as a sudden increase in heart action which causes trembling, shaking, etc. This affliction, it is stated, frequently follows polio attacks. The rumor then outlines that Dr. Lahey was insistent that the President build up his physical condition, as a result of which the President went to Warm Springs, Georgia for a stay of ten days, which has been lengthened to twenty days, in order to build up all possible resistance. Dr. Lahey allegedly has demanded that the operation be performed at the Lahey Clinic in Boston because it is alleged Lahey feels that the advertising value of his operating upon the President in Boston will be "worth millions of dollars to the Lahey Clinic." Dr. Lahey is supposed to reason that even though the operation is unsuccessful and the President dies, most people would conclude that Dr. Lahey and his clinic must be preeminent if the President went there for an operation. Accordingly, it is alleged that the rumor has spread throughout New England that the President is to be operated upon in Boston, the operation to take place about the first of the year or possibly even sooner.

The rumor states that Dr. Lahey performs many of his operations at the Baptist Hospital in Boston and that on or about December 8th, a United States Secret Service man from Washington, whose name is Barker, was in Boston checking upon the facilities, etc., at the Baptist Hospital in Boston.

The story alleges that Dr. Lahey has recently been interviewed concerning the President's health and has stated that the President "has no organic disease" and is "OK physically." Dr. Lahey is supposed to have stated that in so far as he knows, there is no reason for the President coming to Boston for an operation and that he "is not coming." The rumor-spreaders scoff at the statements of Dr. Lahey and point out that the statement that the President is suffering from no organic disease is subterfuge and that even if the President were going to Boston, Dr. Lahey would not admit it.

Congressional discussion has emphasized the fact that Dr. Lahey has recently been in Washington reviewing medical charts with Admiral McIntire and has also placed considerable credence in the stories that Barker of the Secret Service has been inspecting the Baptist Hospital in Boston.

Secret Service agent W. W. Barker subsequently became the source of much investigation, all of which eventually proved unrewarding. Agent Barker was the chief of the Secret Service bureau in New England at that time and therefore would have been responsible for the safety of FDR whenever the president entered this region. Hoover's letter to Early raised the possibility that Barker might have had some knowledge of FDR's physical condition, especially if the president had visited the New England Baptist hospital in Boston. Because of the years that had passed, I assumed Mr. Barker had died but hoped that his family might have heard him mention his connections and observations of FDR. I called the U.S. Secret Service offices in Boston and Providence with the hope that I might locate someone who actually knew or had heard of Agent Barker. Unfortunately, no one had ever heard of Agent Barker, and agents who worked with him in the 1940s were all deceased.

While carrying out investigative research in Washington regarding the Secret Service, I had become friendly with Mrs. Dorothy Jacobson, the U.S. Secret Service archivist at the time, who proved especially helpful. Mrs. Jacobson put me in contact with FBI Special Agent Jack A. French, who also tried to track down information about Secret Service Agent Barker, using his contacts at FBI headquarters. This also proved unsuccessful. Eventually my quest was referred to Mr. Robert R. Snow, the assistant to the director of the United States Secret Service. Mr. Snow wrote a letter on my behalf to Roland T. Wilson, director of the Government Record Center in Suitland, Maryland, where records are stored of all former members of the United States Treasury Department, of which the United States Secret Service is a part:

Dear Mr. Wilson:

This letter authorizes Dr. Harry S. Goldsmith of Dartmouth access to Secret Service records held in the Central Reference Division, as well as the public records contained in the General Archives.

Dr. Goldsmith is currently researching a survey made of hospitals in the Boston area for President Roosevelt in 1944 by an "Agent Barker." This individual may or may not have been a Secret Service employee.

Dr. Goldsmith has already contacted the National Archives regarding the general topic of President Roosevelt and medical arrangements and has received a document entitled "The Hoover Memorandum," which mentions Barker conducting the survey. He would like to obtain more specific information if possible, and would greatly appreciate your assistance from an archivist on your staff.

Thank you for helping Dr. Goldsmith with his research.

I went to Maryland with the hope and expectation that I would locate Agent Barker's records, but got caught up in a government "Catch-22" situation. The government record center in Suitland stated that it was impossible for them to locate Agent Barker's records without his social security number while the Secret Service office in Washington said that the only way they could get Barker's social security number was from his record.

Though the search for Barker proved unrewarding, the Hoover-to-Early memorandum contained a statement which sounded familiar:

[Lahey] allegedly demanded that the operation (on FDR) be performed at the Lahey Clinic in Boston because it is alleged Lahey feels that the advertising value of his operating upon the President in Boston will be "worth millions of dollars to the Lahey Clinic." Dr. Lahey's reasoning was that even though the operation was unsuccessful and the President died, most people would agree that Lahey and his clinic must be preeminent if the President went there for an operation.

This statement was closely reminiscent of a story that I had heard earlier regarding Dr. Lahey's wishes to have famous patients operated upon in Boston for the prestige that it would bring to his clinic.

One evening, while having dinner in London with Dr. L'Etang, we began to discuss the impact Prime Minister Anthony Eden's poor physical condition might have had, between 1953 and1956, on England's withdrawal from the Suez Canal in 1956. Anthony Eden's illness began in 1953 while he was the British foreign secretary under Prime Minister Winston Churchill. Eden entered a London hospital for routine gallbladder surgery, and during the operation, his common bile duct, the tube connecting the gallbladder to the intestine, was accidentally disrupted, a disastrous complication in biliary surgery. When bile began to flow from the foreign secretary's right upper abdominal wound soon after surgery, it presaged a very serious surgical complication. Eden's British surgeons then operated again, but all that was done was the placement of a drain into his abdominal cavity so that leaking bile could drain to the outside; they could not locate and repair the defect in the bile duct. Dr. Richard Cattell, who was soon to become the director of the Lahey Clinic upon the death of Lahey, was in London at the time to give a lecture at the British Royal College of Surgeons. His lecture was, ironically, on the repair of bile duct injuries, for which he was world-renowned. Cattell was asked to see Mr. Eden in consultation, and he advised that surgery be performed in the very near future in order to repair the injured bile duct. Dr. Cattell called Dr. Lahey in Boston to explain the situation. Dr. L'Etang told me that Dr. Lahey instructed Cattell to bring Anthony Eden to the Lahey Clinic in Boston so that both he and Cattell could perform the operation on the foreign secretary at the New England Baptist Hospital. Lahey also advised Dr. Cattell to invite one of the British surgeons who had originally operated on the foreign secretary to assist at the operation in Boston. Dr. Cattell reported to Anthony Eden and Winston Churchill the decision that had been made by Dr. Lahey. Churchill strongly argued that Eden's operation be performed in London and stated that, if necessary, he would personally turn a room at 10 Downing Street, the prime minister's residence, into a hospital operating suite. The prime minister further offered to send a plane to pick up any medical personnel or equipment that was needed by Dr. Cattell. Churchill felt very strongly that the British foreign secretary should be operated on in Britain.

Dr. Cattell called Dr. Lahey to apprise him of Winston Churchill's sentiments, but Dr. Lahey allegedly insisted that, because of the prestige and money Eden's presence would bring to the Lahey clinic, Anthony Eden had to be operated on in Boston. This information adds credibility to Hoover's memorandum to Early in 1944 that Dr. Lahey wanted FDR to have his operation in Boston because of the prestige it would bring to the Clinic.

On February 29, 1972, Dr. Robert M. Goldwyn, an eminent plastic surgeon from Boston, wrote to Dr. L'Etang in London about information he had learned regarding FDR's health. Dr. L'Etang included Goldwyn's letter in the file on FDR he sent me in 1980. The following is an excerpt from that letter:

I have heard from quite reliable sources that Dr. Frank Lahey, who was medical advisor to Roosevelt during the war, saw him professionally for what is rumored to be *carcinoma of the prostate.*

On December 20, 1979, I received a letter from Dr. Robert W. Pritchard, who was professor and chairman of the Department of Pathology at the Bowman Gray School of Medicine at Wake Forest University. He asked:

> Have you ever spoken with Dr. Shields Warren of Boston about the Roosevelt matter since he was in effect Dr. Lahey's pathologist, he would likely have looked at any material taken from Mr. Roosevelt even if it was removed elsewhere. Dr. Warren was in the Navy during World War II and retained close government ties for years thereafter. He is a laconic man and might well say nothing even if he knew everything, but it would do no harm to ask. Though he is in his eighties he continues to publish and from correspondence with him he is as sharp as ever.

Even before receiving Pritchard's letter, I had previously asked Dr. Warren for information about Roosevelt's health but he said that as far as he was aware, FDR had no malignancy. However, a week after receiving Dr. Pritchard's letter, another interesting letter arrived on December 28, 1979, from Dr. Richard Gipson of Torrance, California, concerning FDR's prostate. Dr. Gipson stated:

> In the fall of 1960, I was a resident in plastic surgery at the Veterans Administration Hospital in Jamaica Plain, Massachusetts. The Chief of Pathology at the hospital was Dr. John Holton. On one occasion he told a group of us that some time in the early 1940's he was sent a slide to review from the Lahey Clinic. Dr. Holton was a very respected anatomic pathologist who often received slides from other pathologists for his opinion. He said that it was his understanding that *the slide was a biopsy of the prostate from Franklin Roosevelt and that it showed carcinoma of the prostate.* [Author's emphasis.]
>
> I am actually certain in my memory of the above events. However, I cannot be sure how certain Dr. Holton was in the origin of the slide. Unfortunately, I believe that Dr. Holton may no longer be alive.

I looked into this matter and found that Dr. Holton had died in 1968, and I found no further information regarding his reviewing the slide of the prostate of FDR.

Approximately a month later, Dr. Gerald Brickner from Dearborn, Michigan, related an experience he had had in Havana, Cuba, in February,

1958, when he became acquainted with a Cuban travel agent at the Riviera Hotel in that city. He wrote:

> At the time of FDR's death, the travel agent was a bellboy at the National Hotel where he had attended to FDR's naval aide on several visits. On one such occasion, my friend found FDR's aide in a state of horror and dismay. He was crying and drinking heavily. The naval aide told him that *FDR had cancer of the prostate* which had spread and was causing him pain to the point where morphine was no longer helping.
>
> My impression at the time that I heard this story was that it was true. It seemed that my Cuban friend really did go through this experience and had no reason to doubt the naval aide. Dr. Pack's diagnosis of terminal malignancy may have been prostatic.

The lack of any follow-up from anyone regarding the pigmented lesion over Roosevelt's left eye, plus the growing evidence of prostate cancer, sharpened my interest in accelerating the search for more information on FDR's prostate gland. In the Hoover-to-Early memorandum, Hoover stated that the urologist who had seen the president in consultation, Dr. "Pete" Sterling, felt the president needed an operation but that he (Sterling) did not want to "jeopardize his entire future in the medical practice by being known as the man who had killed the President." To learn whether this story had any validity, I felt it important to locate the family of Dr. Sterling to learn of the relationship between Dr. Sterling and FDR.

The Washington, D.C., telephone directory contained no listing for either Dr. or Mrs. William Sterling. I knew there was little chance that he might still be alive, and I thought the best opportunity to get a lead would be to locate someone in Washington who might have known Dr. Sterling during his lifetime. I obtained the names and addresses of every urologist in Washington over the age of sixty and began telephoning them. No one had heard of Dr. Sterling until Dr. Dabney Jarman was contacted. He stated that he not only knew Dr. Sterling quite well, but prior to his serving in World War II, had actually worked as a young urologist in Sterling's office. Dr. Jarman was absent from Washington during the war and had no knowledge of Dr. Sterling's relationship with FDR during that period. However, he knew of Dr. Sterling's family, and he gave me the address of Sterling's son, who was a practicing lawyer in Washington.

I telephoned E. Killman Sterling and told him the reason for my call; Mr. Sterling was not familiar with his father's professional life since he was in his teens when his father would have seen FDR in consultation. Sterling suggested that his sister might be of more help. After I sent him my published article on Roosevelt, he wrote to me on January 5, 1981:

I read with interest your article on President Roosevelt and a memo from J. Edgar Hoover. I forwarded them to my sister with your letter. I hope she can shed some light on whether our father did ever see the President in his professional capacity. I'm sorry that I have no recollection of my father ever mentioning that he had seen the President.

I do know my father was on the surgeon general's staff during the war and was a good bridge playing friend of Steve Early. I would enjoy reading anything further you might write on the subject.

Having established Dr. Sterling's close acquaintance with Stephen Early, FDR's personal secretary, I now turned to Sterling's sister, Mrs. Marguerite Allardice, who lived at Grosse Point, Michigan. She stated she worked for her father when his regular office secretary was ill or was on vacation, and that she was aware that her father was seeing President Roosevelt. I told her of my article on FDR's health and hoped that after she read it she might recall any details concerning her father and FDR. On January 24, 1982, I received the following letter from her:

I enjoyed very much your article regarding Franklin D. Roosevelt. I wish I could be of more help to you. I do remember that *my father treated the President for prostate problems* [Author's emphasis] sometime around 1940 I think. However, my father and I lost touch with one another when I was married in October 1943 so I do not know how or if he was involved after that time. I assume my father was aware of the President's health problems because he did express concern about the appropriateness of a fourth term considering how ill the President was.

I worked in my father's office for brief periods when his secretary was on vacation but I have no medical knowledge so I paid no attention to medical information.

I would certainly be interested in any further information you discover. It does seem unbelievable that all medical records have disappeared."

I called Mrs. Allardice after receiving her letter to ask if she would contact me if any new thoughts or old memories arose. In August of 1983, she wrote me once again:

My father was a friend of Steve Early and they often played golf together. I specifically remember my father criticizing Roosevelt for running for a fourth term. He said Roosevelt knew he was seriously ill and would not live out another term. I did not know the nature of the illness although I assumed that it had to do with general urinary problems because my father was involved. However, I know there were other doctors involved too; so my assumption might have been inaccurate.

Mrs. Allerdice's memories gave plausibility to the account relayed in the Hoover-to-Early memo that Roosevelt had a urological problem and was treated by Dr. Sterling for several years. The clinical problems that are most common in an elderly man with general urinary problems are prostatitis, benign prostatic hypertrophy, or prostatic cancer. It is difficult to imagine that prostatitis or benign prostatic hypertrophy were conditions that were slowly weakening the president. If such a urological illness existed, it is more logical to suspect that Roosevelt might have had a slow-growing prostatic malignancy.

Dr. Pack had told me that FDR had a malignant tumor, and Dr. Lahey had told FDR that even if elected to a fourth term as president, he would not live to serve his term in office. Earlier information I had received from Dr. Kiely of California stated that FDR's tumor was metastatic from his prostate. This and other information that had been accumulated made a diagnosis of prostatic cancer seem reasonable. In order to get an expert's opinion on this clinical possibility, I sent FDR's medical information to a friend, Dr. W. Scott McDougal, professor of urology at Harvard Medical School and chairman of the Department of Urology at the Massachusetts General Hospital in Boston. Dr. McDougal replied:

> I read with interest chapter 15 of your manuscript entitled "Prostatic Cancer" in which you detailed information which would suggest that President Franklin D. Roosevelt had carcinoma of the prostate. Since there is no biopsy evidence nor documentation of FDR's physical findings with respect to his prostate, the supposition that he had prostate cancer must be circumstantial. However, I do believe that you have gathered a fair degree of evidence which would support this theory.
>
> First, you have gathered numerous references which refer to the diagnosis of prostate cancer. Second, the association of Dr. Sterling with FDR would tend to support the contention that the President had a urologic disease. Although the fact that FDR saw an urologist periodically does not establish the diagnosis of prostate cancer, it certainly would suggest that the President suffered from a urologic abnormality requiring continued care.
>
> Further support for the diagnosis of prostate cancer, particularly its gravity and extent, is suggested by the letter describing the comments of FDR's naval aide in which he stated that the amount of pain that the President was having was no longer responsive to morphine. This in fact is consistent with metastatic prostate cancer. Moreover, the evidence you gathered which noted that the President's non-protein nitrogen was 100

suggests renal failure and is consistent with prostatic obstruction due to cancer. The reason I would suggest cancer rather than benign prostatic hypertrophy is that catheters were clearly in wide use at this time and the President's symptoms could have easily been relieved and his general health improved had one been placed if his condition were due to benign prostatic hypertrophy. However, prostatic cancer which invaded the bladder and obstructed the ureters would not respond to simple placement of a urethral catheter. I suspect Dr. Sterling would have employed a catheter had the President's condition been amenable to its use.

Since the President had poliomyelitis, a condition known to affect the motor function of the bladder, it is also possible that FDR had a neurogenic bladder and it was for this reason he was seeing Dr. Sterling, the urologist. Although renal deterioration could also have occurred due to the neurogenic bladder, which would also explain the elevated nonprotein nitrogen, had this been the case one would have anticipated that a catheter might have been placed with a significant improvement in the President's condition. Apparently, there was no history which you could gather of any catheters being used in the President's care.

I found your research of the health of Franklin D. Roosevelt fascinating. I think the supposition that he had prostate cancer is very tenable although it cannot be proved without a doubt on the evidence at hand.

I was enormously pleased when E. Sterling Tillman sent me several pictures in which Dr. Frank Lahey and Dr. Richard Cattell were shown as surgical consultants to the surgeon general of the U.S. Navy (i.e., Admiral McIntire) and was especially surprised to identify Dr. Sterling in a photograph as part of this select consultant staff. It was now possible to see for the first time a direct relationship between Admiral McIntire, Dr. Sterling, Dr. Lahey, and Steve Early; a small group who had knowledge of FDR's general health, specifically his genitourinary status which may have played a role in the deterioration of FDR's health near the end of his life.[2]

---

2. There have been several books written about FDR that claimed I believed the president's death was caused by either cancer of the stomach or a melanoma. I never believed FDR had cancer of the stomach, and I initially considered melanoma to be a cause of his death, but this latter belief never was substantiated. Most disturbing was a statement written in a major book on FDR erroneously stated I believed FDR had a cancer which originated "in a wen that had been removed from the back of his head earlier in the year and then metastasized to his stomach." This statement was especially embarrassing to me since all doctors know that a wen (sebaceous cyst) is a benign lesion that has no capacity to metastasize.

Admiral McIntire's naval surgical consultants,
Dr. Lahey (lower left, first in front row),
Dr. Cattell (upper left, first in third row),
Dr. William Calhoun Sterling (directly between and behind two naval officers
in front row on right side of picture)
United States Navy photograph

CHAPTER 14

FDR'S DEATH

Much has been written about FDR's deteriorating health during the last year of his life. Little purpose is served in reiterating information that has been well documented by many historians over the past several decades. Bishop, in his book based on his interview with Dr. Bruenn, clearly stated the situation: "[H]e [FDR] had been failing in health—dying to be precise—for at least a year."

When President Roosevelt returned from Yalta in 1945, it was obvious that his physical state had deteriorated considerably during the past two years, yet no special incident had occurred to focus public attention on questions concerning FDR's health.

As the end of FDR's life was approaching, he began to show more openly the warm feelings he had for Lucy Mercer Rutherfurd. Their love story is well known. In May 1943, Mrs. Rutherfurd asked Madame Elizabeth Shoumatoff, the artist, to paint a non-commissioned portrait of FDR. Madame Shoumatoff, whom I was able to locate when she was living on Long Island, New York, told me FDR allotted her only one day in which he could find the time to sit for his portrait. After this single sitting, a substitute thereafter sat in Roosevelt's chair while she completed the necessary details of the painting. The finished portrait was considered to be exceptionally good. It was hung in the White House with a copy of the painting sent to Winston Churchill, which Madame Shoumatoff believed still hangs at Chartwell, the former prime minister's home. Another copy of the portrait was sent to Stalin, which she also believed still hung in Moscow. She said that at the time she painted Roosevelt in 1943, he looked extremely vigorous.

In 1945, Mrs. Rutherfurd asked Madame Shoumatoff if she would paint another portrait of the president. She agreed but at this time asked that the painting be commissioned. Mrs. Rutherfurd traveled to Warm Springs in early April of 1945 to be with the president at the invitation of FDR's daughter, Anna Boettiger, who was there with FDR and was acting for the president in extending the invitation (Mrs. Roosevelt was unaware of the invitation). Mrs. Rutherfurd brought Madame Shoumatoff with her to Warm Springs along with Nicholas Robbins, a photographer, whose photos Madame Shoumatoff frequently used while creating a portrait. Madame Shoumatoff said that when she saw FDR in 1945, she was shocked by the changes in his appearance that had occurred during the two years since she had last painted him.

On April 12, 1945, FDR awoke in the morning and saw Dr. Bruenn at 9:20 AM. According to the doctor, the president "slept well, but complained of a slight headache and some stiffness in his neck. He described this as a soreness of the muscle and relief was experienced with slight massage."

The president remained busy during the morning going over governmental papers. As lunchtime was approaching, FDR was in the living room with Mrs. Rutherfurd, who was busily knitting while Madame Shoumatoff was sketching the president. Daisy Suckley and Polly Delano, FDR's cousins, were also in the room at the time. At 1:15 PM, FDR clutched the back of his head and complained of a severe headache. Bruenn stated in his 1970 paper, "[H]e became unconscious in a minute or two later." After the president collapsed, the women in the room and others quickly realized the enormous impropriety that would be conceived should it be learned that Mrs. Rutherfurd was present at the Warm Springs "White House." Mrs. Rutherfurd and Madame Shoumatoff were instructed by the Secret Service to leave the compound at once. Madame Shoumatoff's photographer, Robbins, who was in the Warm Springs Hotel swimming pool, was notified to come to the compound with his belongings to meet the two women and leave immediately. It is interesting how such a chain of events could be reported so incorrectly. On the following day (April 13, 1945), the *Los Angeles Times*, in detailing the president's death, wrote that an artist was painting a portrait of FDR at the time of his attack:

> The name of the artist was given only as N. Robbins of New York. Robbins left President Roosevelt's cottage when he complained of his fatal headache. Robbins returned to the village hotel at Warm Springs outside the Infantile Paralysis Foundation grounds but left it before reporters could interview him. Mayor Frank W. Alcorn of Warm Springs said that Robbins left by automobile.

No report was made by any newspapers that Mrs. Rutherfurd was with FDR at the time of his fatal attack.

Madame Shoumatoff related how, after she, Mrs. Rutherfurd, and Robbins left the Warm Springs compound, they intermittently listened to the radio as they drove but heard no information as to the president's condition. After several hours, Mrs. Rutherfurd could no longer contain her concern; she asked Robbins to stop the car and requested Madame Shoumatoff to call Warm Springs to find out the condition of the president. The artist learned from the telephone operator at the Warm Springs compound that FDR had died that afternoon. She returned to the car and informed Mrs. Rutherfurd of this tragic news, following which Mrs. Rutherford became inconsolable and endured long periods of hysteria. After reaching her home in Aikin, South Carolina, Mrs. Rutherfurd was taken directly to her priest, who provided some degree of spiritual and emotional comfort, which she so desperately needed at this moment in her life.

President Roosevelt's death was the result of an acute cerebral hemorrhage that killed him in two-and-a-half hours. FDR's last hours have been described in Bruenn's paper in 1970. Prior to that publication; Admiral McIntire supplied additional details of the events surrounding Roosevelt's death.

FDR's attack occurred at 1:15 PM, after which he became unconscious and was carried back to his bed and undressed. Dr. Bruenn was immediately called (he was at the hotel swimming pool) and was at the president's bedside at 1:30 PM. Bruenn stated, "It was apparent that the president had suffered a massive cerebral hemorrhage" and that after examining the president he "immediately called Washington on the private telephone line and contacted Dr. McIntire and informed him of the catastrophe. He [McIntire] told me [Bruenn] that he would call Dr. Paullin in Atlanta immediately."

Dr. Paullin later stated that he received a call from Dr. McIntire "about 1:45 PM, and he was asked to go to Warm Springs to see the president of the United States for a pretty severe headache which occurred quite suddenly." Bruenn had told McIntire over the phone that FDR had suffered a catastrophic cerebral hemorrhage, but surprisingly McIntire told Paullin that FDR only had a severe headache. Apparently McIntire had difficulty in stating FDR's true physical state.

Paullin stated that following McIntire's call, he "left Atlanta at 2:00 PM and at exactly 3:28 PM I drove up in front of the Little White House at Warm Springs." Bruenn wrote in his 1970 paper that "at 3:31 PM breathing suddenly stopped and was replaced by occasional gasps." This meant that Paullin was with the president for only three minutes before he stopped breathing and for only four more minutes before FDR was pronounced dead by Bruenn at 3:35 PM.

During the year following Roosevelt's death, McIntire was frequently questioned about the health of FDR during the last year of his life. More than a year after FDR's death Admiral McIntire wrote Drs. Bruenn and Paullin asking them to summarize their medical experiences with FDR during the last few months of his life. Bruenn was the first to respond on August 1, 1946, but gave no specifics on FDR's death:

Dear Admiral:

I am terribly sorry that it has taken me this long to answer your request for my impressions about President Roosevelt during the last three months of his life. A combination of pressing domestic and official duties have combined to cause this delay.

As you know, it was my good fortune to be with the President for almost *two years before he died.* [Author's emphasis.] Because of this, a valid basis of comparison exists for me. There is no question but that the President was physically tired. The crushing burden of the war and the domestic front, together with an election campaign in the preceding months had sapped his strength. Yet he made the journey to Yalta in February, 1945 in extraordinarily good fashion. This trip, you may recall, employed practically all forms of transportation known to man except, possibly, oxcarts. And at Yalta, he gave freely of his time not only to the main conferences, but also devoted himself to the encouragement and advice of the several members of the party in their individual responsibilities.

Despite the demands made upon him, his mental clarity was truly remarkable. His memory for past and recent events was unimpaired and his recollection of detail was such as to continually impress me when compared with some of his associates ten and twenty years younger than himself. His vitality and sense of humor remained excellent and only on one occasion, if you remember, did I see him depressed i.e., when the Russians were proving to be more difficult than usual. The morning afterwards, however, he was his usual buoyant self.

The return trip proved to be most enjoyable, and he seemed to relax and rest so that I felt much relieved about him. He was greatly saddened, as were we all, by the death of "Pa" Watson [FDR's military aide and appointment secretary], but his tremendous sense of destiny and his almost inexhaustible reserve of strength of character enabled him to take this shock without faltering.

It was not infrequently his custom when he retired at night, to relax and speak in very general terms of events and people. During the last six weeks of his life, his trend of thoughts, his appraisal of situations and his evaluations of circumstances were just as clear and contemporaneous and he maintained his superiority to the end. I can recall one incident which might illustrate this. The overwhelming wish of the President at this time was for an enduring peace and a workable United Nations. He was insistent upon going to the West Coast on April 25, 1945 for the first meeting of the United Nations. All of us pleaded with him not to make the trip because of the stress of a trans-continental journey for the purpose of making a 15 minute speech. It was suggested that if his presence were needed later, he might then go. He finally explained why he felt that the trip must be made as he had planned. He hoped, he said, that by starting the conference off on the right note, it might accomplish its purposes more readily. Whereas, if he were to appear later in case difficulties should arise at the meeting, it would appear to be unilateral action on his part.

The speech which he had prepared by his own hand for presentation at the Conference in San Francisco was written just a few days before he died. All doubt as to the man's mental powers can be answered in its expression of purpose, conciseness of phraseology and stirring appeal. I truly believe that had he been spared, this nation and the world would now be immeasurably further along the road to a lasting peace and a mutual respect and understanding.

Sincerely,
Howard G Bruenn, M.D.

Bruenn's letter is strikingly non-specific regarding FDR's physical condition during the last months and hours of his life and also devoid of any personal warmth towards McIntire. Also quite puzzling is Bruenn's comment in his letter that he had been with the president for almost two years before he died, yet in his 1970 paper he claimed that he saw FDR for the first time on March 28, 1944, just over a year before the president's death. If Bruenn did see the president for almost two years, this would support the likelihood that FDR's deteriorating cardiac status had been present for a longer period than has historically been acknowledged.

On August 12, 1946, Admiral McIntire's reply to Bruenn's letter was also devoid of any medical specifics:

Thanks very much for your helpful letter. It strengthens my own belief that we were not too close to the picture to get a good estimate of the man.

I had a very good talk with Mr. Hiss of the State Department, whom you may remember as being Secretary Stettinius's right hand man at Yalta. I told him that I was writing something on the President and that the Yalta episode was something I had attempted to cover in some detail, regarding the President's clarity of mental processes. He was most emphatic in his belief that he had never seen the President conduct himself in any better fashion than he did there. He said that he felt the President was tired on many occasions, but that never stopped him from being on the beam. In fact, he cited two or three occurrences that were quite pointed.

I am not sure how this book will appeal to many of our immediate party, but at least it is factual. I will see that you get a copy just as soon as the first are off the press for I will want your opinion.

I am glad to know that things are going along well with you. I hope that your work will soon become adjusted in a way that you can plan for the years ahead, as many of us have been able to do in the Service over the years.

I want you to know again how much I appreciate all the fine things you did through the past years, both in Service and in your additional capacity with the White House family. I know that you will look back on most of the things that came about, and I am sure that all of your friends will watch your future programs with sincere interest.

With kindest regards.

In contrast to Dr. Bruenn's brief letter to Admiral McIntire was that of Dr. Paullin who, on August 24, 1946, wrote a relatively detailed report on FDR's death even though he had been with the president for only minutes before the event:

Dear Admiral McIntire:

In order that the record might be complete concerning my visits and consultations with you to see the President of the United States I would like to report as follows:

I first consulted with you concerning the President's health on April 2, 1944. As a result of this conference it was thought that he had a moderate degree of arteriosclerosis with a variable hypertension, some electrocardiographic evidence of coronary artery disease, some cloudiness in his sinuses and some evidence of bronchial irritation from a recent attack of influenza, which he had had. At this time it was my impression that he should take a vacation and go south for at least a month and that he should stop smoking in order to get rid of the irritation in his nose and sinuses. I understand from you that shortly thereafter he went to South Carolina for his much needed rest.

He was seen again later on in the year. At this time he had recovered from his infection in his sinuses and chest. He was feeling quite well, active, but he was still doing entirely too much work and at this time Dr. Lahey[1] and I insisted that he have a period of rest after the noon meal and

---

1. Dr. Bruenn's letter to Dr. Loyal Davis (page 55) said Dr. Lahey saw FDR "on only one occasion some two weeks after I had first examined the President."

that he have his evenings free, certainly after 9 PM, so that he could get some relaxation and recreation.

When he was last seen he was most jovial. We talked to him at least an hour or longer and at that time I stressed upon him the importance of moderation in all things, explaining to him that he had driven his automobile tires quite hard but they would go another ten thousand miles if he would not take the rough places in the road at too great a speed, and if he would also reduce his speed to 25 or 35 miles per hour, which was then the speed established for safe driving of all cars and for the conservation of tires.

I did not see Mr. Roosevelt again professionally until you called me on April 12, 1945, about 1:45 PM, and asked me to go to Warm Springs to see the President of the United States who has a pretty severe headache and that you had just been informed by Commander Bruenn that the onset of the headache was quite sudden. Curiously enough I had just talked to you a few minutes before to find out when you were coming to Georgia. You stated that you had already planned to come and visit with me a day or so before going to Dublin but that you had been held up because of matters relating to the budget of the medical Department of the United States Navy. It was tentatively agreed that you were to come down on Sunday, the 15th of April, and spend the day with me and Monday we would look at Emory University Medical Department and fly down to Dublin to see the Naval Hospital and spend the night in Marshallville and go to Warm Springs the next day.

After receiving your message I stopped all my work at the office and left for the garage, got in my car, left Atlanta at 2 PM and at exactly 3:28 PM I drove up in front of the Little White House at Warm Springs. I was immediately ushered into the room where the President was ill and with him was Commander Bruen [*sic*], Lt. Commander Fox, and the President's valet.

The President was in extremis when I arrived. He was pale, in a cold sweat, ashy gray, breathing with difficulty, numerous rhonchi in his chest. He was propped up in bed. His pupils were dilated. His hands were slightly cyanosed and Commander Bruen had just started artificial respiration.

On examination upon my arrival his pulse was barely perceptible. His heart sounds could be heard, and about 3 1/2 minutes after my arrival his heart sounds disappeared completely. I gave him an intracardiac dose of adrenaline in the hope that we might stimulate his heart to action. However, his lungs were full of rales, [sounds due to fluid in his chest] (author's brackets) both fine, medium and coarse, and his blood pressure was not obtainable. There was no effect from the adrenaline except perhaps for two or three beats of his heart, which did not continue. Within five minutes after my arrival in the room all evidence of life had passed away. At 3:35 PM, CWT, Dr. Bruen and I went out into the next room and announced his death to his cousins.

Immediately after this *I looked over Dr. Bruen's notes* [Author's emphasis.] on what had occurred on Thursday, April 12th. They are as follows:

The President woke about 9 o'clock. He felt well and had no complaints (Bruenn said FDR awoke with a slight headache and some stiffness in his neck). He had his breakfast and conversed with the maid for a few minutes, and he was then seen by Commander Bruen on his morning visit. Commander Bruen stated that he had no complaints that morning. He had had a good night's sleep; his blood pressure was 160 to 170 over 80 to 90. His pulse was normal, and the Commander left. Shortly after this the President got up, dressed and went into his living room, signed numerous papers and letters and felt quite well. While sitting in his chair, having sketches made for his portrait, at about 1:20 o'clock (Bruenn said 1:15) he complained of a sudden onset of very severe pain in the back of his neck which was so severe that it caused him to put his hand to his head, and to complain, bitterly of the discomfort. He was immediately lifted from his chair, carried to his room and undressed. *Commander Bruen arrived and saw him about 1:30 O'clock. At this time according to Commander Bruen's notes he found the President with his hand an the back of his neck, still complaining of intense pain.* [Author's emphasis.] His neck was a little stiff. His blood pressure was over 300. His pulse was 71 or 72 to the minute. The pupils were contracted. He was breathing normally. His heart sounds were very loud and snapping. Dr. Bruen immediately gave him a dose of Papaverine intravenously and in the course of a short time the blood pressure had dropped to 250/120. At this time he was unconscious. His breathing was good. His heart rate was excellent. He continued to have other medication, aminophylline, and various other remedies, including nitroglycerine, but his blood pressure continued high until 3:00 when it began falling. With failing respiration, he developed a cough. His heart rate increased, the moisture in his chest became evident, and from this time onward his respiration seemed to increase. The edema [fluid] in his lungs became more marked and I arrived at the time when his respiration was quite bad and there was a great deal of gurgling in his throat and cyanosis developed.

As best as I could make out from a hurried examination the facts were as stated above. The remainder of the story is a matter of history, Commander Bruen and I reported to you concerning the President's death at 3:35 PM which was an hour and fifty minutes after you called me. After reporting to you, I remained around the house conversing with Dr. Bruen, Mr. Haslett, Miss Delano, Miss Grace Tully, the servants and all.

The story of the onset of the President's illness, as gathered from all of them, is as reported to you. As to the diagnosis there is only one that I know of which would fit into this picture. He had either a massive inter-cerebral hemorrhage which ruptured into the subarachnoid space, giving him his intense pain and stiff neck. [Paullin didn't mention his other pos-sibility.] I discussed the possibility of an autopsy on the President with the idea in mind of bringing the matter to your attention. As you know, at the Georgia Warms Springs Foundation, they have a small hospital but there were no facilities whatever for performing an autopsy on the President, and since he had expressed a wish which was conveyed to me by Miss Delano that he did not care to be embalmed, that he did not wish to be embalmed, I felt that there was nothing further we could do until after the arrival of Mrs. Roosevelt.

It is a great regret that I was unable to do any more for The Chief. I am convinced in my own mind that even had they been present with him at the onset of his attack they could not have done any more than Commander Bruen did during his stay with the President.

Very respectfully,
James E. Paullin, M.D.

Several aspects of this letter are of interest, a minor one being Dr. Paullin didn't know the spelling of Dr. Bruenn's name. Of greater interest is that the letter was not written with a style or organization to suggest Paullin understood the historical sig-nificance of his account. In fact, it appears that the letter was not even edited.

Shortly after FDR expired, arrangements were begun for his funeral. That evening, on April 12, at 7:40 PM, Fred W. Patterson, owner and manager of the Patterson Funeral Home in Atlanta, Georgia, was informed of the president's death. At 9 PM he left hurriedly for Warm Springs in his private car accompanied by his chief embalmers, Hayden Snodderly and George Marshman. They arrived at Warm Springs at 10:45 PM but were told that Mrs. Roosevelt had not yet arrived and were advised that her consent was necessary prior to the initiation of any procedure.

Mrs. Roosevelt arrived about midnight from Washington accompanied by Admiral McIntire and presidential secretary Stephen Early. Doctors McIntire, Bruenn, and Paullin agreed that there was no need for an autopsy because they all felt comfortable with the diagnosis of a cerebral hemorrhage. Mrs. Roosevelt went into the bedroom and spent five minutes with the president, after which she exited from the room and requested that the body be embalmed even though Paullin had been told by FDR's cousin, Miss Delano, that FDR had requested that he not be embalmed. However, the embalming began at 12:35 PM. The procedure was difficult because of severe arteriosclerosis within FDR's major blood vessels, making these structures unsatisfactory to withstand the pressure of the injected embalming fluid.

In the late 1980s I tried to locate the individuals who were directly involved with FDR's embalming. I called Mr. Snodderly's home and was told he had died. I then spoke to Mr. Brannon Lesesne in Atlanta, who at the time of the president's death was assistant manager at the Patterson Funeral Company. He stated that although he was not an embalmer he did view the president's body, and he said he noted no marks or bruises on the body. He did remark, however, how "emaciated" the president had become. Mr. Lesesne suggested I contact George Marshman who actually performed the embalming procedure. Mr. Marshman was extremely cooperative and gave me all the information he recalled. He said the thing that impressed him most was the president's tremendous weight loss. He had seen many pictures of FDR over the years, and he couldn't believe how much weight the president had lost. I specifically asked him if he noticed any distinguishing features on FDR's body, thinking of melanoma and enlarged lymph nodes; but as far as Mr. Marshman could recall, there were none. He did add that after the president had died, his jaw must have been supported with a bath towel to prevent it from sagging since terry cloth marks from the towel were present on the skin of FDR's chin where the towel had been removed.

Dr. Paullin's letter to Admiral McIntire in 1946, a year after FDR's death, claimed an autopsy was not performed on the president because the room in which he died in Warm Springs Cottage was small, with no facilities for the procedure. However, in order to embalm the president, it had been necessary to bring an operating table into his room and a pressure pump, which was required to infuse embalming fluid into FDR's body. An autopsy requires the observation of the exterior and internal appearance of the body with removal of small samples of tissue taken from the heart, liver, kidneys, etc. for microscopic examination. No greater space is needed to perform an autopsy than is needed to embalm an individual. If the space was too small, the president could have been taken to the local hospital in Warm Springs or to a larger medical facility in nearby Atlanta for the procedure. It is unfortunate that an autopsy was not carried out that night. However, there is every likelihood that, even if an autopsy had been performed, the results of the procedure would have disappeared along with FDR's other medical records.

Certain aspects of FDR's death that were reported separately by Bruenn and Paullin deserve careful analysis. Bruenn's paper on FDR was written in 1970 and describes the last two-and-a-half hours of the president's life with specific information regarding heart sounds, pulse rate, blood pressure recording, etc. Twenty-five years had passed since the president's death, and all his health records had disappeared. It therefore seems reasonable to assume that, for Dr. Bruenn to have written his paper in such detail, he must have reported his medical data from personal notes he had retained since 1945.

What is difficult to understand is why Dr. Paullin's letter of June 24, 1946, to Admiral McIntire, written a year after FDR's death, reports details of the president's final hours that are different from those presented by Bruenn in 1970. Paullin states explicitly in his letter that what occurred in FDR's final hours came from Bruenn's notes, which seems obvious since he was with FDR only minutes before his death while Bruenn had been present during the entire period. Therefore, it is difficult to explain the discrepancies in the two doctors' versions of FDR's death—if they came from a single source.

For example, Paullin said that when Commander Bruenn arrived and saw FDR about 1:30 PM, "He found the President still conscious, with his hand on the back of his neck complaining of intense pain." However, in Bruenn's 1970 paper, he states that when he first saw the president, "[H]e was pale, cold and sweating profusely. He was totally unconscious with fairly frequent generalized tetanic contraction of mild degree." Why, if Bruenn said the president was unconscious when he first saw him, would Paullin state that he was conscious?

Bruenn stated in his 1970 paper that "the pupils of the President's eyes were at first equal but in a few minutes after his attack the right pupil became widely dilated." A dilated right pupil is a strong indication that FDR had suffered a right-sided cerebral hemorrhage. However, Paullin, in his report, said FDR's pupils were contracted. Bruenn further stated that between 1:30 and 2:30 PM FDR's lungs were clear, but between 2:45 and 3:30 PM his breathing had become irregular. But Paullin's letter to McIntire said that by 3:00 PM the president had developed "moisture in his chest and at this time respiration seemed to increase. The edema (fluid) in his lungs was quite bad and there was a great deal of gurgling in his throat and cyanosis" [blue coloration of lips and nailbeds].

Another area that raises speculation concerns the treatment given to FDR immediately before his death, as reported by both Bruenn and Paullin. A question could be asked as to why no one made immediate arrangements to transfer FDR to a hospital. Atlanta was only sixty miles away. It is rare for a doctor to allow a patient to die in his bed at home for several hours period in the presence of an acute medical emergency, unless the doctor has already concluded through close contact over time (as with FDR and Bruenn) that no medical intervention could prolong or save the patient. Common practice would have dictated that

Bruenn get FDR to a medical facility for sophisticated care, unless Bruenn believed the president's death was inevitable—which was probably the case.

There is no question that the president was deeply cyanotic (lips and nailbeds were blue) for at least an hour before he died and, as Paullin noted, the president had developed pulmonary edema (fluid in lungs) with "marked gurgling in his throat." When a doctor deals with a cyanotic patient in extremis (near death), especially someone like FDR who was on digitalis for congestive heart failure for over a year, the treatment always includes the administration of oxygen. Oxygen therapy in 1945 was, as now, standard treatment for such a condition. The cyanosis that FDR exhibited during the last hours of life was of extreme degree. Bruenn stated directly in an interview with Bishop, for the latter's book on FDR during the last year of his life, that preceding the president's death, the "lips and fingernails were deeply cyanotic—concord blue."

The bluish coloration of lips and nail beds confirms a diagnosis of insufficient oxygen in FDR's circulation. There is nothing specific in a patient with a cerebral hemorrhage to cause him to be cyanotic; cyanosis is simply an indication of insufficient oxygen that can be caused by a number of conditions. Oxygen is required for treatment that can be delivered by nasal catheter, facemask, or in an oxygen tent. This is standard treatment for a cyanotic patient, especially for a patient with a history of congestive heart failure. I found no reports of any attempts by the Secret Service to procure, or by Dr. Bruenn to administer, oxygen to the president. Additionally, one would have expected a suction apparatus to have been immediately requested in order to aspirate accumulated fluid and mucous from the back of FDR's throat, which were further decreasing his ability to breathe and oxygenate his body.

It is possible that these measures were performed, but there is no recorded evidence of such actions, which leads me to suspect that FDR received no oxygen and had no suctioning of his tracheobronchial secretions prior to his death. These observations are in no way intended as criticism; most physicians, myself included, forego routine therapeutic measures when a terminal situation exists prior to the actual death of a patient. Bruenn may have already decided that FDR's life was close to the end. Heroic treatment at such a time does not extend life but simply prolongs the mechanisms of death.

Beyond the accounts already presented about FDR's deteriorating health and heart failure over the last year of his life, additional information exits to suggest a certain desperation about his health, possibly early in 1945. Sometime during the early 1980s, I was at the Roosevelt Library in Hyde Park studying the appointment schedules of President Roosevelt in order to discover the names of all doctors who had visited him during the last four years of his life. I knew the majority of the doctors officially listed would not be doctors of medicine but of philosophy, law, economics, etc. I reasoned that if a medical doctor was listed who saw the president on a frequent basis, but was not a member of McIntire's medical team, an important new lead might develop.

During the process, I came across the name of Harry Setaro, who saw FDR at the White House on January 3, 5, 8, and 18, 1945, and again on March 12, 15, and 19, 1945, appointments immediately before and after the Yalta meeting. I subsequently learned that Setaro also saw FDR on seven occasions at Hyde Park. What was curious about the entries was that Setaro saw the president for several hours at night between 9 and 11:45 PM. It seemed unusual that a person not previously recorded in official White House logs was seeing FDR for such long periods, late at night, and all shortly before his death. I examined telephone books in the Washington, DC, area and telephoned people with the name Setaro—but with no success. I was also unsuccessful in finding leads from people named Setaro who were listed in old District of Columbia phone books. The Roosevelt Library in Hyde Park at that time also had no further information regarding Harry Setaro. James Roosevelt in California and Dr. Emerson, director of the Roosevelt Library, said they had never heard of a Harry Setaro. Although Setaro might be an important lead, there were no further investigative paths to pursue. Then on May 6, 1987, I received a package from Dr. Emerson accompanied by a note that simply identified the contents as "the newly uncovered material on Harry Setaro."

A feature article in the *Philadelphia Enquirer* (May 11, 1953) stated that Setaro was one of nine boys who grew up in Philadelphia and became a prizefighter at the turn of the century using the name Harry Lenny. He apparently had a mediocre fighting career and withdrew from active boxing in 1910 to become a fight trainer. Setaro claimed he saw President Roosevelt in order to use his unique method of "hand healing." He said, "I just have a way of touching the nerves," which he claimed he learned from his grandmother who allegedly had a gift of using her hands as healing agents. Dr. Emerson's package also included a description by Setaro of his relationship to President Roosevelt. Setaro claimed that Admiral McIntire knew he was treating FDR near the end of his life. We know that Setaro did not see the president simply to give him massages since FDR always used his naval aide, Commander Fox, as his masseur. Setaro had been called in to "lay" his hands on FDR. The conclusion to this is that the president of the United States was being treated near the end of his life by a faith healer— with the tacit approval of Admiral McIntire—even though FDR had the opportunity to be treated by the finest medical people in the country. This suggests that McIntire was aware that FDR was chronically ill, with little more that could be done for the president using conventional medical methods. Perhaps any opportunity to make FDR more comfortable seemed reasonable, even faith healing. (Further information on Setaro has been recently uncovered.)[2]

When Roosevelt went to Yalta in February 1945, some individuals in high governmental positions believed FDR was physically deteriorating. Opinions ranged from his being considered very ill (suggested by Winston Churchill and his personal physician, Lord Moran) to being never stronger nor more decisive than in his activities and deliberations with Stalin and Churchill at Yalta (the opinion of Alger Hiss, one of FDR's major advisors at Yalta, told to me during a personal telephone conversation in 1991).

In 1972, Rear Admiral Clarence E. Olsen, United States Navy (retired) was asked by the United States Naval Institute in Annapolis, Maryland, to give an oral historical reminiscence of Roosevelt at Yalta since Admiral Olsen attended the conference as a member of the United States delegation. He stated,

> Roosevelt was a very sick man when he came over. As a matter of fact, they (Stalin and Churchill) had their first joint meeting in the ballroom there, in the center of the room they had a big round table. You've probably seen pictures of it with spaces for the Americans and for the British and Russians. We were all in there and we asked to stay on the side lines to line the two walls of the ballroom. The door was down here and the table was where that paper is. First Churchill came in the door and marched right down the center with his cigar, talking like this and the little bull dog look he always had. He was definitely on display and he with his staff following went and sat down. Then Roosevelt came in his wheelchair with a big shawl over his shoulders and looked, very, very tired and drawn and this big Negro, Pleasant [Prettyman] was pushing him. Of course he was a great big burly husky fellow and this little old man looked like a dried up old lady sitting there and he had to go through and was put into his other chair. And then Stalin came down, just glaring and looking as if he was expecting to have knives thrown at him at any minute from either side. But the contrast between the physical fitness of Churchill and Stalin versus Roosevelt was very, very striking and of course all through the conference we had the feeling that Roosevelt was not holding up our interest to the best, that he was giving way, giving into the Russians on almost everything. The comments made by Chip Bohlen (future US Ambassador to Russia) when he came out sometimes indicated that that was what was going on.

---

2. Ward, *Closest Companion.*

Photographs taken of Roosevelt at Yalta show a dying man. Because of careful screening of pictures before their release for publication, his physical condition was even worse in reality than what the public was shown.

Years after FDR's death, when there was still interest and speculation concerning the circumstances surrounding the event, James A. Farley, FDR's former close associate and cabinet member, stated in the *Washington Star*, on March 1, 1951, that it was widely known among political leaders that FDR was a dying man in 1944. On March 10, 1951, McIntire responded to this disclosure by writing a letter to the editor:

> As far as President Roosevelt himself was concerned he had a clear understanding of his own physical condition at all times. To say that he deliberately practiced calculated deception in this regard is completely false. If this is an accusation against me, then I take it as one against all the doctors who worked with me. I do not believe that the Star cares to make such a statement.

These editorials indicate that major Democratic leaders in Washington knew before the 1944 Democratic Convention that FDR was a dying man. This will be subsequently shown to have had a major political implication on the selection of Harry Truman in 1944, leading to the thirty-third presidency of the United States.

Public interest in FDR's health in 1951 was intensified by the Farley/McIntire editorials because of the escalation of the Cold War between the United States and Russia and the increasing controversy over FDR's alleged concessions to Stalin at Yalta. This situation finally forced Admiral McIntire to hold a major press conference on March 13, 1951, six years after FDR's death.

As the press conference began, a specific medical question about FDR was addressed to McIntire. He stated:

> I can look at my notes and be sure of the exact dates; he picked up one of these influenza virus infections and it went on over a period—he developed bad bronchitis which made him cough and cough through February and March of that year (1944).

This statement showed that McIntire still had medical records of Roosevelt, yet none of this information is in McIntire's memorabilia at the Roosevelt Library. His donations to the library include among other things, material concerning his naval career and his functions as the surgeon general of the navy. But there is very little regarding the president's health even though McIntire attended FDR as his personal physician for twelve years on a day-by-day basis.

Another reporter at the 1951 press conference asked the admiral specifically if FDR was ill in February and March of 1944, at the time we know the president was in cardiac failure. McIntire responded, "No, he wasn't seriously ill." The illness during these months, he said, was minor, with FDR simply having a cough, bronchitis with thick mucous, etc.; but at no time did McIntire say the president showed signs of what he knew to be congestive heart failure, which required digitalis during the remainder of FDR's life.

When Roosevelt returned from Yalta in 1945, he addressed the joint houses of Congress in a sitting position. This was the first time he had done this, and he apologized, blaming the weight of his leg braces and his long trip from Yalta. McIntire made this statement at his press conference in 1951:

> I was responsible for him (FDR) giving his address to Congress sitting in his chair. I knew that this was a long address, and for him to stand 45 minutes or longer was just too much. And again, one thing that I was deeply concerned that was asked, Were you concerned about his health?

McIntire answered, "I was concerned about his reserve strength."

Another question:

> Let me ask you now about some of these other rumors—there was a large assortment of them—that he [FDR] had cancer of the prostate, a bad heart, something wrong with the main artery of the heart, his mind was failing—you probably know a lot more of them. Was there anything to any of these rumors?

McIntire denied the president had any of the above medical problems.

Again: "Was FDR ever treated for any major illness or disease or anything that the people never heard about?" McIntire's response: "That's right, not one. In fact, I hope I can always be as honest as I was with all of you people."

McIntire always spoke of FDR's "strength" rather than his health. There were many instances, and especially during this press conference, where he completely misrepresented the facts of FDR's medical condition. One reporter at the press conference asked McIntire if he had even been present at Roosevelt's death: "You did go down with him (to Warm Springs) and then come back, didn't you?"

McIntire answered, "Yes—no, I don't think I did. I'm not sure, maybe I did. But I didn't stay, there was nothing alarming."

McIntire's uncertainty as to his own whereabouts at the time of the president's death is difficult to believe; in truth, seems inconceivable.

McIntire ended the press conference with, "I can say honestly to you that he (FDR) never had any heart symptoms."

Admiral McIntire was the White House physician and Navy Surgeon General (1933–1945)

CHAPTER 15

LAHEY AND BOYD— EXTRAORDINARY MEN

Dr. Frank Howard Lahey, founder of the Lahey Clinic, was born in 1880 in Haverhill, Massachusetts, and died in Boston on June 27, 1953. He was educated in the Haverhill School system, Harvard College, and Harvard Medical School, from which he was graduated in 1904. Following graduation, Dr. Lahey interned at the Boston City Hospital and within a few years began practicing surgery in Boston. Early in his career he joined the Harvard Medical School faculty where he eventually became clinical professor of surgery. He also obtained the title of professor of surgery at the Tufts College Medical School. By 1922 his reputation had grown to the point where he and three other doctors founded the clinic named after himself.

By the time FDR entered the White House in 1933, Dr. Lahey had proven himself to be an outstanding surgeon, a keen businessman, and an exceptional administrator. Admiral McIntire appointed him honorary surgical consultant to the Navy Department prior to World War II. Shortly thereafter, on October 30, 1941, FDR appointed him chairman of a six-man commission called the "Procurement and Assignment Agency." The function of the agency was to study the availability of medical professionals and to assign to the various branches of the military the services of every physician, dentist, and veterinarian should a national crisis arise, which it did following the Pearl Harbor attack on December 7, 1941.

As discussed earlier, Mrs. Louise M. Poe, Dr. Lahey's personal secretary, had declined in 1980 to relate any information to me concerning Dr. Lahey's personal and professional relationship with FDR. However, I persisted over the years, with infrequent and very brief phone calls. On January 12, 1982, almost five years after our first contact, I received the following letter from Mrs. Poe:

In accordance with your telephone call to me, Dr. Lahey, to my knowledge, saw President Roosevelt only once at the request of Admiral McIntire. If Dr. McIntire's secretary is still alive, she may have some information about this. Her name is Claire Murphy and her home is or was in Worcester, Ma. She and I became quite friendly during the war years, but I have since lost track of her.

Dr. Lahey died June 26, 1953 having suffered a coronary on June 11. He did not dictate anything to me about the Roosevelt examination so if there is a memo of any kind it will be in his own handwriting.

I was unsuccessful in locating Claire Murphy.

Two weeks later Mrs. Poe sent me a copy of a letter she had sent on January 25, 1982 to Dr. David P. Boyd, a senior Lahey surgeon, who was writing a history of the Lahey Clinic:

He (Dr. Lahey) did examine Roosevelt at the request of Admiral McIntire and when he came back he told me that he advised him not to run and that he would not live through the term.

According to the letter I received from Mrs. Poe, Dr. Lahey saw FDR on only one occasion. Dr. Bruenn, in his letter to the editor regarding my FDR paper in *SGO*, also claimed that Dr. Lahey saw Roosevelt only once "some two weeks after I [Bruenn] had first examined the President on March 27, 1944." And yet in his earlier paper, printed in the *Annals of Medicine* in 1970, Bruenn said that Dr. Lahey saw FDR on March 31 and April 1, 1944. Further confusing the issue is that Paullin's letter to Admiral McIntire in 1946 said he and Dr. Lahey saw FDR on April 2 and then "later on in the year." These discrepancies indicate that Dr. Lahey saw the president more than once for medical reasons. A major reason for believing this is based on an undated newsletter I located that had been printed privately by the Bald Peak Colony Club located on Lake Winnipesaukee in New Hampshire where Dr. Lahey spent his summers. Dr. Lahey was a member of the club, and the newsletter told brief anecdotes of each member. This particular newsletter mentioned that Lahey had been summoned to Washington by President Roosevelt in 1943 to serve as his personal consulting surgeon. Dr. Lahey agreed to the appointment after reciting several conditions which were quoted in the publication and had to have been supplied by Dr. Lahey:

He would accept no "undue remuneration."
He would not be made an admiral or a general.
He had never voted for FDR and didn't plan to in 1944.

He considered FDR the most important person in the world, so his health was of great concern to him.

"Do you still want me as your personal consulting surgeon?"

Lahey asked, and Roosevelt laughed and replied, "Thank you, Dr. Lahey, for your frankness. I will send my plane for you every Monday morning."

One can also detect a faint familiarity between the two men as evidenced in a letter from Dr. Lahey to the president dated December 31, 1943, long before their alleged first medical meeting of March 28, 1944. The letter concerned the formation of a commission, but the last paragraph in the letter is of special interest:

> I hope that you have recovered from your cold and while this may represent Hibernian sentiment, I would like to express to you my admiration for what you have recently accomplished and for your capacity to take the physical hardships which I know went with it.

When Admiral McIntire asked Lahey to act as surgical consultant to the president, he must have insisted, as he had done with Bruenn and unquestionably other doctors, that Lahey observe strict secrecy on matters pertaining to the president and his family. All persons involved apparently accepted this restraint, and Dr. Lahey honored this oath of silence. However, Dr. Lahey, with far-thinking astuteness, recognized the inevitability of future scrutiny of FDR's medical management. In order to show that he personally didn't wish to be involved in a cover-up of FDR's health before the election of 1944, he recorded his concerns regarding the president's health in 1944 in a personal document that has become known as the Lahey Memorandum, which I will discuss shortly.

By the early 1980s, I had exhausted all leads regarding FDR's health. Fortunately, at about this time I became acquainted with David Preston Boyd, M.D., former chief of Thoracic and Cardiovascular Surgery at the Lahey Clinic, former president of the American Society of Thoracic Surgery, and a trustee of the Lahey Clinic.

My first contact with Dr. Boyd began when I first called members of the Lahey Clinic staff who had been mentioned in Dr. Lahey's will, in the hope that they might have knowledge of Lahey and FDR. At that time I told Dr. Boyd of my interest in the health of FDR and the difficulty I had encountered in uncovering any medical information regarding FDR in the records at the Lahey Clinic. He showed no surprise at hearing this since he also had searched for and found nothing on FDR. He made a few suggestions as to where I might seek further information, but these proved unrewarding.

Over the next few years, Dr. Boyd and I remained in touch, and I soon realized that he was a devoted student of medical history. He held the position of historian for the Lahey Clinic; belonged to the American Association of the History of Medicine and the Massachusetts Historical Society; was a past president of Countway Library Associates; served as historian of the American College of Chest Physicians (1978 to 1985); and was past president of the Benjamin Waterhouse Medical History Society in Boston. The more time we spent together, the more I appreciated his character, sensitivity, and wisdom. He encouraged me to continue my medical study of FDR.

Dr. Boyd was a strong individual. At times, when sitting in his living room in Wellesley, Massachusetts, or having lunch at his Harvard club in Boston, I would see a twinkle in his eyes because of what he was doing to help me. He felt he was "tweaking the beaks" of some people who, he felt, were knowingly withholding historical information since they knew of the existence of the Lahey Memorandum, which was unknown to me. Yet at the same time he understood and respected the doctors who maintained a pact of secrecy regarding FDR. Such a pact was clearly shown in a personal experience I had with a very close friend and associate of Dr. Boyd's.

At the Roosevelt Library in Hyde Park, I located a scheduled appointment FDR had in the White House on November 11, 1943, from 2:00 to 3:30 PM with a group comprised of Secretary of War Henry Stimson; Undersecretary of War John J. McCloy; the honorable Paul V. McNutt, chairman of the War Manpower Commission; Major General Norman T. Kirk, surgeon general of the army; Rear Admiral Ross T. McIntire; and, surprisingly, Dr. Frank Lahey. Of great interest was the discovery that, just preceding this apparently important meeting, the president had another appointment between 1:45 and 2:00 PM with Dr. John W. Norcross, who had been the chief of Internal Medicine at the Lahey Clinic before the war and at one time was the doctor Lahey wished to succeed him as the director of the Lahey Clinic.

Dr. Norcross was the internist involved in the post-operative care of Sir Anthony Eden in 1953 when he was operated on at the Lahey Clinic for complications resulting from his gallbladder surgery in London. By coincidence, just weeks before, I had been discussing the same Dr. Norcross with Dr. L'Etang in London since I hoped in the near future to discuss Anthony Eden's (Lord Avon) case with Dr. Norcross. The reason I wanted the interview with him was because Eden's widow, Lady Avon, had recently given me permission to publish her husband's case. I told Dr. Boyd about my discovering Norcross's visit with Roosevelt at the White House in 1943, which surprised Boyd very greatly, since Dr. Norcross, who was one of Boyd's closest friends, had never mentioned FDR to him. After our discussion, Dr. Boyd sent me a letter on March 29, 1983:

After talking to you this morning I decided it would be better for you to go down to see John Norcross than call him. He is one of the most honorable men I know but he is reserved. He is a close friend and you may use my name if you think it might help.

I called Dr. Norcross who, I found, was retired and living in Nashua, New Hampshire, and told him I was a good friend of David Boyd, who had suggested that I call to make an appointment to see him. I told him I was planning to write a paper on Anthony Eden's surgical complications, which had been my original reason for wanting to contact him; we discussed Eden's medical problems at length.

I sensed that, as a retired physician, Dr. Norcross was delighted to speak to another doctor about medicine. After about ten minutes, I asked Dr. Norcross if he would mind if we switched from Anthony Eden to another subject and he said, "Not at all." With no further preliminaries, I simply asked, "Did you ever see Franklin Delano Roosevelt in consultation?" After a pause of about twenty seconds on the telephone, Dr. Norcross said in a rather hesitant manner, "No, no, I don't believe that I've ever seen the president in consultation." It seemed that no one has to think hard, as the hesitation indicated, to remember whether or not one has seen a President of the United States in consultation. I then gently asked, "If what you say is true, Dr. Norcross, why is it that you are listed in the White House appointment schedule as seeing President Roosevelt between 1:45 and 2:00 PM on November 11, 1943?" Again, another long pause and then he answered, "Oh wait a minute, wait a minute, it's starting to come back—yes, I do remember, yes, I did see the president but it was not in consultation."

I sensed that Dr. Norcross was very uncomfortable and wished to terminate our conversation but, being the gentleman that he was, didn't know how to do it without seeming rude. I then again quietly asked, "Under what conditions did you see the president between 1:45 and 2:00 PM, and who set up this appointment?" Quite clearly nervous, Dr. Norcross replied, "I was able to get an appointment to see President Roosevelt because I was a great admirer of the president, and I had a patient whose life I saved who was able to get me such an appointment." This statement seemed rather odd to me since it is rare for a doctor to tell another doctor that he "saved a patient's life." I then asked, "Who was this patient that got you the appointment?" Dr. Norcross answered, "Mr. Myron Allen." [Allen, at one time, was the chairman of the board of the United States Steel Corporation and later appointed by FDR to be the first United States envoy to the Vatican.] My next question was whether Mr. Allen had been with him at the time he saw the president. Though Dr. Norcross replied that Allen had been with him at the meeting, I knew by FDR's official appointment schedule that Dr. Norcross had been alone with FDR.

By now Dr. Norcross's voice had become unsettled, and I did not wish to cause him further anxiety. I thanked him for his time and mentioned that I hoped it would be possible for me to visit him in New Hampshire at some later date for further discussion. Several weeks later, I called Dr. Norcross and asked to meet him; but he said there was nothing further he could add to what we had already discussed.

When I told Dr. Boyd of my conversation with Dr. Norcross, he felt it clearly illustrated the integrity of a person like Norcross, who still maintained a covenant of silence regarding President Roosevelt that must have been made many years earlier between himself, Dr. Lahey, and Admiral McIntire.

Dr. Boyd encouraged me to continue my search regarding FDR's health; to assist in this endeavor, he sent me by mail, sometime in 1983, a chapter from a book he was currently writing on the history of the Lahey Clinic. The chapter was entitled, "The Roosevelt Episode:1944–1945." It was twenty-two pages in length and liberally marked with editorial changes indicating that Dr. Boyd was still in the process of revising the book. Some of the things Dr. Boyd had written were quite startling:

> The strange disappearance of these historical documents (FDR's medical records) is only one of the enigmas surrounding the President's last illness. It says to all the world in thunderous tones: "Much was hidden."

I knew Dr. Boyd had the greatest respect and admiration for Dr. Lahey and that he deeply loved the Lahey Clinic. Yet, he stated that the oath of secrecy (taken by FDR's doctors) apparently transcended professional responsibility and that he was surprised that "a man as resolute as Frank H. Lahey, a man so accustomed as he by this time to the society of captains and kings, would go along with this outright deception." He continued:

> To contemplate Frank H. Lahey as a partner to a cover-up is almost beyond the capability of those who knew him best and are still here to justify; but all can see that the circumstances were unique. That Lahey would certify as fit and well a man who he considered a threat to the country's economic life and to the safety of the world and in whom he found a terminal malignancy is to pull the snout of reason. But he may have done it.

Ending his writing on Roosevelt, Dr. Boyd raised the question of accountability regarding FDR's health: "It lies at the door of the tragic figure of Franklin D.

Roosevelt and the star-studded galaxy of physicians who served him not wisely but too well."

Boyd's chapter on FDR also referred to Linda Strand, the executrix of Dr. Lahey's estate. There was a letter reported in the chapter, from Harold Willcox (Linda Strand's lawyer in her lawsuit against the Lahey Clinic from 1958–1962) to Edward B. Hanify, the lawyer for the Lahey Clinic in the case. The letter had been sent at the time of the settlement of the lawsuit between the two parties. This Willcox-Hanify letter stated:

> [T]he plaintiff (Mrs. Strand) has a fairly large number of miscellaneous papers that can be considered to have no contemporaneous importance to anyone. There were certain other papers which were delivered to the plaintiff by Dr. Lahey because of their supposed confidential character. All of these have, according to the plaintiff, been delivered to me and with an exception to be noted below, these documents have been destroyed. The plaintiff has gone over these documents with me sufficiently for me to be able to tell you that there were none that would be of any help in the treatment of a living patient today.
>
> The document excepted from the foregoing is a document written by Dr. Lahey in relation to the health of a well-known former statesman whose identity is known to both you and me. Plaintiff was given this document by Dr. Lahey with instructions that *if Dr. Lahey should ever be posthumously criticized for his conduct in relation to his consultation and his failure to make public report thereof, the document was to be published if the plaintiff saw fit.* [Author's emphasis.] That document will be delivered to this firm to be held by this firm until such time comes, if it ever does come, that the document should be redelivered to the plaintiff in order that she may carry out the conditions upon which it was given to her. *In the event of the plaintiff's death, the document will be destroyed if it is still in our possession.*

Dr. Boyd died in the early months of 1989 before his book on the history of the Lahey Clinic was published. He was a wonderful man who helped me immeasurably, and I shall always be indebted to him. He pointed the way to finding undisclosed facts of FDR's health that might be present in the document (Lahey Memorandum) that had been entrusted to Mrs. Strand by Dr. Lahey.

If Mrs. Strand were still alive, she had to be found if the FDR quest was to continue.

CHAPTER 16

THE SEARCH FOR
LINDA STRAND

I picked up the threads of my earlier unsuccessful attempt to locate Mrs. Strand, Dr. Lahey's business manager, who had moved years earlier to Mt. Dora, Florida, from Sudbury, Massachusetts. I began by calling the post office at Mt. Dora to ask if box 195 was still in use under the name of Linda Strand. The postal employee I spoke with said it was but would give me no further information. I then called Mrs. Dorothy Jacobson, the United States Secret Service archivist in Washington, and asked if a Secret Service or a FBI agent could go to the Mount Dora post office to obtain Mrs. Strand's address. She told me that this would be an invasion of Mrs. Strand's privacy, and if it were attempted, both the Government and I would be in violation of her civil rights.

Mrs. Strand had not answered letters I had sent her years earlier, and it appeared that contacting her was going to be a challenge. I considered going to Mt. Dora, sitting in the post office, and watching PO box 195 until someone picked up the mail from it; I would then simply ask the person if he or she would be kind enough to tell me where Mrs. Strand lived. That seemed rather aggressive, so I modified it to waiting at the post office until someone picked up the mail from box 195, and then I would follow that person in my car to their final destination, hopefully the home of Mrs. Strand. Fortunately, friends at the Secret Service and the FBI persuaded me that my plans were completely impracticable. I abandoned the post office approach.

I telephoned the Mt. Dora fire and police departments, also without success. Then I inquired at the Mt. Dora town hall if Linda Strand was on their tax roll, but she was not. The clerk explained, however, that this did not necessarily mean that Mrs. Strand had died, only that perhaps someone in her family might be paying her taxes. Possibly she didn't even live in Mt. Dora but simply used that post office as a place to receive mail. The several utility companies in the area, whom I called, advised me that even if Mrs. Strand were being billed, it would be illegal for the company to give out information regarding her location.

The regional government center (the county seat) for Mt. Dora is in Tavares, Florida, and I called to inquire if Mrs. Strand was on the county tax rolls. She was not, and I was transferred to several other offices where everyone tried to be helpful; yet all leads proved unrewarding. One last suggestion was to contact the deeds office and ask if Mrs. Strand possessed land in her name. A pleasant woman in the deeds office came on the phone with initially disappointing word that it would be impossible to get a name from a deed without first knowing the location of the property involved. Sensing my disappointment, she offered another idea; she would look up all Strand listings in the region, and perhaps one of those might be the Mrs. Strand I was looking for. After several minutes, she came back on the phone with information concerning three people named Strand, together with information to help locate them. Apologetically, she also proffered a fourth name; she had no information about this person named Strand except that the individual with this property listing had a mailbox located in the Mt. Dora post office, box 195. My excitement was perceptible.

Obviously pleased to realize she had found the Mrs. Strand for whom I was searching, this helpful individual said Mrs. Strand's property was located in Eustis, Florida, Rainbow Ridge, building D, lot 4. Eustis was the town next to Mt. Dora. The description of building D, lot 4 at Rainbow Ridge suggested that Mrs. Strand was probably living in a housing complex with various units listed alphabetically, as is frequently done in many governmental and military facilities. I still didn't know if Mrs. Strand was alive, but at least I now knew where she and/or her family might be found. I cannot describe my elation at finding the person who might have direct and personal information regarding FDR's health. I was certain I could find the home Mrs. Strand had lived in for the past thirty years; but I feared that when I located it, I might learn she was deceased.

Two days later I took an afternoon flight to Orlando, Florida, and stayed the night at a motel. On the following morning I rented a car and drove approximately sixty miles northeast to Mt Dora. When I reached the area around Mt. Dora, I asked at several gas stations for directions to Rainbow Ridge, but no one had ever heard of the place. I pulled into a large gas station on one of the main highways, where an old man was sitting in a rocking chair in the sun, and asked him if he knew where I might find Rainbow Ridge. He laughed and said he hadn't heard the area called that in several decades. He told me to continue on the road I was traveling for several miles, after which I would come to a former gas station that had been converted to a small aluminum company. I should turn left at this point and go a mile or so until I reached a lake that previously had been known as the Rainbow Ridge area. I thanked the man and followed his directions without any difficulty. I drove for a mile to the area that I now believed was Rainbow Ridge. On several occasions, I stopped the car when I saw people outside their homes either gardening or walking. No one had ever heard of Rainbow Ridge.

For the first time I was becoming concerned about locating Mrs. Strand's home. I couldn't even find the Rainbow Ridge area, much less building D, lot 4. Driving farther, I noticed an older woman, approximately one hundred yards from the road, who was working in the garden close to her home. I stopped and started walking up toward her garden, which was elevated above the road. Since I didn't want her to think I was some sort of intruder, I quickly greeted her from a distance. I told her I was looking for a Mrs. Linda Strand who lived at Rainbow Ridge, but I couldn't locate the area. She told me that she knew of Rainbow Ridge but hadn't heard the area called by that name in many years. She instructed me to turn around and drive on the opposite side of the lake for approximately a mile, at which time there would be a slight rise in the land's elevation. This heightened area had been known years previously as Rainbow Ridge.

Following her directions, I was soon driving along the left side of the lake. No one area, however, looked more elevated than any other, and I stopped twice to ask people in their backyards if they knew of Rainbow Ridge. They had never heard of it. I drove to a slight hill on the left where several houses were being built. There were construction people there, and I thought they might be familiar with any building in the area entitled "D," which had been constructed on "lot 4"; but none of them had ever heard of that kind of designation.

Somewhat disheartened, I was leaving the construction sites when I noticed a large garbage truck operated by a single garbage collector. I walked up to him and asked if he had ever heard of Rainbow Ridge; he had not, but he asked whom I was looking for. He didn't recognize Linda Strand's name, but he went to the cab of his truck and took out a two-inch stack of three-by-five-inch index address cards to see if she was on his garbage route. I remember thinking, as he started going through the "S" cards, that the chance of his finding Mrs. Strand and her address seemed almost nonexistent.

Looking over his shoulder, I felt unbelievable excitement when the name "Linda Strand" appeared on a card. Under her name was written the unnumbered location of her house. I asked where this was and received directions. I thanked the driver profusely, telling him he could not imagine how helpful he had been. He smiled and said he was pleased to have been of service.

I returned to my car and drove to the area. There I found four houses at an intersection; two larger homes were situated below the intersection and two smaller homes on the upper side of the street. I reasoned that since Mrs. Strand had probably moved into the area from Boston in the 1950s, she likely would be living in one of the larger houses. I went to the first house and rang the bell; no one was home. I then went to the home on the opposite side of the street, and an elderly woman came to the door. I asked if she were Mrs. Strand. She not only wasn't Mrs. Strand, but she said she had never heard of a Mrs. Strand.

With growing unease I walked up the hill, approaching the next house above the intersection, and could see an elderly woman sitting inside the screened porch. As I drew nearer, she noticed me and asked, "Can I help you?" I answered that I was looking for a Mrs. Linda Strand and she replied, "I'm Mrs. Strand." She then asked who I was and what I wanted. I introduced myself and explained my mission regarding Dr. Frank Lahey. At that moment, the full implication of my discovery hit me full force. There before me, alive and well, was the woman who, within a short time, could prove pivotal in my search for information on President Roosevelt's health in his final years.

Mrs. Strand invited me in and introduced me to her sister. It was quickly apparent that Mrs. Strand was in her eighties, was short, overweight, extremely alert, and feisty. We then went out on the porch for a pleasant conversation that lasted several hours. She wanted to know why I was looking for her and how I had found her. I told her of my interest in Franklin D. Roosevelt and that I knew of the memorandum regarding FDR's health that Dr. Lahey had given her. I told her I believed that it might have historical importance as to whether FDR was aware of his poor health and possible impending death when he ran for office in 1944. I also told her I was aware of Dr. Lahey's admonition that if she learned of any criticism of his conduct relating to FDR's health, she was to publish the Lahey Memorandum.

It was apparent that Mrs. Strand was very adept at asking questions and getting answers and that she still harbored a great deal of animosity toward the Lahey Clinic, dating back to her lawsuit with that institution from 1958 to1962. She repeatedly asked me if I had anything to do with the Lahey Clinic, and I continued to reassure her that I did not. She wanted to know the details of how I learned of the Lahey Memorandum. I told her I had learned of its existence from Dr. David Boyd, whom she instantly remembered from the Lahey Clinic, causing her to become defensive. She then cautioned me that even if she did agree to retrieve the Lahey Memorandum from her law firm, this would not ensure that she would let me see the document, much less obtain a copy of it. Explaining that I understood this, I tried to reassure her that all I wanted was first-hand information regarding Roosevelt's health. Perhaps the Lahey Memorandum would confirm that FDR was aware he was either dying or at least was not a well man. This fact in itself was important since it might establish FDR's condition during the last year of his life, including his performance at Yalta in February 1945.

Mrs. Strand asked to see the written criticism of Dr. Lahey that I had brought with me. I felt obliged to first tell her that I personally believed Dr. Lahey to have been one of the great American surgeons. I explained that the only critical thing I had ever written about him concerned an act of his that I simply termed "awkward" in the FDR paper I had written in *Surgery, Gynecology and Obstetrics* (*SGO*) in 1979. This comment was in regard to Dr. Lahey's withholding medical information in 1944 from a reporter from the *St. Louis Post-Dispatch* concerning the physical condition of the president. I showed her Dr. Boyd's chapter concerning Dr. Lahey's relationship with FDR, particularly Boyd's written reference to the same *St. Louis Post-Dispatch* letter that I had just mentioned:

> Dr. Goldsmith calls it [the letter Lahey sent to McIntire] "awkward," which is a generous verdict. In fact, it is tortuous and convoluted. Worse, it is evasive, disingenuous and intellectually less than honest; unless Lahey was oblivious to the evidence of his clinical senses as was Admiral McIntire.

Dr. Lahey's concern about future criticism of his medical conduct with FDR had now been realized in the eyes of Mrs. Strand, and Lahey's faith in her was now to be tested.

After learning the facts I presented, Mrs. Strand said she now felt she had to obtain the Lahey Memorandum so she could carry out Dr. Lahey's instructions. What seemed incredible to me, however, was she expressed doubt that her law firm in Boston would return the Lahey Memorandum to her. She also felt it was going to be extremely difficult, if not impossible, for her to fight for her document, citing her advanced age, the long distance between her home in Florida and Boston, and an earlier request she had made for the Lahey Memorandum that had resulted in a "runaround" from her lawyers.

I offered to initiate the steps necessary for her to gain the Lahey Memorandum. She replied that it would be perfectly all right for me to do this, but again reminded me that this was no guarantee I would be allowed to see the document even if it were returned to her. I must admit, however, I felt that if I did recover the Lahey Memorandum for her, she would allow me at least a glimpse of it. I reassured her I had no wish to own the document; I only wanted to know its contents.

I asked Mrs. Strand simply to write a short note informing her law firm (Herrick and Smith) that I was acting as her agent and requesting the firm to return the Lahey Memorandum to her in Florida. Mrs. Strand agreed to this; but because of her poor eyesight, she requested I write the note, which she would sign and date. I removed a six-by-nine-inch notebook from my briefcase and pulled out a single page. On this lined piece of paper I wrote:

To Herrick, Smith, Donald and Farley:

I would appreciate it if you would send to me immediately all papers given to you by me (Mrs. Strand) pertaining to Dr. Frank H. Lahey and the Lahey Clinic.

Thank you.

She signed the note, "Linda M. Strand April 21, 1983." Because I believed this was a simple matter, neither I nor Mrs. Strand thought to ask her sister to sign the letter as a witness.

We then talked for an additional half-hour, beginning a very nice relationship. I was enormously impressed with her astuteness, clarity of thought, and great sense of humor that was closely admixed with a sharp degree of crustiness. She was really great fun. I felt certain at that point that her law firm would send the Lahey Memorandum to her in the near future and that she would be hearing from me quite soon.

The day following my return to Boston, I called Herrick and Smith and told a secretary I had a note written by Mrs. Strand which I would send the firm requesting that the Lahey Memorandum, which they held, be returned to her. The secretary said the document was kept in their depository used to store old legal records and that after receipt of the authorization written by Mrs. Strand, the document would be sent to her as requested. Several weeks passed and I heard nothing. I again called Herrick and Smith and asked the status of Mrs. Strand's document. I was transferred to a lawyer named Michael Austin who stated that it would be impossible for Herrick and Smith to send anything to Mrs. Strand without a release written by her. I told him such a release had already been sent but I would be happy to send another; which I did. Several weeks passed with still no word from Herrick and Smith. On May 19, 1983, I again called the law firm and strongly urged Mr. Austin to send Mrs. Strand the material she had requested; he replied that his firm could not respond to Mrs. Strand's request since it had been made by me. What they needed was more information including Mrs. Strand's telephone number so they could confirm what I had already told then over the telephone. The next day (May 20, 1963) I wrote the following letter:

Dear Mr. Austin:

I am responding to our telephone conversation yesterday in which you wished confirmation of my role as intermediate between Mrs. Linda Strand of Florida and your law firm.

Since I am in the northeast area, Mrs. Strand has asked that I request that your firm send to her her papers which she left in your custody pertaining to Dr. Frank H. Lahey and the Lahey Clinic. When I first spoke to you several weeks ago mentioning that Mrs. Strand wished this material to be sent to her, I gave you her telephone number (904-357-6881) since you requested it would be necessary for you to call her to confirm the request that I was making in her behalf. I was quite surprised yesterday when I spoke to you to learn that you had not called her and that you had said there might be some material that could not be given to your former client.

I therefore am requesting that you do send Mrs. Strand's material to her at your earliest convenience and that you call her to confirm any information that I have now given you, both by telephone as well as by letter.

After waiting several months and still hearing nothing from Herrick and Smith, I now advised Mrs. Strand to write a request to her law firm that was more formal than the one I had handwritten on her porch in Florida months before. Her new request said:

This is to authorize Dr. Harry Sawyer Goldsmith to obtain my papers which are in the possession of the law firm of Herrick and Smith whose offices are presently located at 100 Federal Street, Boston, MA.

These papers are my property and I wish to obtain them through Dr. Harry S. Goldsmith. Due to my age and place of residence, I am authorizing Dr. Goldsmith to act in my behalf in order to procure these papers.

For any further reference as to my standing concerning my papers in the possession of Herrick and Smith, see superior Court Case Docket #539688 of Linda M. Strand versus Lahey Clinic.

It was signed Linda M. Strand and witnessed by her sister, Francis M. Young. The date was September 8, 1983.

After waiting several more weeks, Mrs. Strand and I knew that nothing was going to be done by Herrick and Smith. I once again called the law firm and asked to speak to Mr. Austin but was told that Mrs. Strand's request had been transferred from the desk of Austin to that of John French, a senior partner at Herrick and Smith. I requested an appointment with Mr. French, and within a few days we had a meeting. He was a pleasant individual who quietly, but clearly, informed me that neither Mrs. Strand nor I would ever receive the material she was seeking. I told Mr. French that I believed the Lahey Memorandum relating to FDR was of great historical importance and that, if necessary, Mrs. Strand might be forced to seek legal help in order to obtain her document. I was then told that it wouldn't make any difference what legal action she might contemplate; under no circumstances was Mrs. Strand to have the Lahey Memorandum returned to her. He gave no reason for his position.

As I left the office of Herrick and Smith, I was totally confused; everything concerning Mrs. Strand had seemed so straightforward. Dr. Lahey had left a memorandum in the hands of the executrix of his estate with the stipulation that, if any criticism was ever made of him regarding his medical relation to FDR, she was to publish the document as she saw fit. Why would Herrick and Smith not return to their former client a document that they were simply to hold for her?

That evening I called Mrs. Strand and told her of my conversation with Mr. French. I told her that he said she would never receive the Lahey Memorandum. Mrs. Strand was not surprised but believed that the actions of Herrick and Smith clearly were improper and unfair. Equally distressing was the stipulation made by Mrs. Strand's law firm (but vigorously denied by her) that if the Lahey Memorandum were not published during Mrs. Strand's lifetime (and she was eighty-nine) the document would be destroyed upon her death.

I asked Mrs. Strand if she wished to do anything further. She once again told me she would like to but because of her age, distance from Boston, and other factors; she felt she was not in a position to become involved in a lawsuit.

I told her how historically important I felt Dr. Lahey's document might be, and I asked if she wished me to act as her agent in seeking a legal remedy to her problem. She said I was perfectly free to go ahead; she advised, however, that based on her past relationships with her lawyers and those of the Lahey Clinic, she felt any chances of getting the Lahey Memorandum were highly unlikely. Her language during our conversation had become quite earthy when expressing her personal opinion of certain members of the legal profession.

Mrs. Strand wished me good luck. I had no idea that a major episode in my life was about to begin.

Linda Strand

CHAPTER 17

LEGAL BATTLE BEGINS

Clearly, Mrs. Strand's law firm intended to withhold the Lahey Memorandum from her. The question arose as to whether it might be possible to obtain a copy from another source. Could the document be referenced in the court records of Strand vs. Lahey Clinic (1958–62)? A search in the Suffolk county courthouse to obtain the court file of the case revealed that the entire record had been impounded following the trial in 1962.

I again contacted Assistant District Attorney Arthur Tiernan who had earlier helped me obtain Dr. Lahey's will. He explained various legal procedures I could use to obtain the Lahey Memorandum, the easiest of which was a *pro-se* (for self) petition, meaning an individual simply requests a judge to make a ruling. With Mr. Tiernan's help, I wrote *pro-se* petition #539688 asking the judge of the Suffolk County Equity Court in Boston to order the law firm of Herrick and Smith to return Dr. Lahey's memorandum to Mrs. Strand. As time drew near to present the petition, Mr. Tiernan convinced me that there could be complicated legal circumstances making my *pro-se* petition not in Mrs. Strand's best interest. He suggested I seek legal assistance if I felt the Lahey Memorandum was of such historical importance. I knew nothing about lawsuits, never having been involved in one, and I wasn't even sure what type of lawyer would be needed for such a case. The thought of becoming entangled in a legal action was uninviting.

One evening while having dinner with my sister and her family, who lived in Needham, Massachusetts, she mentioned a highly regarded lawyer who headed his own Boston law firm and who had been elected Needham town moderator for twenty-seven consecutive years. I made an appointment to meet him.

Tall and strikingly handsome, Richard P. Melick, senior partner in the Melick and Porter law firm in Boston, was personable and easy to talk to. I explained the possible historical importance of the Lahey Memorandum and that Mrs. Strand's law firm refused to return the memorandum to her. He agreed that legal pressure might be the only solution and wrote Mrs. Strand on December 16, 1984, outlining his overview of the case. He felt there were sufficient legal grounds to institute proceedings to pressure Herrick and Smith to return the Lahey Memorandum to her.

Mrs. Strand requested that I be her agent so I was named as the plaintiff in the lawsuit that was filed on May 31, 1984. The defendants in the case comprised all forty-one lawyers of Herrick and Smith. Being the sole plaintiff against an entire law firm was somewhat unnerving, but there appeared to be no other recourse.

One of our concerns was the possible destruction of the Lahey Memorandum by unknown parties since all of FDR's medical records had already been lost. It was agreed that every effort had to be taken to safeguard the document while its final disposition was being decided. Melick described proposed legal protective devices in a letter on May 31, 1984, to Mrs. Strand in Mt. Dora:

> In order to attempt a means of assuring that your papers are not destroyed I have urged Dr. Goldsmith to request of the Court that the papers be reserved in their present condition. Dr. Goldsmith agreed with me that every effort should be made to preserve those papers awaiting your return to Massachusetts. Therefore, on May 31, I obtained an order that the papers be preserved. This was done without the knowledge of Herrick and Smith, and that firm will have an opportunity to object to such a court order on June 6. I am enclosing a copy of the order to keep you fully informed.
>
> I would hope that on June 6 the order would be continued against Herrick and Smith and even further that the papers may be ordered to be placed in the custody of the Court.
>
> In any event, we are making every effort to preserve these documents pending your return and further instructions.

The written complaint in the equity court petitioned the judge to deliver the Lahey Memorandum and any other of her papers held by the law firm to Mrs. Strand, or as an alternative to place them in the custody of the clerk of the court, where they would be "secured and sealed by said Clerk until further order of this honorable Court." It was also requested that a preliminary injunction be issued whereby "no harm, damage, or destruction would come to the Lahey document." The memorandum was unique and had to be preserved.

The hearing in the equity court was scheduled for June 6, 1984, before Judge James Lynch. It was very warm and humid that morning when I arrived and quietly took a seat in the back of the courtroom. Mr. Melick was already in the courtroom, and he told me that Richard Gelb of the law firm of Gelb and Heidlage would represent Mrs. Strand's former law firm, Herrick and Smith, the defendants in the case.

The hearing was to begin at 10:00 AM. Just before it commenced, a prepossessing man, accompanied by an associate, strode into the courtroom and requested that his law firm, representing the Lahey Clinic Foundation, be allowed to intervene in the lawsuit. The individual was Edward B. Hanify, chief counsel for the large and powerful law firm of Ropes and Gray; his associate was Roscoe Trimmier, Jr. Amazingly to me, Judge Lynch told the courtroom he was honored to have someone of Mr. Hanify's legal stature and skills present in his court that morning. The Judge's remark seemed highly inappropriate as far as I was concerned, but Mr. Melick assured me that a judge might demonstrate a high regard for a lawyer without its influencing his subsequent legal decisions. I hoped this would hold true in our case.

Dr. Boyd had told me that Hanify, a Lahey Clinic trustee with Boyd, was the Lahey Clinic's lawyer in Mrs. Strand's lawsuit against the clinic (1958–1962). I wondered why Hanify's prestigious law firm was now intervening in a case that was in all appearances a straightforward matter; the return of a personal document that had been placed for safe keeping in another law firm forty years earlier. I now realized I had become the plaintiff in a lawsuit challenging three prominent Boston law firms: Ropes and Gray, Gelb and Heidlage, and Herrick and Smith. This seemed to me to be an inordinately large amount of legal artillery to be arguing what I still believed to be a straightforward case.

Mr. Hanify's appearance that morning was a surprise, but it was not the first time I had had contact with him. Several months earlier we had a far from pleasant telephone conversation. I had read of Hanify in John Tolland's book, *Infamy*,[1] which dealt with the Japanese bombing of Pearl Harbor. Tolland recounts the story of Admiral Husband E. Kimmel, the United States naval commander of the Pacific Fleet at the time of the attack, who was later court-martialed in Washington for dereliction of duty. Admiral Kimmel assembled a legal team to clear his name, and one of the bright young naval lawyers on this team was Lieutenant Edward B. Hanify of Boston. Hanify, in preparation for Kimmel's trial in Washington, D.C., read through volumes of intercepted Japanese messages indicating that the "surprise attack" on Pearl Harbor was no surprise to some in Washington.

Tolland indicated, in an account in *Infamy*, that Hanify was highly displeased at being denied naval intelligence material that might have been used in Admiral Kimmel's defense. These passages, about the legal unfairness of Hanify's being denied information that could aid his client, seemed applicable to Mrs. Strand's lawsuit, i.e., her being denied possible medical documentation of historical importance pertaining to President Roosevelt. More than a quarter of a century had elapsed since Mrs. Strand's legal battle with Hanify and the Lahey Clinic. I naively thought a simple phone call to him might result in his allow-

---

[1]. J. Toland, *Infamy* (New York: Doubleday, 1982).

ing Herrick and Smith, after forty years, to return the Lahey Memorandum to Mrs. Strand.

I called Mr. Hanify at his office at Ropes and Gray, explained my thoughts on the release of important historical documents, and asked if he might help in the effort to gain firsthand knowledge regarding FDR's health. If for nothing else, I thought he might do it for the sake of history. He became immediately incensed at my request, yelling over the phone and wanting to know what right I thought I had to try to gain this information, that I should "let sleeping dogs lie," etc. Shocked by his response, I quickly thanked him for his time and hung up, briefly reflecting that he either possessed a hair-trigger temper or had an unusually intense personal interest in a case he had tried many years earlier.

On that morning of June 6, 1983, in the equity court, I was as yet unaware of Hanify's formidable legal reputation. Now in his presence for the first time, I thought him a commanding presence: tall, robust, with a strong face, and an articulate speaker. I later learned that he had represented many powerful and famous clients and was the lawyer who led Senator Edward M. Kennedy's legal team at Martha's Vineyard in 1968. In Damore's book about the tragic death of Mary Jo Kopechne at Chappaquiddick, there is a description of Hanify's legal stature and skills[2]:

> Whenever the Supreme Court of the United States wishes to hear a lucid description of elements of law, there is no one they would rather hear it from than Edward B. Hanify of Boston.

Hanify represented other members of the Kennedy family, being the lawyer who filed John F. Kennedy's will, and subsequently was named the agent for the slain president's widow. I learned that he was an intimidating opponent in the law courts and continued to hear that Mr. Hanify didn't lose lawsuits.

The first legal skirmish for the Lahey Memorandum was over almost before it began. Judge Lynch, who had received a handwritten motion filed by Hanify (without Melick's knowledge), immediately stated that "Goldsmith" could not be the legal agent for Mrs. Strand since it was she who was petitioning the court for the return of her property. Judge Lynch ruled "all proceedings are stayed for 45 days during which time Linda M. Strand may move that she be substituted as the real party in interest under Massachusetts law, civ. P. 17(A)."

I promptly called Mrs. Strand with this information and asked if she would be willing to become the plaintiff in the case. She readily agreed.

---

2. Leo Damore, *Senatorial Privilege: The Chappaquiddick Cover-Up* (Washington, D.C.: Regnery Gateway, 1988), p. 126.

Melick wrote Mrs. Strand a week later, on June 14, 1984:

Since the writing of my before-mentioned letter I did appear in Court, according to plan, on June 6. Several things occurred on that day:

(a) None other than a senior partner, Edward Hanify of the firm of Ropes and Gray representing the Lahey Clinic, appeared and filed a request to intervene. This means that the Lahey Clinic wished to be permitted to address the Court and argue that your papers should not delivered to you. I cannot provide you with a copy of that motion filed by Attorney Hanify because apparently it was handwritten by him and given to the Clerk without my knowledge. The request by the Lahey Clinic was not acted on because of the other action taken by the Court.

(b) Attorney Gelb appeared for the law firm of Herrick and Smith and filed an Affidavit by Attorney John B. French, partner in the firm of Herrick and Smith. A copy of the Affidavit is enclosed herewith. You will see that *Herrick and Smith is taking the position that the law firm has the right to determine whether the particular medical documents should be released to you even though the so-called Settlement Agreement states"If Mrs. Strand saw fit."* [Author's emphasis.]

It is apparent that both the Lahey Clinic and Herrick and Smith will resist all of efforts made to release these documents.

(c) The Court (Judge Lynch) found that Dr. Goldsmith, even though you have authorized him to obtain these documents on your behalf is not the true party in interest and that it is you and you alone that should be the petitioner. Therefore the Court has continued the temporary order (which orders that the documents should not be altered or changed in any way until further order of the Court) until July 23.

(d) The Court further ordered a stay of the proceedings (meaning that nothing further should be done) for forty-five days, until July 23, in order to provide you the opportunity to, as the real party who is the owner of the documents, to be substituted as the petitioner. A copy of this order is enclosed herewith.

After speaking with Mrs. Strand over the phone, Melick clarified questions she raised with another letter, which he sent on June 28, 1984:

The Order of Judge Lynch of June 6 which I enclosed in my letter to you of June 14 stated that "All proceedings are stayed for 45 days during which time Linda M. Strand may move that she be substituted...." This means that in order to obtain the documents it is necessary for me to draw a motion, which is a one-page piece of paper, requesting that you be substituted for Dr. Goldsmith.

Your appearance would not be required in court at the time that I make that motion. It is conceivable that some pretrial discovery might be undertaken by Herrick and Smith such as written questions being submitted which would require answers; which would of course be handled through our office.

We now know that Herrick and Smith together with the attorneys representing them, Gelb and Heidlage. as well as Attorney Edward Hanify from Ropes and Gray are anxious that your papers not be returned to you. [Author's emphasis.] If you are as anxious as I understand you are to have these papers returned, then I am enclosing an additional copy of this letter, together with a return envelope, in order that you might sign your name in approval of my going forward on your behalf.

The next hearing was on July 20, 1984, in the equity court. Presiding at this hearing was Judge Andrew R. Linscott (judges in the Massachusetts court system periodically rotate between various courts.) Mrs. Strand was now the plaintiff, Mr. Gelb continued as the attorney for Herrick and Smith, and Mr. Trimmier represented Ropes and Gray for the Lahey Clinic since Mr. Hanify was on vacation. Mr. Trimmier began the proceedings. He argued that the Lahey Clinic opposed Herrick-Smith returning the memorandum to Mrs. Strand because she had failed to live up to the terms as set forth in the settlement letter between her attorney, Harold Willcox, of Herrick and Smith, and Mr. Hanify of Ropes and Gray. The Willcox-Hanify letter, written on October 19, 1962, was soon to become the key issue in Mrs. Strand's lawsuit.

Mr. Gelb said Herrick and Smith would be happy to return the Lahey Memo to Mrs. Strand, but he feared that if this were done, Herrick and Smith would be sued by Ropes and Gray for breaking their written agreement. For this reason, and perhaps others, Gelb apparently did all he could throughout the subsequent legal proceedings to prevent the return of Mrs. Strand's personal property, the Lahey Memorandum.

Mr. Trimmier said the matter was not simple, and for the first time he introduced to the court the name of Franklin D. Roosevelt as being the main issue in the Willcox-Hanify letter. I was deeply concerned by this new turn of events, as I had always wanted the lawsuit to be free of any reference to FDR so that there would be no publicity. Now that Trimmier had mentioned it in open court, I feared that Roosevelt's name would attract the attention of the media.

Mr. Melick then presented a strong case for returning the Lahey Memorandum to Mrs. Strand, giving reasons why the law firm of Ropes and Gray had no standing in the matter, and that it was the duty of Herrick and Smith to honor the request of their former client. Melick further asked that the Lahey Memorandum be removed from Herrick and Smith's custody and placed in the custody of the court due to its possible invaluable historical contents. However, Trimmier felt that placing the Lahey Memorandum in the court's custody was inappropriate since he "did not wish to place an added burden on the court related to the difficulty in storing such a document." The court did not rule on the issue so the Lahey Memorandum remained in the possession of Herrick and Smith. Trimmier, very unfairly I thought, raised the question of the mental competence of Mrs. Strand, although he had never met her and had no way of knowing how extremely astute she was (see Appendix A).

The alarming condition in the Willcox-Hanify letter to destroy the Lahey Memorandum upon the death of Mrs. Strand motivated me to contact Dr. William R. Emerson, director of the Roosevelt Library in Hyde Park, to ask for his assistance in preserving the document. He agreed that we must try, to the best of our ability, to prevent the permanent loss of the document. On July 18, 1984, Dr. Emerson wrote to Judge Linscott. He sent the letter to me for delivery, and I gave it to Mr. Melick on the morning of July 20. He then presented it to Judge Linscott just before the hearing began. The letter read:

Dear Judge Linscott:

I am informed that you will have before you on Friday, July 20, a case involving the papers and personal effects of a Mrs. Linda M. Strand who for many years was personal secretary [*sic*] to the late Dr. Frank Lahey of the Lahey Clinic in Boston. I understand Mrs. Strand's papers include inter alia a memorandum by Dr. Lahey, and possibly other pertinent materials, which arise from a consultation he performed for the late President Franklin D. Roosevelt in late 1943 or early 1944.

As Director of this Library, the designated depository of President Roosevelt's material, I *write to apprise you of the great potential significance of these materials of Dr. Lahey for the historical record and of my concern that they be preserved at all costs.* [Author's emphasis.] If it please you, may I suggest that they now be abstracted from Mrs. Strand's other material and confided to Dr. Harry S. Goldsmith of the University Hospital in Boston, for transmission to this library. Dr. Goldsmith is a medical man but is also a leading student of President Roosevelt's health and medical problems. I believe this to be Mrs. Strand's wish. Speaking on behalf of the National

Archives and of the Franklin D. Roosevelt Library, I can say unequivocally that such action on your part would be greatly in the public interest and it is on these grounds that I respectfully petition you to do it.

After hearing the arguments and having read the letter from Dr. Emerson regarding the historical significance of the document, Judge Linscott said he would take all the information under advisement and hoped that he could make a decision in a relatively short period of time. Judge Linscott was very sensitive to Mrs. Strand's advanced age, especially in view of the stipulation in the Willcox-Hanify letter that the Lahey Memorandum be destroyed after her death. He ruled that the case be expedited as quickly as possible with pleadings and depositions completed by early August with a trial to begin in September. Since I had been told that a case of this nature could be in the courts for years, and since neither Hanify nor Gelb had shown any interest in accelerating the legal process, I was very pleased with Judge Linscott's decision. The case was to be jury-waived and decided by a judge.

Mrs. Strand's deposition was taken on August 14, and I was deposed on August 20, 1984. The manner in which Mrs. Strand confronted Hanify is especially informative (see Appendix A).

APPENDIX A

It was quite apparent during the deposition of Mrs. Strand that she was in no way intimidated by Mr. Hanify who, she knew, had the reputation of being a controlling influence on legal matters.

Question (Mr. Hanify)	"And in Cambridge, do you live with the member of your family?"
Answer (Mrs. Strand)	"A member of my family lives in the same house with me, yes, my sister."
Question (Mr. Hanify)	"And what is her name?"
Answer (Mrs. Strand)	"Well, what she got to do with this?"

Mr. Melick "That's all right, why don't you tell him, Mrs. Strand."
After establishing the role Mrs. Strand was to play in the legal action, the next maneuver carried out by Mr. Hanify was to establish the health of Mrs. Strand.

Question (Mr. Hanify)	"How old are you, Mrs. Strand?"
Answer (Mrs. Strand)	"88"
Question (Mr. Hanify)	"Are you hard of hearing?"
Answer (Mrs. Strand)	"Yes"
Question (Mr. Hanify)	"Can you hear me now?"
Answer (Mrs. Strand)	"Yes"
Question (Mr. Hanify)	"Have you heard my questions this far?"
Answer (Mrs. Strand)	"Yes"
Question (Mr. Hanify)	"Is your sight good?"
Answer (Mrs. Strand)	"No"
Question (Mr. Hanify)	"What's the trouble with your sight?"
Answer (Mrs. Strand)	"Just can't see."
Question (Mr. Hanify)	"What's the condition of your general health?"
Answer (Mrs. Strand)	"Not too bad."
Question (Mr. Hanify)	"Other than your eye sight and your hearing, you're in good condition?"
Answer (Mrs. Strand)	"That's right."

This type of questioning obviously showed that Mrs. Strand not only was physically up to the task of instituting a lawsuit, but it was quite obvious that her mental faculties were extremely sharp.

The next part of the deposition was Mr. Hanify establishing the fact that Mrs. Strand was aware that Dr. Lahey had seen FDR in consultation and that a stipulation had been made between Dr. Lahey and Mrs. Strand regarding the memorandum that he wrote pertaining to the president's physical condition.

Question (Mr. Hanify) "If the former statesman (FDR) died on or about April, 1945, the consultation that Dr. Lahey had took place prior at least to April, 1945, is that not right?"

Answer (Mrs. Strand): "I can't tell you. I don't know. I don't remember those dates."

Question: "At some time subsequent to the consultation, did Dr. Lahey make a memorandum with respect thereto?"

Answer (Mrs. Strand): "Just let me have that again."

Question: "At some time prior to his decease and subsequent to the consultation, did Dr. Lahey make a memorandum with respect to the consultation?"

Answer: "That's right."

Question: "And did he give you certain instructions with respect to this custody of that memorandum?"

Answer: "That's right, he gave it to me personally."

Question: "And at the time he gave it to you personally, what if anything did he say to you with respect to its safekeeping?"

Answer: "I was told to keep it and use it when my judgment told me I should."

At this point in the deposition, Mr. Hanify raised an extremely important point pertaining to the letter written by Mr. Harold Willcox of Herrick and Smith to Mr. Hanify in 1962. It was this letter that Hanify was using in his attempt to establish that Mrs. Strand did not have the right to the memorandum that was given to her by Dr. Lahey.

Question (Mr. Hanify): "Do you remember in October of 1962 Mr. Harold Wilcox of Herrick and Smith wrote you a letter with respect to this document?"

Answer:	"Not that I recall, what did the letter say?"
Question:	"I show you what purports to be a copy of the letter. Could you read it? Let's mark it as Exhibit A to the deposition (witness examined Exhibit A)."
The witness:	"I have never seen this before."
Question (Mr. Hanify):	"Do I understand your testimony to be that you never received the original of the letter which is Exhibit A for identification?"
Answer:	"Who signed that letter?"
Question:	"It purports to be signed by H.M. Willcox."
Answer:	"No, I don't recall ever seeing it."

Mrs. Strand never understood why Hanify, the Lahey Clinic, and Herrick Smith had anything to do with the agreement that had been made between Dr. Lahey and herself regarding the Lahey Memorandum.

Question (Mr. Hanify):	"Did you authorize Mr. Melick to represent you in this case?"
Answer:	"Yes."
Question:	"When?"
Answer:	"Oh, I don't know. I think your questions are ridiculous."
Question:	"Why do you resent my questions?"
Answer:	"Because I think it's none of your business. In the first place, I don't understand why you're in on this right now. It's none of your business. Those papers belong to me, and you should have nothing to do with them."
Question:	"You do not recognize that you had any obligations under the settlement to turn those papers over to Herrick Smith?"
Answer:	"No."

I was deposed several days following Mrs. Strand's deposition. When my deposition of 3 hours ended, the conference room in which it was held began to empty. Mr. J. Bryant Fritz, the registered professional reporter and notary public who had taken the stenography of the deposition that morning, came to where I was sitting and told me that he had been taking stenography for 12 years and this was the most interesting deposition that he felt he had ever recorded. He asked if I would send him a copy of the paper that I had written in 1979 concerning

President Roosevelt. I told him that I was pleased by his request and that I would send him the article as soon as I returned to my office.

Another event of interest that occurred after my deposition dealt with Mr. Hanify. Everyone was in the process of leaving or had already left the room. Mr. Hanify and I were sitting at the end of the conference table directly opposite each other, being separated by no more than two and a half to three feet. Suddenly our eyes met. Looking directly at me and with no emotion showing on his face, Mr. Hanify brought his right hand above his right eye in a sharp military salute. I, in turn, also showing no emotion and still focusing directly on his eyes, returned the salute. I have never been certain what was in Mr. Hanify's mind when he did this, but I hoped at the time that the reason for his salute was that I had stood my ground in a gentlemanly and intelligent manner against one of the foremost leaders in the legal profession.

CHAPTER 18

THE TRIAL

The trial was scheduled for Friday, September 28, 1984, to be heard before Judge Jeremiah J. Sullivan in the Middlesex Superior Court, Cambridge, Massachusetts. Melick and his associate, George E. Wakeman, Jr., were present to represent Mrs. Strand; Hanify and Trimmier represented the Lahey Clinic Foundation; and Richard M. Gelb represented Herrick and Smith.

Melick presented first. He detailed how Mrs. Strand had been entrusted with a memorandum from Dr. Lahey with specific instructions that if there should ever be criticism of his medical relationship to FDR, it was to be made public. Melick explained that Mrs. Strand had placed the document in the custody of her law firm, Herrick and Smith, for safekeeping with the understanding that it would be returned to her at any time she wished. He argued that Mrs. Strand knew nothing of and had never seen, much less signed, the Willcox-Hanify letter of October 19, 1962, the letter the opposing attorneys claimed warranted Herrick and Smith's retaining her document.

Mr. Hanify then rose to discuss the position of the Lahey Clinic Foundation that he claimed was a defendant-intervener in the case. He described the settlement of the litigation that occurred between Mrs. Strand and the Lahey Clinic in 1962, and he read the entire Willcox-Hanify letter as though the case now revolved almost solely around this document. He stressed the key paragraph in the document:

> Mrs. Strand was given this document by Dr. Lahey with instructions that if Dr. Lahey should ever be posthumously criticized for his conduct in relation to his consultation and his failure to make a public report thereof, the document was to be published if Mrs. Strand saw fit. That document would be delivered to this firm to be held by this firm until such time comes, if it ever does, that the document should be redelivered to Mrs.

Strand in order that she may carry out the conditions upon which it was given her. In the event of Mrs. Strand's death the document will be destroyed if it is still in our possession.

Sitting next to me in the courtroom, Mrs. Strand said quite audibly that all this was a lie, she had never seen the Willcox-Hanify letter, and she had never considered at any time that the Lahey Memorandum be destroyed at her death.

Mr. Hanify ended his opening statement with the following:

> It's our position that there had not come to our attention anything of the nature of the kind of substantive criticism of Dr. Lahey; that this matter has been stirred up by Dr. Goldsmith who was the original plaintiff in this case, who has, what my brother [Mr. Melick] has described, a hobby with respect to unearthing this kind of information. So all the Lahey Clinic is trying to do as an intervener here is preserve the privacy of that patient's record which we have attempted to preserve by virtue of the special arrangement made in this said letter integrating into the basic settlement agreement, giving that law firm the custody of the letter subject to its release when the conditions took place.

The first witness Hanify called was Charles C. Cabot, Jr., a former lawyer in the firm of Herrick and Smith who had been involved in the litigation involving the Lahey Clinic conducted by his firm for Mrs. Strand. He was asked simply to confirm the signatures of Linda M. Strand and the late Harold M. Willcox, Mrs. Strand's lawyer in her lawsuit against the Lahey Clinic from 1958 to 1962.

Hanify introduced for identification the Willcox-Hanify letter of October 19, 1962, written by Harold M. Willcox to Hanify. The Judge asked specifically to whom the letter was sent and Hanify stated, "To me, which I represent to the court comes from my file."

When asked if the signature on the letter was Willcox's, Cabot replied, "I don't remember his signature, but I believe that it is." He said the signature looked like Mr. Willcox's but because twenty years had elapsed since he had seen the letter he could not be positive. Hanify continued:

> Now its true it's some twenty-odd years ago and naturally he (Cabot) is somewhat reserved about identifying, with precision, a signature on a document that purports to come from the firm. I will be prepared if necessary to present testimony from my own office that I received this letter, and have had it in my files through all the intervening years, and was a letter

delivered to me as part of that settlement agreement along with the settlement agreement.

Prior to the trial, I had obtained a copy of the Willcox-Hanify letter from Herrick and Smith. The signature on the Willcox-Hanify letter I had received from the law firm was completely different from the signature on the letter Hanify had just presented to the court, which he stated had been in his files for over twenty years. Not only was the signature of Willcox different between these two letters, but the letter I received from Herrick and Smith was preceded with a hieroglyphic and followed by the words "By Harold M. Willcox." Melick called attention to the discrepancies in the signatures when he stated to the court:

> I find it strange. I don't know how many lawyers sign "By." Lawyers just sign their names and when I see "By" it seems to indicate more that someone else has affixed someone's signature, and in this case we have a witness who can't identify the signature. *I could not explain how an original letter written from one law firm to another law firm could have been signed by someone other than the originator of the document.* [Author's emphasis.]

I subsequently researched the question of the authenticity of the signatures. After visiting the archive section in the law library in the Suffolk County Court Building, I found Willcox's original Massachusetts Bar Association registration card, complete with signature, requesting the privilege to practice law in the commonwealth. Willcox's signature on the Massachusetts registration card matched that on the letter originating from Hanify's office. Surprisingly, Willcox's signature on the letter sent to me by Herrick and Smith was not Willcox's signature!

After Melick's presentation, Gelb, representing Herrick and Smith, produced a document for the court and said, "Let me show you a memorandum dated 1962 from the Herrick and Smith files." He also said, "I have copies of the settlement agreement, the Willcox letter, and agenda I have extracted from Herrick and Smith's files." Obviously, Gelb had gone through Herrick and Smith's files on Mrs. Strand, which he had carefully studied and was well aware of information pertaining to Mrs. Strand and the Lahey Memorandum. (His knowledge of Mrs. Strand's file will be shown later to be of great importance.)

Melick joined Mrs. Strand and me during the lunch recess. He told us that we would not have to testify since he had obtained, subject to our approval, an agreement with the opposing lawyers that Mrs. Strand's and my depositions would be introduced into evidence without either of us having to take the witness stand. We had already given full testimony during our depositions; Melick was greatly concerned that Mrs. Strand's combativeness toward Hanify and Herrick and

Smith might cause her to say something explosive that could prove detrimental to our case. I personally felt Mrs. Strand's mental competency and loyalty to Dr. Lahey would favorably impress the judge, but I said nothing. When the court reconvened, Melick said no further witnesses were necessary and that the remainder of the trial could be carried out in closed session, deliberated among Judge Sullivan and the law firms involved.

The opposing lawyers, especially Gelb, were clearly elated that Mrs. Strand was not to testify, and observing this, Mrs. Strand and I had grave misgiving that our side had made a bad decision. However, Melick apparently made the right decision. Judge Sullivan requested that all necessary exhibits be submitted to him by both sides for his deliberation in order that he be informed at the time of closing arguments. He hoped these final arguments would take place within the next month or two. Court recessed.

Just over two months later, the closing arguments were held in the Suffolk County Courthouse on Wednesday, December 5, 1984, in a closed meeting. The only persons in attendance were Melick, on behalf of the Plaintiff, Linda Strand; Gelb, on behalf of the defendants Herrick and Smith; and Hanify and Trimmier, on behalf of the defendant-intervener, the Lahey Clinic Foundation. The following account is from the official record taken by the court stenographer.

Hanify spoke first, outlining the case as it had developed, including how I had become involved and ultimately how Mrs. Strand had become the plaintiff. Hanify commented:

> It is too late in the day to advance the contention that Mrs. Strand did not know about this letter when the agenda shows she was present at the settlement agreements, when counsel who witnessed her signature has testified and when you have the statement of a deceased lawyer, made in good faith to me, that she knew about the contents of the letter.

Mrs. Strand had told me personally and had earlier testified at her deposition that she had never seen the letter written by Willcox to Hanify. She also told me that under no condition would she have allowed such a letter to pass between lawyers without having signed it. She had been Dr. Lahey's business manager for many years and well knew the importance of documenting by initials or signature any letters or business matters of significance. The Willcox-Hanify letter would certainly have required her initialing if she had seen it.

Mr. Hanify pleaded, based on the Willcox-Hanify letter, that Mrs. Strand should not have the Lahey Memorandum returned to her because the conditions in the document, concerning the posthumous criticism of Dr. Lahey, had not been met. Hanify asserted the Lahey Memorandum should therefore remain with

Herrick-Smith who would determine whether the criteria of the criticism had been met or not. Additionally, upon the death of Mrs. Strand, it was not to be left to her executor or representative to dispose of the document; Herrick and Smith was to be empowered to destroy the document. Hanify further commented:

> That was the deal the parties made with respect to this particular document. It was obviously not intended that at any time in the future at her complete discretion she could get the document back to do with it as she would. What would be the purpose of the bailment of the document to Herrick and Smith with those specified conditions if the next day she was entitled to have it back regardless of whether the conditions had developed. The whole arrangement would have been ridiculous if it did not have the objective of interposing between her recovery and disposition of the document, a judgment that we, as counsel for Lahey, could trust; the judgment of her counsel with respect to existence of the occurrences which were to release the document back to her for the exercise then of her discretion as to whether she published it. That was the essence of the agreement; it makes no sense to construe it otherwise.
>
> We are here to defend the interest of the Lahey Clinic against the intermeddling of a medical entrepreneur who is looking for publicity and who has, in my judgment, manipulated this poor old woman into becoming his cat's paw in his effort to make a notorious first.

I was somewhat surprised that Hanify attacked me personally and openly since he knew my search for historical information on FDR had the sanction and support of James Roosevelt, the Roosevelt Library, and the National Archives in Washington. Mr. Melick was also disturbed by Hanify's personal comments about my motives as he showed at the beginning of his own arguments:

> I would first make comment your honor of I suppose, amazement of some of Mr. Hanify's comments. I have known Mr. Hanify for a long time. I've heard Mr. Hanify speak on a number of occasions. I am aware that he has a reputation as an eloquent speaker and in fact has a great command of the English language. I do not know how often Mr. Hanify gets into court anymore. Perhaps he is misjudging his after-dinner speaking with his comments in open court, but I am surprised to find him attacking Dr. Goldsmith as a medical entrepreneur. I'm surprised to hear him saying that he has exhibited an appalling disregard for medical ethics. I find these comments unworthy of Mr. Hanify and out of place in this courtroom. I am surprised to hear him characterizing me as someone who has exhibited

a cavalier indifference. I'm surprised to hear him say that my client, Mrs. Strand, is a manipulated poor old woman who has been manipulated into being a cat's paw. Those comments I feel are inappropriate. I feel they are absolutely contrary to the circumstances before your honor.

Hanify's rhetoric had not overwhelmed Mr. Melick in any way. Melick stressed that Dr. Lahey entrusted only Mrs. Strand with the Lahey Memorandum, with instructions to publish it if there were ever any criticism of him concerning FDR. There were no stipulations as to types of criticisms, written or oral, and Mrs. Strand alone had the right and the obligation to publish his memorandum. Melick established that Mrs. Strand left the Lahey Memorandum with "her attorneys in full confidence that any such time that she asked for her personal papers back she could have them." He stated again that Mrs. Strand said she "never saw this letter from Willcox." He referred to the Lahey Memorandum's historical importance and added:

The issue [Lahey Memorandum] really is whether Mrs. Strand is entitled to have a document that she was given as a personal piece of paper.
Ropes and Gray (Hanify) does not have any authority to be here. They are
here, they refer to themselves as defendant. They are not a defendant. They
are an intervener and they came before the court and said "we have a stake
and because we have a stake let us enter and we will tell you what our stake
is." It is interesting what they have told us as to what their stake was as evidenced by these documents. They say "let us come in and tell you," but
they did not represent Dr. Lahey, they do not represent President
Roosevelt, they do not have any standing to talk about this document, if
Your Honor please. If these papers, or if one paper was a part of the Lahey
Clinic record, that would be a different story but this is a personal one.

Nearing the end of his plea, Mr. Melick discussed the Willcox-Hanify letter as an agreement that lacked legally enforceable specifics:

If anybody—Herrick-Smith, Ropes and Gray, the Lahey Clinic had
intended that somebody other than Mrs. Strand would make that determination (criticism) of Lahey they certainly would have at least put it in
the letter. I submit that they would have provided it someplace in one of
the documents but they did not put it in the letter and if one simply reads
this, it says if there was criticism it was to be published, says it was to be
published if Mrs. Strand saw fit. There is nothing here that indicates that
Herrick and Smith makes the determination of criticism; there is nothing

that says that Lahey Clinic makes that determination or that Ropes and Gray makes that determination. It is strictly if Mrs. Strand sees fit.

Melick then went on to explain the different forms of criticism that had been raised against Lahey, including:

> The most interesting comments [criticism] come from the gentleman who Mr. Hanify has passed over rather quickly, a Dr. Boyd, who the transcripts indicate is presently a Trustee of the Lahey Foundation. Now this is not some obscure writer in some distant state. This is a gentleman who is a physician and a fellow Trustee along with Mr. Hanify at the Lahey Foundation.

Melick concluded by noting that Lahey's memorandum on FDR was not a part of any hospital record but was a personal paper and therefore not subject to any of the Lahey Clinic Foundation's interest:

> He [Lahey] gave it to a personal friend in whom he had entrusted it to be used to protect his own reputation if at such time she found there was criticism. He left the judgment to her. She is 88 years old. She is not half blind and half deaf as Mr. Hanify suggests. She has very poor sight and she is hard of hearing but she has all her faculties. If it was not otherwise, the defendants in this case would be coming in and suggesting that and offering medical proof to the court. The lady knows what she is doing and she wants to protect the man who entrusted her with that document.

When the trial before Judge Sullivan had been completed, I felt confident that he would instruct Herrick and Smith to return the Lahey Memorandum to Mrs. Strand. Melick warned against overconfidence; one could never be certain of the outcome of litigation until the final decision. Nevertheless, I could sense that he felt Mrs. Strand would get her document. Yet his admonition turned out to be correct. On January 10, 1985, we were all amazed to learn that Judge Sullivan had ruled against Mrs. Strand. Not only did she lose her case, she lost it "with prejudice," meaning the case could never again be tried in court (the exception being a court of appeals). An additional and unbelievable decision by the judge was his directive that Hanify's law firm, which had entered the case completely on their own, were to have their legal fees paid by Mrs. Strand; their fee—$25,000.!

I studied carefully Judge Sullivan's written rulings of law, which were the basis for his decision. His writings were almost identical to the rulings of law submitted by Hanify in his legal brief. In fact, the Judge had accepted, almost word for word, Hanify's case against Mrs. Strand, even to the point of copying Hanify's misspellings and improper punctuations.

Shortly after learning that Mrs. Strand had lost the case, Melick called me with the news that Trimmier, Hanify's associate, had advised him that if we did not appeal the case, Trimmier's law firm would not request the legal fee Judge Sullivan had ordered Mrs. Strand to pay.

The ruling in favor of Herrick and Smith and Ropes and Gray (representing the Lahey Clinic) was an appalling setback. It continued to raise the question of the safety of the Lahey Memorandum, a document by a credible source that might explain FDR's health during the last year of his life. It also bespoke a concerted effort by these law firms to interpret Dr. Lahey's instructions themselves and to prevent the disclosure of his memorandum at any cost. The offer by Trimmier that Ropes and Gray would drop the court-mandated payment of their fees, if we did not appeal the case, emphasized this effort to suppress the memorandum. The question of whether or not to continue our efforts was carefully discussed and deliberated. There was no question. We would appeal the case back to Judge Sullivan.

CHAPTER 19

THE APPEAL

Mr. Melick wrote a letter to Mrs. Strand stating that Judge Sullivan "finds that Herrick and Smith has the right to determine whether there has been criticism of Dr. Lahey, which we find inconsistent with the evidence." Melick also wrote a letter to me on February 1, 1985, that stated:

I regret to be writing this letter to you but must report that Judge Sullivan has found against us. I'm enclosing a copy of his decision. As you will see, he finds that Herrick and Smith had the right to determine whether there was criticism of Dr. Lahey. While I realize that this is the defendant's position, it is not substantiated by the evidence.

All of us here are shocked at his report. None of us expected it.

I would like to talk to you about your feelings in regard to appeal and would hope that we could get together for this purpose. I know of no evidence known to us which was not represented in its most favorable light to Judge Sullivan; further, I conclude that nothing could have been done that was not done.

The strong legal defense which had been mounted to continue to deprive Mrs. Strand of the Lahey Memorandum seemed unusually aggressive, even suspect. Concern for the security of the memorandum had already been expressed, and it seemed clear that there would be much criticism leveled at the Lahey Clinic in the future by historians if it allowed the destruction of the Lahey Memorandum. In fact, there appeared to be no reason for the Lahey Clinic to be involved in the case since there was no record of FDR ever having been a patient at the Lahey Clinic. Yet Hanify claimed the reason the clinic wished to suppress the Lahey document was to protect the privacy of one of its patients.

Believing that the decision of the court should and could be challenged and changed, Melick filed a motion for a new trial. Reasons for the appeal were: 1) the judgment entered by the court is against the weight of evidence; 2) the judgment of the court in favor of the defendants is predicated upon findings of facts and rulings of law which are clearly erroneous; 3) the judgment of the court in favor of the defendants is clearly erroneous in light of the court's improper denial of plaintiff's proposed findings of facts and rulings of law which are expressively incorporated herein by reference; 4) to prevent a gross miscarriage of justice.

Melick was visibly upset at the previous ruling against Mrs. Strand. He expressed his dismay with the legal system itself, which he felt had been abused by the methods employed against Mrs. Strand. These concerns were expounded in his opening remarks at the appeal that began on March 7, 1985, again before Judge Sullivan:

> I would say, your Honor, that this is the saddest day of my life as a practicing attorney, absolutely the saddest. I am non-plussed by your Honor's findings. I don't understand them. I can only assume that I totally failed in my position. I guess my feeling of disappointment is that I obviously have failed to convince the court of my client's position. There was never any question, any question in my mind, for what Mrs. Strand not only had a meritorious case but would succeed. I can only say to the court that I obviously failed.

Melick further reminded the court that if the fate of the Lahey Memorandum were to be decided by Herrick and Smith's definition of criticism of Lahey, there would have to have been:

> ... terms, conditions, circumstances, possession to which they would have had to comply in the course of that obligation ... There is nothing in any documentation that says what Herrick and Smith is supposed to do. Even if Ropes and Gray [the Lahey Clinic] wanted Herrick and Smith to make a decision whether there was criticism of Dr. Lahey, Ropes and Gray would have spelled out what Ropes and Gray on behalf of the Lahey Clinic through Herrick and Smith would have to do.

Melick pointed out that he felt it odd that Hanify was arguing so strongly against Mrs. Strand rather than Gelb, who represented Herrick and Smith, the law firm Mrs. Strand was suing. Melick emphasized:

> The Lahey memo is not a Lahey Clinic medical record. This is not a document that belongs to the Clinic. This is a document that Dr. Lahey

provided for his personal self-protection. He wanted to protect his own reputation. He gave this FDR memo not to the Clinic, not to Ropes and Gray or Herrick and Smith; he gave it to the one person in the world that he thought he could trust the most. He gave it to Linda Strand to hold and to protect for his reputation if it is criticized.

Finally, Melick protested the Judge's decision that Mrs. Strand pay the legal fees of Ropes and Gray, Hanify's law firm. He argued that Ropes and Gray not be awarded legal fees since they were not a defendant, only an intervener in the case. Mrs. Strand had not sued Hanify's firm, and if they didn't sue Mrs. Strand, "why should an intervener be permitted to voluntarily come into a case and then ask for financial relief against a person who they didn't sue?" Melick expressed complete disbelief that anyone could even think of asking Mrs. Strand to pay legal fees to Hanify's firm. When Melick had concluded, Judge Sullivan addressed him in the following terms:

> Thank you Mr. Melick, I want to make it clear Sir, that as you know I have been in and out of these courts now for thirty-three years and I have never seen a case tried better than the one you tried. It was excellent.

On March 12, 1985, Melick wrote Mrs. Strand the following letter:

> On Thursday, March 7, 1985, I appeared in Suffolk Superior Court for the purpose of arguing all post trial motions which had been filed by us on your behalf and also on behalf of the defendants by their counsel. This was the most difficult time in my practice of law because I frankly cannot conceive of the rulings which have been made by the trial judge in this case.
> Judge Sullivan was, however as always, thoughtful, attentive and polite. Whether I convinced him to reverse his rulings we will not know until we have his order. Frankly, I would doubt it. We may however, find that he is helpful to us in his rulings in respect to those motions filed by the defendants.
> As soon as I have received the orders of Judge Sullivan relative to these motions, I will communicate with you immediately.

We received the new ruling of Judge Sullivan on April 11, 1985. His original judgment was upheld; but he did concede that the legal fees demanded by Ropes and Gray of Mrs. Strand seemed excessive, and he instructed "the plaintiff [Mrs. Strand] to pay the *defendant* (Ropes and Gray) as a contribution towards its attorney fees and expenses, the sum of $5,000 and cost of $795.85." Again it must be stressed that Ropes and Gray was not a defendant in the case.

This new legal decision, although still inexplicable to those of us trying to gain the Lahey Memorandum, was not entirely unexpected. Mr. Melick and I had already determined that our only recourse in case of losing was an appeal to the Massachusetts Court of Appeals. The settlement in the lower court only served to amplify the possible importance of the Lahey Memorandum; we felt obliged to fight for its preservation to the very end.

Melick filed a notice of appeal two weeks later, on April 25, 1985. Preparations for the new trial began in earnest by all the firms involved. Melick called on Robert Powers, a junior member in his law firm (now a senior partner) to write the arguments that would be presented to the second-highest court in the Commonwealth of Massachusetts. Powers—young and intense—was particularly pleased to participate, at such an early stage in his legal career, in a case to be tried before the Massachusetts Court of Appeals against Edward B. Hanify, the prominent Massachusetts lawyer.

Melick's brief to the appeals court rested upon two basic questions: the first, substantial, the second more technical: 1) whether Linda Strand was entitled to the prompt return of the Lahey Memorandum from her former law firm that had no explicit grounds upon which to retain the document; and 2) whether Judge Sullivan's award for attorney fees from Mrs. Strand was proper since the court had failed to follow the statutory mandate to set in order the specific facts and reasons upon which the award was based.

The arguments outlined in Melick and Powers's brief were written specifically for the appeals court, based in law and facts supporting the following argument:

1) Herrick and Smith is under legal and ethical duty to return the Lahey Memorandum to Mrs. Strand because they were given permission solely to safeguard the document;

2) the Lahey Clinic had no legal or equitable right to interfere with the arrangement which resulted in Dr. Lahey giving his memorandum on FDR to Linda Strand because they were not a party to this agreement;

3) the settlement agreement between Linda Strand and the Lahey Clinic did not affect her control of the Lahey Memorandum;

4) even if the letter (Willcox-Hanify) was part of the settlement agreement, it did not establish that judgment of Herrick-Smith had anything to do with whether or not the Lahey Memorandum was to be returned to its lawful owner, Linda Strand;

5) even accepting the Lahey Clinic's arguments, Herrick and Smith must return the document to Linda Strand because Dr. Lahey has been posthumously criticized;

6) historical considerations compel the return of the Lahey Memorandum to Mrs. Strand so it will not be destroyed upon her death;

7) the award of attorney fees must be reversed because the trial court did not establish any facts or reasons for the award nor did it specify the method by which the award was computed.

Melick and Powers's brief, dated September 20, 1985, concluded with:

> Counsel for the Lahey Clinic stated "we are not anxious to obstruct history." Unfortunately, that is exactly what will happen if they prevail. They are not entitled to historical considerations. For all the foregoing reasons, Linda M. Strand requests that this court reverse the decision below and order the return of the Lahey Memorandum together with any and all remaining papers of hers that Herrick and Smith may possess.

The legal brief submitted on October 18, 1985, by Hanify and Trimmier argued against all the points mentioned in Melick and Powers's brief. Their conclusion stated:

> The defendant Lahey Clinic Foundation Incorporated prays that the judgment on the merits be affirmed and that the case be remanded for the necessary findings for the award of reasonable attorney fees and costs to the Lahey Clinic Foundation incurred in connection with this action, including this appeal.

When the date of the hearing before the appellate court was drawing near, I enlisted outside sources to impress the court of the possible historical importance of preserving the Lahey Memorandum. I wanted the judges to appreciate that there was no reluctance on the part of the Roosevelt family to preserve the Lahey Memorandum. James Roosevelt submitted an *amicus curiae* (friend of the court) brief to John E. Powers, clerk of the appeals court, requesting that the Lahey Memorandum be preserved. The National Archives and Records Administration, Washington, DC, sent another Amicus Curiae brief to the Massachusetts Appeals Court. The brief was from William F. Weld, United States attorney (later governor of Massachusetts); Richard K. Willard, acting assistant attorney general; William F. Leonard Schaitman and Marc Johnston, attorneys on the Appellate Staff-Civil Division of the Department of Justice in Washington, DC. Their brief stated:

The National Archives and Record Administration (National Archives) is charged with the responsibility for preserving historically valuable records and other materials pertaining to the Government. By statute, the National Archives has special authority to collect and preserve "in the public interest" historical materials relating to the Presidents of the United States, 44 U.S.C.211, 2112. The instant brief Amicus Curiae is being submitted to advise the court of the National Archives belief that a document of unique historical importance, relating to former President Franklin Deleno Roosevelt, is at issue in this case ... it would be tragic if preservation of a document about which the parties are arguing is not ensured.

They continued:

It is not altogether clear to us why the parties in this case seemed to have reached an impasse that jeopardizes preservation of the Lahey Memorandum. We are informed about the privacy interest that is attached to a patient's record. However, we also understand that the Roosevelt family already has written to this court to put on record its concern that the document be preserved at all costs for the historical record and made public when circumstances permit.

The brief ended with a single-sentence conclusion: "The Lahey Memorandum is a unique and important historical document; there is substantial public interest in ensuring its preservation."

CHAPTER 20

THE SUPREME JUDICIAL COURT OF MASSACHUSETTS

On September 20, 1985, the legal brief written by Melick and Powers was submitted to the Massachusetts Court of Appeals. The case, initially listed in the lower court under my name, was now "Linda Strand vs. the Law Firm of Herrick, Smith." Without Roosevelt's name on the court's listed docket, the case had gone unnoticed during the past year by the local courthouse press who are in the pay of major newspaper bureaus seeking interesting cases for newspaper publication. I was grateful for the lack of media attention.

That was soon to change. On the morning of October 14, 1985, I bought the *Boston Globe* to read while having breakfast in a small restaurant near my home. After ordering, I opened the paper to see pictures of FDR and Dr. Lahey glaring out from the top of the front page. The headline read: "A Memo—and a Mystery: Documents Sought in Court Case May Hold Clues to FDR's Health." The article was extensive, requiring seven columns printed on two pages. It told of Mrs. Strand's attempts to gain the Lahey Memorandum from her law firm and the firm's refusal to release it to her. Hanify was quoted:

> We realize the historical implication and *we are not trying to be obstructive to history.* [Author's emphasis.] All we are doing is making that decision considerately and not from the sole view of an archivist who would like to have a first for his papers—they (hospital trustees) do not want to be in the position of having the world say and having patients say what protection do you give us?

Then the following sentence in the article caught my eye, one that I had been fearing as it could bring unwanted media attention:

It wasn't Strand who first went to court to get the document, but Dr. Harry S. Goldsmith, a Boston Surgeon and Medical School Professor, who asked her permission to get the document for her.

The *Boston Herald* carried the story the following day with a picture of Roosevelt under the headline, "Feds Want FDR Memo Public: Note Could Peg 4th-Term Health Issue."

Someone had leaked the story to the Boston newspapers, so there was now the added burden of unwanted publicity. A day or two later, however, Melick called with an exciting message. The Supreme Judicial Court of the Commonwealth of Massachusetts had become aware of the case and considered it of significant importance to try it in this highest court of the commonwealth. My anxiety, generated by the discomfort of publicity, was quickly dispelled by the news that the top jurists in Massachusetts would impartially evaluate the rulings of law as written by Hanify and copied by Judge Sullivan.

The case was scheduled for December 5, 1985. In the legal brief submitted by Melick and Powers, they highlighted the criticism that Hanify directed against me, and stressed that Mrs. Strand never made any prelitigation commitments regarding the Lahey Memorandum:

> The Lahey Clinic spends page after page in their brief talking about Dr. Goldsmith. Nearly three pages out of seven of their statement of the facts is spent on Dr. Goldsmith's involvement in this matter. The clinic's argument spends an inordinate amount of time attacking Dr. Goldsmith's involvement. (This action was commenced and fostered by Dr. Harry Sawyer Goldsmith, a medical publicist). This preoccupation with Dr. Goldsmith serves no useful purpose. It needlessly clouds the issues and is for the most part, irrelevant to the resolution.... The clinic's attempt to paint this case as one of medical sensationalism is particularly disingenuous. A litigation so motivated was oriented to tomorrow's headlines. The record reflects, and the Lahey Clinic is well aware, that Linda Strand made no prelitigation promises about the Roosevelt Memorandum. She made clear her intentions with respect to that particular document.
>
> She wants it back in order that she may make a considered decision about how to best effectuate those wishes expressed to her alone by Dr. Lahey when he gave her the memorandum.

The case was tried in the impressive courtroom of the state supreme court, Chief Justice C. J. Hennessey presiding. He and Associate Justices Wilkins, Liacos, Abrams, and Nolan were seated on a dais with the lawyers sitting directly below and in front of them. Protocol allowed each lawyer to speak for twelve-to-fifteen minutes into a microphone centrally located before the judges, who would ask questions during and after the legal arguments. Both Hanify and Melick delivered impressive presentations. Melick spoke first, arguing that the decision made by Judge Sullivan was:

> … no independent work by the trial court and that the rulings as adopted by the trial judge are a mirror image of those submitted by the Lahey Clinic. You will undoubtedly find that the findings were clearly erroneous and have a firm conviction that an error has been made.

Melick further stated that the trial, which had been ongoing for a year and a half, was not "frivolous," as claimed by the opposing attorneys. He argued that there was no justification for the court's order that Mrs. Strand pay the legal fees of Ropes and Gray, whose role was simply as an intervener in the case. He stressed that Hanify, representing Ropes and Gray, knew that the clinic was not a "defendant" and that being an "intervener" did not entitle them to punitive awards.

Mr. Melick emphasized that the Lahey Memorandum was given to Mrs. Strand to carry out Dr. Lahey's wishes concerning any possible future criticism of him *vis-à-vis* his relation to FDR. Obviously, Mrs. Strand was to make the decision as to what criticism would justify action. To establish that such criticism had been raised against Dr. Lahey, Melick stated:

> [I]f the average citizen of this Commonwealth heard him or herself spoken of as being tortuous, convoluted and evasive, intellectually less than honest, a partner to a cover-up-the ultimate in chicanery, and outright deception; these are the words that had been used about Dr. Lahey, and Mrs. Strand is properly concerned about them even though the trial court [Judge Sullivan] found that these words did not represent criticism.

Speaking without notes, Melick continued that the Willcox-Hanify letter was not part of the settlement agreement between Mrs. Strand and the Lahey Clinic (which Mrs. Strand always claimed):

> [A]ll of the papers of the settlement were put together at a meeting of all parties on a Friday evening to be held in escrow until they were to meet again at 2 PM on Monday. This letter (Lahey Memorandum) was not among those papers. It was not held in escrow, in fact it was delivered to Lahey Clinic's attorney on Monday morning and therefore it was separate from the agreement.

Melick asked if the letter from the now deceased Willcox to Hanify in 1962 was signed by Willcox and remained in Hanify's files for thirty years, why was the copy held in Willcox's office signed by someone other than Mr. Willcox? Melick finished his presentation:

> [T]here is no evidence, it is pure speculation whether the Lahey Memorandum even contains medical evidence. It's argued by the Clinic that it relates to the medical condition of Roosevelt. The fact of the matter is that the evidence shows that it was drawn by Dr. Lahey for protection and explanation of his actions which may just as easily, by way of speculation, relate to something that is non-medical.

I found this statement to be astute since it raised the question as to how the attorneys opposing Mrs. Strand were so certain of the medical contents of the Lahey Memorandum, which was in a sealed envelope—unless someone had opened the envelope and knew the contents of the document!

Hanify then argued that there had been no posthumous criticism of Dr. Lahey and said, "[T]he Clinic is anxious to protect the doctor/patient principle as would be violated by returning the Lahey Memo to Mrs. Strand." Then he presented a major surprise by implying doubt about the existence of the Lahey Memorandum: "[N]either the Clinic or its Counsel had seen that Memorandum nor have we ever seen it ... this raises a serious question in my mind as to the authenticity of whatever it is that is in this sealed envelope; it would be a shame if a bogus document was treated as the work of Dr. Lahey because the Clinic assented to its preservation."

This was the first suggestion, after a year and a half in the courts, that there might not be a Lahey Memorandum. The back of attorney Powers's neck actually turned conspicuously red, betraying his surprise and befuddlement when Hanify insinuated that the document over which he and Melick had been fighting so strenuously might be a bogus document. Hanify's attempt to denigrate the authenticity of the Lahey document at this late stage in the proceedings was odd.

In the lower court proceedings, Hanify had derided my association with Mrs. Strand, but both Melick and Powers assured me there would be no such personal attack before the state supreme court, whose function was solely to evaluate points of law and legal decisions. Hanify, however, surprised us:

> This action was commenced by a Dr. Goldsmith who had thought, as the records show unsuccessfully, to pry the secret of the document from the deceased doctor's operating room nurse and from his private secretary, and had not been successful. He was more assiduous than ingenuous. He

then commenced this litigation with the apparent authorization of the plaintiff, making it appear that it was a simple case of an agent for a client attempting to retrieve that client's papers from a custodial attorney and that still seems to be the gist of what has been said.

Hanify finished his presentation:

> The Lahey Clinic has no vested interest in the destruction of the paper, all the clinic was attempting to do your Honor, in this case, was to prevent the immediate delivery to Dr. Goldsmith or the plaintiff of this document under conditions which would violate the terms under which it was given to Herrick and Smith and unfortunately result in its present exploitation. We suggest therefore that the decision of the Superior Court be affirmed.

After almost two-and-a-half months, on February 18, 1986, Chief Justice C. J. Hennessey wrote a unanimous decision. The state supreme court ruled that the failure of the lower court to appreciate the posthumous criticism made against Dr. Lahey was "clearly erroneous." The twelve-page opinion ended with the following:

> In essence, the evidence presented suggested that Dr. Lahey was part of a *conspiracy of silence* [author's emphasis] regarding President Roosevelt's health. These opinions, regardless of their validity, constitute partial criticism of Dr. Lahey for his conduct in relation to his consultation and his failure to make a public report thereof. The condition preceding to Herrick and Smith the redelivery of the Lahey Memorandum. To order attorney fees to the Lahey Clinic was improper. As the foregoing analysis indicates, Strand's action clearly was not wholly insubstantial, frivolous and not advanced in good faith.

And finally:

> The judgment for the defendants and the order granting them attorney fees are reversed. A judgment shall be entered which requires Herrick and Smith to deliver the Lahey Memorandum to Strand.

We had won. Melick and Powers had done a superb job in preparing and presenting the case. What was ironic was that it had all been done to preserve a document whose contents still remained unknown. But, as I was later to learn, the legal struggle to preserve the document had been worth the effort.

CHAPTER 21

THE LAHEY
MEMORANDUM

Mrs. Strand was at her home in Florida when the Supreme Court of Massachusetts ruled that the Lahey Memorandum belonged to her and ordered Herrick and Smith to return it immediately to her. In order to retrieve the document, Melick and Powers went to the law offices of Herrick and Smith. Melick carried a letter opener in his briefcase because Mrs. Strand had requested that after he received the sealed envelope, and before he left Herrick and Smith's offices, he open the envelope and examine its contents.

Mrs. Strand's two lawyers were directed to the office of John B. French, the attorney who several years earlier had told me that neither Mrs. Strand nor I would ever get the Lahey Memorandum from Herrick and Smith. His first words to Melick and Powers were, "Where are the television cameras?"

Melick and Powers sat down in front of French's desk. French then took out an envelope from the desk drawer and handed it to Melick, who in turn handed it to Powers. While Melick and French were engaged in conversation, Powers looked down and recognized Mrs. Strand's signature on the envelope. The date written on the envelope was December 12, 1962. Powers knew that Mrs. Strand's lawsuit with the Lahey Clinic had been settled in October of that year and the Willcox-Hanify letter, used by Hanify as the legal basis for trying to keep the Lahey Memorandum from Mrs. Strand, had been dated October 19, 1962.

Written on the outside of the envelope was the following:

This is the personal property of Linda M. Strand, sealed and delivered to Mr. Harold M. Willcox of Herrick and Smith, Donald, Farley, and Ketchum, to be held in the safe of HSDF&K until called for by me, Linda M. Strand.

This memo has been read by the Judge of the Probate court in Boston, Mr. Kevin Hearn, Mr. Charles C. Cabot, and Mr. Harold M. Willcox, all of the HSDF&K. In case of my decease, it is to be turned over to the administrator or executor of my estate who will have instructions from me.

Directly under Mrs. Strand's instruction on the outside of this envelope was a handwritten note, "Opened by John B. French and Shepard Remis. See JBF memo of this date." The date was July 11, 1983. Remis was another Herrick and Smith attorney.

Powers immediately realized that the envelope containing the Lahey Memorandum had been opened previously and initialed by French and Remis on July 11, 1983, a date shortly after I had first asked Herrick and Smith to return the Lahey Memorandum to Mrs. Strand, and one year prior to her lawsuit against the law firm. Powers, with all the intensity of his youth, had a strong reaction to what he had just learned. It was legally and ethically unconscionable to Powers that Mrs. Strand's instructions on the envelope had not been made known to the court before or during the trial. Nor could he believe that Mrs. Strand's sealed envelope containing the Lahey Memorandum had been opened without either her permission or instructions from the court.

Powers, who was twenty-six years old when Melick brought him into the Strand case, had only recently passed the Massachusetts Bar. As a young lawyer, he said he might have been somewhat naive, but he was literally stunned when he realized key instructions written by Mrs. Strand pertaining to the dispensation of the Lahey Memorandum had been deliberately withheld from the court by experienced and well-respected lawyers. Now it was indisputably clear what Mrs. Strand said before and during the trial regarding her ownership of the Lahey document was true; she had only left the Lahey Memorandum with her law firm for safekeeping. It further supported Mrs. Strand's contention that the Willcox-Hanify letter had been written without her knowledge.

As Melick and Powers rose to leave French's office, no courteous pleasantries were exchanged in the chilled atmosphere. The two lawyers stepped into the elevator, and as the doors closed, Powers handed Melick the envelope. Powers later told me that once they were alone and in the privacy of the elevator, he unleashed an outburst of strong language directed toward the outrageous behavior and conduct of the Herrick and Smith law firm. It wasn't until they reached their car that Melick opened the resealed envelope.

What was in the envelope was not the original document written by Lahey, but a photocopy. The original was missing! Melick flipped the photocopy over and saw the signatures of Mrs. Strand and the Judge who presided at the Strand-

Lahey Clinic trial in 1962. Mrs. Strand later confirmed both signatures thus proving the photocopy's authenticity.

Returning to his office, Powers was so upset that he telephoned Gelb, the attorney who represented Herrick and Smith. He asked Gelb why the clearly written instructions of Mrs. Strand had been deliberately kept secret from the court, especially since all documents held by Herrick and Smith pertaining to Mrs. Strand and the Lahey Clinic had been requested by Melick prior to the trial. Gelb gave Powers no explanation for his actions even though Gelb had to have known of Mrs. Strand's instructions since he stated during the trial that he had studied her file very carefully.

After speaking with Powers, Gelb, apparently anxious over their altercation, or perhaps to appease an angry fellow lawyer, inexplicably sent Powers another piece of highly incriminating evidence, which was also withheld during Strand's trial. Written by Mrs. Strand was a letter dated December 14, 1962, two months after Mrs. Strand's settlement with the Lahey Clinic and after the writing of the Hanify-Willcox letter:

Dear Mr. Willcox:

Your letter has finally reached me. All I can say is that the day before I left home in October, I went to the bank vault and the Lahey memo was not there.

You knew before your letter was written that I was of the opinion it was at that time in the custody of HSDF&K and I question any connection between this very personal document and my case. I know copies were made of the one I had and have in my purse by HSDF&K the same day copies were made of the other two memos. I also know we had it with the other two originals when Mr. McFarland was comparing signatures (1953). I cannot recall having the original since that time. Could it be that someone has the original which would be the original of the number #2 memo? Is someone playing tricks?

I did not know nor never did see how this Lahey memo (my personal property) ever had anything to do with my case of the settling of Dr. Lahey's estate, and neither can I understand who it was that is so vitally interested and why even to the extent of asking if I would sell it to them. [Author's emphasis.]

Do you know the answer to this? and if so, I would appreciate it if you would enlighten me.

I have with me the memo I showed to the Judge of the probate court, to Mr. Hearn and to you and Mr. Cabot and in order to show my good faith I am enclosing it in a sealed envelope to be held in safe keeping, sealed and delivered as my personal property by HSDF&K and to be delivered to me on request and to no one else except my administrator or executor. [Author's emphasis.]

This letter showed unequivocally that Mrs. Strand never considered the Lahey Memorandum to be part of her settlement agreement with the Lahey Clinic in 1962 and further shows lack of awareness of so called "conditions" laid down in the Willcox-Hanify letter two months earlier. Mrs. Strand's letter to Mr. Willcox also questioned the ultimate disposition of the original Lahey Memorandum that she had left for safekeeping at Herrick and Smith in 1953 but never saw again. When Mrs. Strand died in 1990, she still had no idea who wanted to buy the Lahey Memorandum and why they were "playing tricks."[1]

According to Mrs. Strand, the original Lahey Memorandum was deposited with Herrick and Smith in 1953 and must have been removed from their safe sometime between 1953 and 1962, without her knowledge or permission. At the end of the Strand-Lahey Clinic trial that went on between 1958 and 1962, Willcox evidently made efforts to obtain from Mrs. Strand any photocopy she had of the original Lahey memo. She did possess one photocopy verified by the court in 1962, which she sent to Willcox in a sealed envelope with her written instructions. This is the envelope Herrick and Smith relinquished to her by the directive of the Massachusetts Supreme Court in 1986.

Melick flew to Florida to personally deliver to Mrs. Strand the envelope with the enclosed Lahey Memorandum photocopy. Based on her signature on the envelope and on the back of the photocopy, she confirmed its authenticity, but she was extremely upset that the envelope did not contain the original Lahey Memorandum. She repeatedly asked Mr. Melick what had become of the original document, but he had no answer.

I felt I should try to help answer Mrs. Strand's question regarding the whereabouts of the missing original Lahey Memorandum. I went to see Gelb and French at their respective offices, but neither could explain the loss of Dr. Lahey's original memorandum from the Herrick and Smith safe. Neither could they explain the reason for withholding Mrs. Strand's explicit written instructions as to the disposition of the Lahey Memorandum. If such information had been

---

1. After waiting a long period to let the Strand case settle and to let Mr. Hanify see that I had no interest in publicity, I called him at his office on April 3, 1990, against the advice of Mr. Mellick. The purpose of the call was simply to ask if he had any idea who was trying to buy a photocopy of the Lahey Memorandum from Mrs. Strand in 1962. I thought if this person could be identified, it might open up a new lead relating to FDR's health. Hanify very gentlemanly denied having any information regarding the matter.

made known to the court, no basis for the court case would have existed, and I didn't believe there would have been a trial.

After waiting an extended period of time, I visited Judge Sullivan at his office in the Middlesex Probate Court and showed him the envelope which had contained the copy of the Lahey Memorandum and on which Mrs. Strand's instructions concerning the document were clearly written. I also showed him Mrs. Strand's letter to Mr. Willcox of December 14, 1962, stating that the Lahey Memorandum belonged to her and no one else. Seeing this evidence, Judge Sullivan said, "I can't believe what you are showing me; I find this unbelievable." I then asked him the legal implications of withholding such evidence from the court, and he replied he couldn't answer my question without giving it a great deal of thought. He asked me to put in writing the exact questions I wished him to answer. I returned to my office and wrote the following letter on December 15, 1989:

Dear Judge Sullivan:

Thank you very much for taking the time to see me.

I would appreciate it if you could write for historical purposes your feelings regarding the Strand case in light of the information we discussed and the enclosed material I am sending you.

1. What is your opinion regarding the position of the defense lawyers which appears to be completely inconsistent with the evidence in Mrs. Strand's correspondence with Herrick and Smith of December 14, 1962?

2. What is your opinion of the failure of the defense lawyers to inform you of the information Mrs. Strand sent to Herrick and Smith following her settlement with the Lahey Clinic? This material unequivocally shows that Mrs. Strand believed she was the owner of the Lahey document and had the right and the responsibility to follow Dr. Lahey's instructions regarding the document. If you had been aware of this information during the trial would it have had any impact on your ultimate ruling against Mrs. Strand?

3. What is your opinion now of the defense lawyers' argument during the trial that there was a pre-existing condition that it was Herrick and Smith who had to determine if criticism of FDR existed before Mrs. Strand could receive the Lahey document? What could be the legal basis for this view of Mrs. Strand's letters of December 19, 1962?

4. What was the legal responsibility of the defense lawyers in making Mrs. Strand's information of December 19, 1962 known to you?

Thank you Judge Sullivan for your interest in this matter.

I waited three weeks and then called Judge Sullivan to ask when I might expect his reply. He told me he had been discussing my letter with his law clerk and that I would hear from him within the next few weeks. I again waited almost a month before calling Judge Sullivan again. He was extremely pleasant but simply said, "Dr. Goldsmith, I am sure you understand the situation I am in and I really don't think that I can respond to your letter." He ended our conversation by saying, "I think you know what I am trying to say."

Approximately a month later I received the following letter from Judge Sullivan:

> The attorneys who tried the matter before me in a jury waived trial are among the most able in Massachusetts. With regard to the queries contained in your letter of December 15, 1989, the code of judicial conduct requires that I respectfully decline to answer specific questions regarding the litigation strategies utilized by any of the litigants. While fully understanding the thrust of your questions to me, it is my opinion that a trial judge, albeit a retired trial judge, must decline to answer such questions and refer them to counsel.

In my letter to Judge Sullivan, I didn't ask for his comments on the "litigation strategies" of the lawyers. What was asked was the "legal implications" of withholding evidence even from the state supreme court in Mrs. Strand's case. Obviously, the judge felt he couldn't respond to my question.

After the trial I remained in touch with Mrs. Strand. She was living in Cambridge, Massachusetts, and one afternoon I took her to lunch along with Mr. Powers and my secretary. During the luncheon we talked at length about Dr. Lahey and his relationship with FDR. Mrs. Strand claimed she had met FDR at the New England Baptist Hospital where he had been a patient listed under a different name. She said he had come to Boston on several occasions for what she believed was treatment, but she did not know specifically what was wrong with him. She also could not be specific as to the dates of the visits. She said she was responsible for secretly making all of FDR's arrangements when he came to Boston. Dr. Lahey ordinarily performed tests on his patients at his clinic and then referred the patient to the hospital for treatment. In FDR's case, however, Mrs. Strand said all FDR's tests were conducted at the hospital where it was easier to maintain tight security. Mrs. Strand said she knew Dr. Lahey had told the president not to run for a fourth term, "that he would not make it." She also said that, as far as she knew, Dr. Lahey never operated on FDR. These were unsubstantiated comments by a ninety-year-old woman, but they certainly seemed believable.

I had never mentioned the Lahey Memorandum to Mrs. Strand after the trial. I knew she would decide on her own, and at the time of her choosing, whether she would show it to me. As our luncheon was ending, Mrs. Strand quietly opened her handbag, took out a copy of the Lahey Memorandum, and gave it to me without a word.

After I returned to my office, I carefully read the document that I had hoped would shed light on the health of Franklin Delano Roosevelt in the last year of his life. It read:

Monday, July 10, 1944

I wish to record the following information regarding my opinions in relation to President Roosevelt's condition and to have them on record in the event there comes any criticism of me at a later date. I want to do this after having seen him in consultation as a private record.

On Saturday, July 8, I talked with Admiral McIntire in my capacity as one of the group of three, Admiral McIntire, Dr. James Paullin of Atlanta, Georgia, and myself, who saw President Roosevelt in consultation and who have been over his physical examination, x-rays, and laboratory findings concerning his physical condition. I have reviewed all of his x-rays and findings over the past years and compared them with all the present findings and am recording my opinion concerning Mr. Roosevelt's condition and capacities now. I am recording these opinions in the light of having informed Admiral McIntire Saturday afternoon July 8, 1944 that I did not believe that, if Mr. Roosevelt were elected President again, he had the physical capacity to complete a term. I told him that, as a result of activities in his trip to Russia he had been in a state which was, if not in heart failure, at least on the verge of it, that this was the result of high blood pressure he has now had for a long time, plus a question of a coronary damage. With this in mind it was my opinion that over the four years of another term with its burdens, he would again have heart failure and be unable to complete it. Admiral McIntire was in agreement with this.

In addition to that I stated that it was not my duty to advise concerning whether or not such a term was undertaken, but to inform Admiral McIntire, as his family Physician my opinion concerning his capacity to do it and that it was my opinion that it was Admiral McIntire's duty to inform him concerning his capacity.

In addition to the above I have told Admiral McIntire that I feel strongly that if he does accept another term, he had a very serious responsibility concerning who is the Vice President. Admiral McIntire agrees with this and has, he states, so informed Mr. Roosevelt.

I am putting this on record, I am asking that it be witnessed, sealed and placed in safekeeping. It is to be opened and utilized only in the event that there might be criticism of me should this later eventuate and the criticisms be directed toward me for not having made this public. As I see my duty as a physician, I cannot violate my professional position nor possible professional confidence, but I do wish to be on record concerning possible later criticism.

Signed: Frank H. Lahey
Witness: L. M. Strand

The simple document showed several things:

1) It was written on Monday, July 10, 1944, after Dr. Lahey had seen the president on Saturday afternoon, July 8. It is unknown why Lahey was called to see the president just a week before the Democratic Convention, but we now know that Dr. Lahey informed Admiral McIntire that if Roosevelt were elected president again, he did not believe FDR had the physical capacity to complete the term and "Admiral McIntire was in agreement with this."

2) FDR's cardiac deterioration is noted, but there is no reference to a malignant tumor. It should be mentioned that Dr. Irving M. Ariel, Pack's closest associate who became director of the Pack Clinic following Pack's death, wrote me a letter on June 26, 1986, in which he stated, "Lahey was called in consultation to see Roosevelt before his last term in office. After his examination, Lahey decided that Roosevelt had metastases to the liver but did not tell Roosevelt that." However, there is no substantiation for this claim.

3) Dr. Lahey clearly noted his concern for FDR's condition and declared "it was Admiral McIntire's duty to inform him concerning his capacity."

4) Dr. Lahey realized the enormous importance of FDR's running mate for the vice presidency and warned that FDR had a very serious responsibility concerning whom he chose as vice president. "Admiral McIntire agrees with this and has," as Lahey states, "so informed Mr. Roosevelt."

When I first read the Lahey Memorandum, I was disappointed that there was no mention in the document that FDR had a malignant tumor. When Lahey wrote the memo, just days before the Democratic National Convention in 1944, it was almost a year before the president's death, and at that time no malignancy may have been present. However, an answer to this possibility will probably never be known.

It would appear from the Lahey Memorandum that both FDR and McIntire knew that the president was very ill. Of equal importance, Lahey emphasized the importance of FDR's choice for his vice president. The likelihood was very high that FDR would win the election of 1944 and die before his term was over. Whoever was the vice president at that time would then become the next president of the United States and inherit a country at war. Information in the Lahey Memorandum regarding FDR's medical condition was of enormous political importance in helping Truman to inherit this position.

CHAPTER 22

AN IMPORTANT CONTACT

Mrs. Strand's court victory in the legal battle to recover the Lahey Memorandum was reported in newspapers throughout the United States. My name was mentioned in the article, which prompted my receipt of a letter marked "confidential," sent by a Joseph Leib, "Washington Political Writer:"

Regarding your attempt to obtain the secret memo written by the late Dr. Frank Lahey of the Lahey clinic regarding President Franklin D. Roosevelt's health. May I advise you that I had a copy of this document which was later stolen by J. Edgar Hoover of the FBI and unless it was altered, would reveal startling information and reveal to the American people the concerted effort to conceal his dangerous condition in time of war and his inability to make decisions in Yalta.

After reading this intriguing letter, my first thought was who was this Joseph Leib and how had he obtained information regarding the health of FDR? I immediately called him at his home in Alexandria, Virginia, and within a very short time realized he had extensive knowledge of FDR's political career and information regarding the president's health. Since Leib later proved my source of much primary information regarding the relation between the Lahey Memorandum and its impact on presidential history, I believe it necessary to show Leib's credentials and experiences related to FDR.

Leib first met FDR in 1928 when he was a seventeen-year-old volunteer page at the Democratic National Convention in Houston, Texas. Young Leib was greatly impressed with FDR, and two years later, during the Great Depression; he became convinced that Roosevelt was the person who could lead the country to economic recovery. Nineteen-year-old Leib requested and received permission from FDR to organize the first Roosevelt for President club; by election time in 1932, he had established ninety-six of these clubs nationwide.

While he was working on behalf of FDR, Leib was frequently asked if FDR's disability from polio might preclude his ability to be president. His answer was a man's mind was more important than the status of his lower extremities. However, Leib did feel it was an issue that should be addressed, and he wrote an article that he sent to Roosevelt for approval. FDR responded on July 8, 1931:

> This is the first chance I have had to thank you for your letter and to read over this suggested story. I have made a number of corrections as to facts. By the way, I don't "suffer". I have no pain and except for weak lower muscles, I am probably in better health than 99% out of a 100.

Leib followed up with the suggestion that, to neutralize critics who claimed that FDR's physical condition would handicap his progress in national politics, FDR should allow one of the national magazines to report on his excellent health.

It so happened that, at the time, Earl Looker, a Boston newsman, had already been working on a story concerning Roosevelt's health. Months earlier (February 23, 1931), Looker had written FDR directly and asked if he was in physical condition to "stand the strain of the presidency." Roosevelt answered:

> This is to acknowledge your letter of February 23rd.
>
> Of course no statement from me as to my physical fitness should really be acceptable to you. Your question, however, is very distinctly a personal challenge to me no matter what my present or future position as a public servant may be—even in the humblest of positions. Furthermore, not being in any sense a candidate for any other public office is equally a challenge to any business or professional worth which I may assume on leaving Albany.
>
> Being assured of your integrity, I am therefore prepared to permit you to make an investigation into my physical fitness, to give you every facility for thoroughly making it, and authority for you to publish its results without censorship from me.

On July 25, 1931, Looker published the story on Roosevelt's health in *Liberty* magazine, which at that time was one of the most widely read national publications. The article was titled: "Is FDR Physically Fit To Be President?"[1] Looker stated that he accepted FDR's challenge and had asked Dr. Lindsay R. Williams, the director of the New York Academy of Medicine, to pick three respected doctors to examine FDR. These doctors later sent Looker a telegram:

We have today carefully examined Governor Roosevelt. We believe that his health and powers of endurance are such as to allow him to meet any demand of private and public life.

> Samuel W. Lambert, M.D.
> Russell A. Hibbs, M.D.
> Foster Kennedy, M.D.

Looker reflected:

It is an amazing possibility that the next President of the United States may be a cripple. Franklin D. Roosevelt, governor of the State of New York, was crippled by infantile paralysis in the epidemic of 1921 and still walks with the help of crutches and a walking stick. Yet, by all the political signs, he will emerge as the Democratic nominee.

Leib's early support of FDR was expressed in a letter Roosevelt sent to Leib on February 29, 1932: "Thank you for your continued confidence in me. I hope I shall always deserve it." But this early support of FDR was simply a prelude to the impact Leib apparently had on Roosevelt's pursuit of the presidential nomination at the Democratic National Convention in Chicago in 1932.

The three leading presidential contenders at the convention that summer were former New York Governor Al Smith, who had lost the nomination in 1928 but was running again; Roosevelt; and John Nance Garner, the Speaker of the U.S. House of Representatives. Though Garner wanted the nomination, he had done little campaigning. Roosevelt had run well in the Democratic state primaries that spring, but in the last primary, which took place in California, he lost to Garner—thanks to a campaign for Garner run by William Randolph Hearst, the wealthy newspaper publisher. Leib realized that the Garner victory in California posed a strong political threat to Roosevelt. He began, therefore, corresponding directly with Garner, hoping to talk him out of running against Roosevelt. Garner responded on May 7, 1932:

I am of course aware of the movement that has been inaugurated by my friends in Texas and elsewhere, but I have no connection therewith. The duties and responsibilities of the leadership require all my time and

---

1. Earl Looker, "Is Franklin D. Roosevelt Physically Fit to be President?," *Liberty* (July 25, 1931): 6–10.

thought and I would be doing an injustice to the country and myself if I permitted anything to distract my attention from these duties.

On May 12, 1932, Garner responded to a second letter sent by Leib:

I am taking no part in any pre-convention campaign and like yourself I am very hopeful that the convention will be harmonious in every respect.

Leib wrote a third letter to Garner asking him if he would withdraw from the presidential race. Garner responded, "I have no intention of throwing my hat into the ring" and reiterated that he was giving his entire time and thought to his duties in Washington as the Speaker of the House of Representatives. Incredibly, Leib, at the age of twenty-one, now considered himself a free-lance newspaperman and gave no indication to Garner of either his age or background.

Two days after receiving Garner's last letter, Leib forwarded all of Garner's correspondence to FDR and to the Associated Press, who published Garner's letters nationally (April 26, 1932). FDR hurriedly returned to New York from Warm Springs, Georgia, to confer with Colonel Edward M. House, once Woodrow Wilson's confidential advisor and now head of the Texas Democratic delegation, whose sixty-forty votes were already committed to Garner. Evidently, FDR was exploring how he might gain some of these votes, if not on the first ballot, at least on subsequent ones.

Leib received a fourth letter from Garner on May 30, 1932:

I read your letter of May 27th and the newspaper clipping regarding our previous letters.

Since I defeated the Governor in the California primaries I would be glad to have him as my running-mate, but if it is the wish of the convention, then I will be pleased to be his running-mate. This is not for publication.

Leib kept the letter secret—but only until just prior to the opening of the 1932 Democratic Convention in Chicago. Then he revealed it to political writers at the *Chicago Daily News*, whose headline on June 23rd asked: "Garner and Roosevelt Deal Reported—Speaker and Governor to be Running-Mates?" There was neither identification of the source nor any details relating to the headlines. This suited Leib's purpose since he told me that all he wanted was the suggestion in print that a possible political deal had already been reached between FDR and Garner.

On the first ballot for the Democratic candidate for president, Garner received forty-four votes from California, Roosevelt none. The New York delegation with ninety-four votes gave twenty-eight and a half to FDR, sixty-five and a half to Al Smith, and none to Garner. On the second and third ballots, Garner kept his forty-four votes from California while New York remained relatively unchanged with sixty-three votes for Smith and thirty-one for FDR.

The voting remained deadlocked throughout the night, without a recess until the following morning at 8:30 AM. In the midst of the tension, Leib realized that a continued deadlock would likely produce a dark-horse candidate. Leib told me (which I had no second source for confirmation) that on his own, he called Garner and asked him why he was "trying to stop Roosevelt" and whether he would live up to the statement in his letter of May 30, 1932, that stated, "[I]f it is the wish of the convention, then I will be pleased to be his [FDR's] running-mate." Leib suggested that Garner become FDR's running mate, and Garner responded, "Hell, no"; but with Leib insisting that he could win the vice presidency if he threw his votes to Roosevelt, Garner said, "See what you can do." Leib immediately contacted Louis Howe, FDR's personal advisor, and repeated his conversation with Garner. Howe called FDR in Albany, who immediately called Garner, and the result was that Garner withdrew from the race and gave his votes to FDR. The rest is history.

This story by Leib was impossible to verify totally. However, to substantiate his role in the 1932 Democratic Convention, Leib showed me a letter from James A. Farley, who at that time was the newly elected chairman of the Democratic National Committee. The letter acknowledged Leib's contribution to FDR's presidential victory. The letter to Leib, dated April 12, 1933:

Dear Joe,

Thank you very much for your letter of congratulations on my appointment. I appreciate it very much and can only say that it was through your assistance and support during the campaign that makes all this possible. One who is familiar with the details of your activities would realize that you are very much responsible for the nomination and election of the President.

With best wishes and kindest regards,
James A. Farley, Chairman

Leib's participation in the political machinations leading to the 1932 election equipped him with a firsthand overview of the machinery of politics. Almost fifty years later, he related a host of events to me that on most occasions I could confirm. He eventually became a comprehensive resource of primary information

DEMOCRATIC NATIONAL COMMITTEE

NATIONAL PRESS BUILDING

WASHINGTON, *May 25, 1933.*

To Whom It May Concern:

This is to introduce Mr. Joseph H. Leib of South Bend, Ind. Mr. Leib is the young man who organized the first Roosevelt-for-President Club in the United States in August 1930.

Very truly yours,

JAMES A. FARLEY, *Chairman.*

STATE OF NEW YORK

EXECUTIVE CHAMBER

ALBANY, *February 29, 1932.*

Mr. JOSEPH H. LEIB,
South Bend, Ind.

MY DEAR MR. LEIB: Thank you for your continued confidence in me. I hope that I shall always deserve it.

Yours very sincerely,

FRANKLIN D. ROOSEVELT.

———

DEMOCRATIC NATIONAL COMMITTEE

NATIONAL PRESS BUILDING

WASHINGTON, D. C., *April 12, 1933.*

Mr. JOSEPH H. LEIB,
South Bend, Ind.

DEAR JOE: Thank you very much for your letter of congratulation on my appointment. I appreciate it very much and can only say that it was through your assistance and support during the campaign that makes all this possible. One who is familiar with the details of your activities would realize that you were very much responsible for the nomination and election of the President. With best wishes and kindest regards I am,

Sincerely yours,

JAMES A. FARLEY, *Chairman.*

———

JOSEPH LEIB

National Press Building, Washington, D. C.

Telephone, Metropolitan 6226

FOUNDER

First Roosevelt-for-President Club in the United States

Joseph H. Leib, of South Bend, Ind., acknowledged by the Democratic national chairman as founder of the first Roosevelt-for-President club in 1930.—New York Times, April 8, 1937.

WASHINGTON, March 12.—Joseph Leib, of South Bend, Ind., president and organizer of the first Roosevelt-for-President club of the United States.—New York Herald Tribune, March 13, 1937.

The organizer of the first Roosevelt-for-President club, Joseph Leib, of South Bend, Ind.—Washington (D. C.) Star, May 10, 1937.

Joseph Leib, formerly of South Bend, president of the first Roosevelt-for-President club organized in 1930.—Washington, D. C., United Press, May 20, 1937.

Leib, who organized the first Roosevelt-for-President club in South Bend in 1930.—Washington (D. C.) Herald, December 6, 1935.

Joseph Leib, of South Bend, Ind., active in the young Democratic movement and organizer in 1930 of the first Roosevelt-for-President club. Leib organized 96 Roosevelt clubs before the 1932 election.—New York World-Telegram, October 28, 1935.

JULY 18, 1941.

Joseph Leib, National Press Building, Washington, D. C.: 1930, organized the first Roosevelt-for-President club in the United States.

1931, advocated the formation of the Young Democratic Clubs of America. It was organized in 1932, and Mr. Leib was one of the founders of that organization.

1933-37, employed in several Government departments.

1937 to date, engaged in independent political writing and political newspaper work. Now also preparing a book.

that eventually supplied me with the link that showed the connection between FDR's health, the Lahey Memorandum, and the 1944 presidential election.

From 1932 to 1936, many in Washington recognized Leib's political ability. On November 24, 1936, his twenty-sixth birthday, an article appeared in the *Washington Times*:

> His [Leib's] glamour is derived from the fact that he is Roosevelt's supporter number one, and was one of the first, probably the very first, in the United States to advocate for Franklin D Roosevelt the seat he now occupies.

Although Leib by this time had begun to wonder if FDR's New Deal policies served the best interest of the country, he remained loyal to the president and worked for his re-election in 1936. He organized a "Re-elect Roosevelt Club" in Washington, made up of members of the cabinet and Congress. It was Leib's hope that FDR would devote his second term in office to restoring further public confidence in America.

By 1937, however, Leib's respect for FDR had vanished. The main issue involved Roosevelt's wish to fill the United States Supreme Court with liberal justices who would uphold his executive decrees, which some legal scholars considered to be unconstitutional. Leib's energy and drive, which had earlier assisted FDR's entry into national politics, were now rechanneled into halting FDR's proposed Supreme Court reform. The first public evidence of his intent was headlined in the *New York Sun* on April 7, 1937: "Number-one Roosevelt Fan Is In City and He Is Out To Be Number-one Foe of New Deal Generally." The article claimed that Leib planned to "organize the nation's opposition to the Supreme Court reform proposal into a pressure group so large and powerful that Congress would be forced to vote it down."

FDR's meddling in the Supreme Court had already resulted in the resignation of Supreme Court Associate Justice Willis Van Devanter. Leib then took it upon himself to write Associate Justice James C. McReynolds and inquire if he also planned to resign under pressure from FDR. McReynolds wrote a personal letter to Leib on May 14, 1933, stating, "You may disregard all rumors regarding my resignation." This letter was published on the front page of newspapers on May 20, 1937, and in the New York Times on May 21, 1937. Chief Justice Charles Evan Hughes later confirmed that he also had no intention of stepping down. Congress subsequently refused FDR's court-packing scheme, which proved to be one of the president's major political blunders.

Somewhat later in 1937, Leib became concerned that FDR was going to run for a third term. To verify the truth of this, he wrote Roosevelt's son (FDR, Jr.)

asking directly if his father planned to run again in 1940. FDR, Jr., answered on October 24, 1937:

> Thank you very much for your recent letter, but I am afraid I cannot give you the answer you desire. In the first place, I think it is not my position to make any statement concerning a third term for my father. And furthermore, the necessity for deciding such an issue has not as yet arisen since what we feel today may have to be revised three years from now in the light of circumstances beyond our control, such as the foreign situation.

Based on this letter from Roosevelt's son, published on the front page of the *New York Herald Tribune* on October 31, 1937, and in the Congressional Record, Leib decided to bring the matter of a possible third term for FDR into the open, much as he had done with FDR's Supreme Court-packing venture. He wrote the Democratic chairman in each state asking if they thought FDR should run for a third term. One of these letters fell into the hands of Lawrence W. Robert, Jr., who was at that time the secretary of the Democratic National Party. Robert wrote Leib requesting they meet immediately in Washington. At this meeting, Leib reassured Robert that he would publish the replies from the state Democratic chairmen exactly as he received them, without any editorializing. When Robert learned that the first six replies were unanimously against a third term for FDR, he demanded that the survey be stopped. Leib refused. This information was kept confidential and was not reported in the nationally read newspapers. However, the *Pittsburgh Post Gazette* on November 11, 1937, learned of the Robert-Leib meeting and published an editorial titled "Bad News Not Wanted," by Raymond Z. Henke. The editorial reported this reaction when Leib refused Robert's request to stop his investigation:

> Robert wanted to know whether there was not some job in the government service Leib would like to have. This alluring bait also failed to bring in the quarry so Robert summarily ended the interview.
> But shortly thereafter the replies from state chairmen suddenly ceased coming in. No Sherlock Holmes needed to produce the surmise that telegrams flew out of Robert's office to every state chairman telling them to ignore young Leib's inquiry. Perhaps what caused Robert to adopt such high handed methods was the reply Leib received from J. B. Hodges, Democratic state chairman of Florida. He suggested that instead of an inquiry to determine whether the people wanted the President to have a third term, it would be better to inquire whether they want "the completion of the president's second term."

Leib was threatened, and his mail delivery was disrupted. Leib's mail situation was subsequently reported on the front page of the *Newark Star Eagle* on December 2, 1937, which stated that postal inspectors had stopped all mail to Leib. Following this report his mail delivery resumed.

Leib's disillusionment with FDR's political policies and his doubt about the president's health intensified, and by 1940 he had resolved to try to prevent FDR's election to a third term. Initially, this effort began with Cordell Hull, the secretary of state. Hull and Leib had been friends for years, beginning in 1933. After Leib had helped FDR during the presidential campaign in 1932, Leib told me (although I had no way to prove it) that he spoke to FDR directly regarding his obtaining a position in his administration. FDR allegedly told him that he would help him get a job in the government, but some positions would be restricted because of his youth. Some arrangement must have been worked out since FDR asked Farley to write to Leib offering him a job with Farley instructing Hull (secretary of state) to contact Leib regarding "a job in the passport office." From that point and over the years, Hull and Leib remained good friends. I asked Leib how this friendship had occurred, and he told me that as an investigative reporter, he had discovered an unfavorable event that had happened early in Hull's young career. Leib never reported this information, which resulted in a bond of friendship between the two men.

Hull, who came from Tennessee, asked Leib to investigate a story published in the Nashville *Tennessean* on March 6, 1940, claiming that FDR would probably not seek a third term. Hull had presidential ambitions and was waiting on FDR's decision about a third term. John Thompson wrote the newspaper article, captioned, "Hull chances for Presidency Excellent—Depends on Roosevelt." Excerpts included:

> Secretary of State Cordell Hull has excellent chances of becoming the Democratic Presidential nominee and carrying the party to victory, Walter Davenport of Colliers magazine said here last night.
>
> The veteran political analyst and writer is so convinced of Hull's prospects that he is down in these parts gathering information for a special article on the subject.
>
> Of course there is one big "if" to it all—what President Roosevelt decides to do about it.
>
> Davenport said he did not think the President wants to run again. "I know he is interested in doing other things, writing for instance, and that his physician, Ross McIntire has told him his health may not stand the strain of another term."

Leib contacted Davenport and asked about the story, but Davenport refused to confirm that he had ever made such statements. Leib then called Thompson, the author of the article, who stated unequivocally that Davenport had said exactly what he had reported in his article regarding Roosevelt's health. Thompson told Leib that he would never have made such statements in his newspaper article if he had not written down direct quotes when he interviewed Davenport.

Believing Thompson's story, Leib sent copies of the newspaperman's article to political leaders in Washington, asking if they thought FDR should run for a third term, focusing especially on the reference to the president's failing health. Leib told me that he also wrote Admiral McIntire on March 8, 1940, asking him if the newspaper report was accurate, but McIntire never answered the letter. Davenport, an associate editor of *Colliers*, became upset by the whole incident and sent a letter on March 19, 1940, to Steven Early, Roosevelt's press secretary, regarding Leib and the matter of the president's health:

Dear Steve:

I have just returned to the office and find the file of the Leib to McIntire to Early correspondence. Of course I never said to anybody, privately, publicly, or "off the record" what the *Tennessean* is alleged to have reputed to me. If I had any such information I would give it to *Colliers*, not a newspaper. Neither can I recall having said anything which might be misconstrued into such a statement. Moreover, I did not say in an interview or otherwise, quoting Mr. Leib's letter, that the editors of *Colliers* are close to Mr. Roosevelt.

I regret a great deal that this has happened. Will you please tell Admiral McIntire, and if you think it is necessary, the President.

Leib again questioned John Thompson about his newspaper article, who responded:

Obviously I would never have published such quotations in the newspaper unless they were completely factorial.

By this time, the White House's concern about Leib's determination to make FDR's health a political issue culminated in a letter sent by Early on May 28, 1940, to Admiral McIntire:

I feel that the time has come when all this Joseph Leib correspondence should be turned over to the Director of the FBI [J. Edgar Hoover] with the request that he assign an operator to call upon Leib and ask him directly whether he is functioning for the deliberate purpose of creating fear that the President and the C&C (Commander in Chief) of the US Army and US Navy, particularly during these trying times, is failing physically and cannot be trusted to carry on, plainly implying that such strategy is subversive in character and closely akin to the fifth column and Trojan horse tactics.

On the following day (May 29, 1940) Steven Early followed up his letter to McIntire with a similar letter to J. Edgar Hoover of the FBI:

Dear Mr. Hoover:

I feel that in view of the present world conditions our entire file on Joseph Leib should be turned over to your department in order that an operator may be assigned to call upon Mr. Leib to ask him directly whether he is functioning for the deliberate purpose of creating fear that the President is failing physically and cannot be entrusted to carry on.

I would suggest the operator make it clear to Leib that such strategy is subversive in character and closely akin to the fifth column and Trojan horse tactics.

The enclosed file also includes letters forwarded to this office by people both in and outside of the Federal Government who were the recipients of letters from Leib.

Hoover rapidly responded to Early's letter; a week later (June 5, 1940), Hoover received a report from H. H. Clegg, chief of FBI field agents in Washington:

Concerning the request of the President's secretary, Mr. Steven Early, for an interview with Joseph Leib, it was observed that Leib had on his stationery a telephone number in the National Press Club building. Earlier in the week, I telephoned that number and they had not seen Mr. Leib for many weeks. Additional letterheads and correspondences indicated that his home was in South Bend, Indiana.

After conference with Mr. E. A. Tarn (an FBI field agent) this morning, we were agreed that neither Mr. Tarn nor I should interview Leib, but that Mr. Carson should do so and Mr. Carson is presently undertaking to find Leib for the purpose of completing the interview today.

On the same day, June 5, 1940, Clegg received a memorandum from FBI agent C. H. Carson that was sent to J. Edgar Hoover:

I attempted to locate Joseph Leib and ascertained that he usually frequents the office of one Paul O. Peters, this being apparently the office of a press representative of some kind of press service. Leib was out when I called, no one knowing just where he had gone. He apparently dropped in and out of his office throughout the day. I waited his return until 2:00 pm when I left due to an appointment to lecture at Bowling Field.

Leib claimed in our long conversations that he was away during this period, during which the FBI was actively searching for him, and he tried to keep his whereabouts unknown by using only unlisted pay phones and secret living quarters. He claimed, however that eventually the FBI did locate his home and files and stole many of them. I had no way to confirm this.

Leib had extensive knowledge of Washington politics prior to World War II and up to FDR's death in 1945. His stories about politicians and government agencies were fascinating, most could be confirmed, but some I found questionable, especially when I could not provide corroborating information regarding his experiences.

One day we were discussing Harry Truman. Leib said he had known Truman for many years, and he said he played a prominent role in helping Truman attain the chairmanship of the Senate War Investigating Committee that later became famous as the Truman Committee. I questioned this because I had read in Truman's memoirs that Truman proposed the idea for the committee February 13, 1941, following his travels around the country in his automobile. However, Leib directed me to information in the Congressional Record that gave some substance to his claim that he played a major role in establishing the Truman Committee.

On May 10, 1943, Senator Styles Bridges of New Hampshire, speaking before the Senate, first alluded to the role played by Leib in the origination of the Truman Committee. Bridges told of Leib's effort to establish a committee to fight war profiteering, but because the Second World War was in progress, Bridges said he couldn't go into details at this time. It was only years after the war ended that Raymond S. Springer, the Democratic congressman from Indiana, speaking on the floor of the House of Representatives on January 27, 1947, discussed Leib's role under the title "Origin of the Truman Committee:"

Mr. Speaker, last week the Upper Chamber of Congress debated at great length the question of whether or not the famous Senate War Investigating Committee should be continued. After the debate came to a close, the

Senate deemed it advisable to grant this committee an additional year in order to complete its investigation of the war period. This committee has been in the public eye for several years, yet very few people know of the incidents that occurred behind the scene to inspire its creation.

It was this committee originally headed by Harry S. Truman that sent him skyrocketing into the Vice Presidency of the United States and then into the White House itself.

In this connection, it would seem apropos to state for the first time the genesis of this committee.

The story dates back to late December 1940, when sensational information concerning a highly placed defense-contract profiteer, came to the attention of Joseph Leib; free-lance writer of Washington, D.C.

Leib took this matter up with Sam O'Neil, who was at that time Washington correspondent of the *St. Louis Star Times*—now publicity director of the Democratic National Committee and they decided to bring the information to the attention of the Department of Justice. On January 4, 1941, they made their first call upon the then Attorney General Robert Jackson, Wendell Berge, Assistant Attorney General, and other officials. They made their calls on January 9, 14, 15, 16, and 23, 1941. However, the Justice Department refused to take action on this case.

Nevertheless, Leib sent the following letter to every Member of the Senate in the hope of bringing the case out into the open:

January 6, 1941

My Dear Member of Congress: Several days ago I conferred with Department of Justice officials relative to profiteering and frauds in defense and war contracts. The Washington correspondent of the *St. Louis Star-Times* assisted me in presenting amazing evidence in connection with this matter.

It is becoming increasingly evident that the Congress should set up an investigating committee to watch over possible frauds against the Government and I trust that you will give this suggestion your careful consideration and attention.

Should you care for further information, please advise. With many thanks.

Very truly yours,
Joseph Leib

This letter was followed up with personal calls upon a number of Senators, including Mr. Truman.

Then on February 13, 1941, Senator Truman introduced his resolution calling for the creation of a defense investigating committee, and the measure was officially approved on April 1, 1941. Senator Truman immediately became chairman of the committee.

I relate this story simply to show that Leib did have credibility, but in searching government records, it became apparent that he was considered by many over the years to be a meddling miscreant.

The most interesting story related to me by Leib concerned the Japanese attack on Pearl Harbor. As mentioned earlier, Cordell Hull and Leib were friends, with Hull allegedly totally trusting Leib since he knew him to be an experienced newspaperman and considered him to have integrity.

Leib told me that in late November 1941, Hull called him and asked that they meet immediately in Lafayette Park across from the State Department. They met on a park bench, and Hull handed Leib an envelope that contained an Army Signal Corps communication. It was an intercepted cable translated into English revealing that the Japanese would attack Pearl Harbor on December 7, 1941. Leib asked if FDR was aware of this, and Hull assured him that he was and that the cable had also been discussed with J. Edgar Hoover of the FBI.

I asked Leib why Hull had shown the Japanese communication to him and he replied, "Hull knew he could trust me to keep the source absolutely secret." Hull had for a long time been excluded from the inner circles of FDR's foreign policy advisors and he felt he was not in a position to go to the news media on his own. He wanted Leib to make public the Japanese communication regarding Pearl Harbor, but he insisted that it had to be done without implicating the source of the story.

Leib told me he immediately went to the office in the National Press Building of Lyle Wilson, the chief of the United Press bureau. Leib showed him the communication foretelling an attack on Pearl Harbor, but (having been sworn to secrecy by Hull) withheld the identity of his source. Wilson said that without a source he couldn't publish the Japanese dispatch. Leib then went to Harry Franz, his friend who was the foreign cable editor of the United Press agency in Washington. Franz believed Leib's story and accepted it for transmission with the understanding that under no circumstance would the source of the information be published. The communication was sent out by the United Press that circulated throughout the world, but because it traveled only on the foreign cable, newspapers in the continental United States did not pick it up. Ironically, the only paper in the world to publish the information that came over the foreign cable by wire from the United States was the *Honolulu Advertiser*, which proclaimed on November 30, 1941, with a headline at the top of its front page, "Japanese May Strike Over the Weekend." There was no explanation; nor was its source identified. The headline simply stated that a Japanese attack was imminent but did not target the location of the attack.

When Leib told me this story, I literally found it incredible. However, once again he led me to sources that gave some degree of credibility to his story. Six months after Pearl Harbor, an article was published in the *Washington Post* on July 19, 1942, written by Gerald G. Gross, entitled "This Capitol of Ours." The story said:

> A city room visitor walked in one day last week with a copy of the *Honolulu Advertiser* dated November 30, 1941, whose eight column banner proclaimed "Japanese May Strike Over Weekend." They did—Pearl Harbor came the following Sunday. No such pathetic story was published in Washington November 30 as far as the search of back files revealed—yet the *Advertiser* piece bore a Washington dateline.

Leib later wrote of the Pearl Harbor incident:

> On the Sunday morning of the Japanese attack I had my big Philco radio right up next to the window of my apartment. When I heard the news flashes I talked to Hull about it. He cried and I cried long afterwards, it was pathetic. I was very hurt that I had failed this very important story. If I had been able to get my story out then, the week before Pearl Harbor, Pearl Harbor would never have taken place.

These comments by Leib at first seemed unbelievable to me, but the fact that this information was reported on the British Broadcasting Corporation (BBC) and in Arts and Entertainment (A&E) television on December 7, 1989, the anniversary of Pearl Harbor, lends support to his story. More recently, on December 13, 1998, Leib, who died in 1990, had his story repeated on the History Channel on cable television. The television program was titled "Sacrifice at Pearl Harbor."

Leib showing front page of *The Honolulu Advertiser*.

APPENDIX B

Lieb informed me that President Truman initiated and signed in the name of Congress (H.J.RES.66) that he receive a civilian Medal of Honor for saving the U.S. government $36 billion during World War II and for "correcting defective production methods of airplanes for the Armed Forces during World War II." Lieb claimed he refused to accept the award because of his continuing anger against Truman who, as chairman of the Senate War Investigating Committee, failed to punish individuals in the Curtis-Wright Company for knowingly selling defective airplane engines to the Army Air Corps resulting in the loss of numerous pilots.

In order to confirm Lieb's claim, I referred the matter to the Library of Congress. I received the following reply:

From:	Marilyn L. Nelson, Senior Reference Librarian
	Congressional Reference Division
Re:	Information on HJ.RES.66 of the 82nd Congress on an
	award to Joseph Lieb because he saved the government
	$36 billion during the war

We found an entry in the Congressional Record Index for the 82nd Congress 1st Session which indicated the introduction of HJ.RES.66, but there was no entry showing any continuing action in the Index for the 82nd Congress, 2nd Session. It appears that no action was taken on this legislation after the initial introduction.

82D CONGRESS
1ST SESSION
H. J. RES. 66

IN THE HOUSE OF REPRESENTATIVES

JANUARY 4, 1951

Mr. SAYLOR introduced the following joint resolution; which was referred
to the Committee on Armed Services

JOINT RESOLUTION

To authorize the presentation of a civilian Medal of Honor to
Joseph Leib.

1   *Resolved by the Senate and House of Representatives*

2   *of the United States of America in Congress assembled,*

3   That the President is authorized to present, in the name of

4   Congress, a Medal of Honor to Joseph Leib, 3908 North

5   Fourth Street, Arlington, Virginia, in recognition of his un-

6   selfish and patriotic work in the passage of certain legislation

7   that ultimately saved the United States Government over

8    $36,000,000,000, and for his tireless efforts that brought

9   about the revamping of the wartime Army Air Corps Safety

10   Bureau, and for his undaunted fight that corrected defective

11   production methods of airplanes for the Armed Forces during

12   World War II.

CHAPTER 23

THE FOURTH TERM

Roosevelt knew it was highly unlikely that the war would be over before the Democratic Convention was to meet in Chicago in July of 1944. He also knew he would be nominated at the convention, and he must have believed that he was politically unbeatable since he was the military leader of the country in the middle of World War II.

Early in 1944, the Democratic national bosses, William Hannegan of St. Louis, Edward Flynn of New York, Frank Hague of Jersey City, and Edward Kelly of Chicago, realized the poor results of the off-year elections in 1942 had markedly reduced the Democratic Party's strength. These political bosses felt it essential that FDR be re-elected for a fourth term, believing this would pull other Democratic candidates along on his coattails. They also felt it imperative to block the re-nomination of Henry Wallace for the vice presidency. Wallace had political strength with support of northern liberals, blacks, and most labor, but he was extremely disliked by the conservative wing of the Democratic Party. This was especially true of the national Democratic leaders who believed, justifiably, that FDR had forced Wallace on them at the Democratic Convention in 1940. Also distasteful to the Democratic hierarchy was their awareness that Wallace was an idealistic left-leaning liberal who had the strong support of the labor movement that the political bosses feared was gaining control of their party.

Wallace was perceived to be personally cold and non-gregarious, undesirable qualities considered rare in a politician. However, he was FDR's dear friend whose thinking ran parallel with FDR's New Deal philosophy. The president knew that he could rely on Wallace to always fight for the political philosophy that both men felt represented the highest political principles of democracy.

Roosevelt began to show signs of illness at least six months before the 1944 Democratic Convention. After he returned from the Tehran conference in November 1943, he was ill for several months with what was described as post-Tehran flu; in retrospect, the "flu" was most likely the beginning sign of FDR's congestive heart failure. He had given little indication up to that time of his feelings related to the upcoming Democratic Convention, but events were now developing that would have a major influence on Roosevelt's choice for his vice-presidential running mate that summer.

Harry Truman had run for re-election to the United States Senate in 1940. He won the Missouri state Democratic primary election but only with an overall plurality of 7,476 votes over his party opponents. This winning margin was gained through the efforts of Robert E. Hannegan, chairman of the St. Louis Democratic Committee who was able to get the ward leaders in that city to switch 8,000 last-minute votes to Truman.

Truman already had a reputation for fierce loyalty to his supporters, and he was indebted to Hannegan following the primary election. After Truman successfully went on to win re-election to the United States Senate in 1940, again with Hannegan's strong support, the senator helped him become collector of Internal Revenue in St. Louis. Again with Truman's help, that attractive post was soon followed by Hannegan's promotion to the position of United States commissioner of Internal Revenue. Four years later, Senator Truman gave Hannegan his most important political plum, a presidential cabinet position.

Frank Walker was chairman of the Democratic National Committee and postmaster general of the United States in 1943. He believed he lacked the time for the duties of both offices and decided to relinquish the chairmanship of the Democratic National Party. He asked Senator Truman if he wanted the job, but Truman declined. Requirements of the Senate left him no time, especially since he was handling the high-profile and powerful chairmanship of the Truman Committee, the Senate watchdog organization created during World War II. Since Frank Walker had earlier helped Truman secure Hannegan's promotion to commissioner of the Internal Revenue Service, Truman now asked Walker to offer the chairmanship of the Democratic National Party to Hannegan. Walker presented Truman's proposal directly to FDR, who interviewed Hannegan before agreeing that he would be acceptable as the new Democratic Party chairman. Hannegan assumed the position on January 22, 1944. As Daniels said in his book, "Certainly Hannegan owed his entire political status to Truman."[1]

[1.] Jonathan Daniels, *White House Witness: 1942–1945* (New York: Doubleday, 1975), p. 233.

Within days after taking his new position, Hannegan joined other political bosses in going to the White House to discuss with FDR who might be his vice-presidential running mate in the up-coming 1944 presidential election. The political leaders could see that FDR was ill, and some knew there was the likelihood that he would not live out his fourth presidential term, which ran to January 20, 1949. It seemed reasonable to believe at that time that whoever was vice president under FDR during his fourth term would at some point become the next president of the United States.

The political bosses strongly urged FDR to drop Henry Wallace as his vice-presidential running mate in 1944, but the politically adroit president said nothing on the subject. Neither did Hannigan who stood to gain the most politically of all the participants at this White House meeting if Truman were chosen. Hannegan had already spoken to Truman about the possibility of his vice-presidential candidacy, but Truman felt:

> The President might not favor his candidacy because his committee had made numerous attacks on war agencies. Furthermore, the Republicans would have a field day because of his association with Tom Pendergast. However, Hannegan told him not to take himself out of the race by making public statements to that effect.[2]

By April of 1944, many names had already been mentioned as possible Democratic vice-presidential candidates. These included Wallace, Byrnes, Kerr, Rayburn, McNutt, Douglas, and Truman. However, Harry S. Truman (HST) is alleged to have said:

> If Bob Hannegan is running me for Vice president, he is doing it without my knowledge and without my consent.

But Victor Meisel, HST's personal secretary, later commented:

> Senator Truman was always politically ambitious. I'm sure he wanted to be Vice president, but he had to pretend he didn't.

By May and into June, FDR wanted Wallace to continue as his vice president. Eleanor Roosevelt also wanted Wallace to remain as FDR's vice president and had written an article to that effect. Roosevelt remained committed to the idea that

---

2. Tully, *My Boss*, p. 275.

no one would follow his New Deal philosophy better than Wallace. As Grace Tully, FDR's personal secretary, said in her book:

> The Boss wanted the Iowan to continue with him in office. I know this because I heard him say so many times.[3]

Moreover, as Bishop said:[4]

> The party bosses made it clear that they would work loyally for an unprecedented fourth term if FDR was willing to drop Wallace. Roosevelt was not willing. Having enjoyed an unprecedented third term, he was certain that he was above Party and represented the only chances of victory against a rising tide of Republicanism. Therefore, he should be permitted to choose a vice-president.

The implication of this is that the Democratic leaders would not support FDR unless he was willing to drop Wallace, an action which sounded threatening but one highly unlikely, in view of the Democratic Party's poor political position at that time. FDR needed the political support of his associates and so he remained silent. At the same time the president knew he was the most influential person in the Democratic Party and represented the only chance the Democratic Party had for victory in 1944. It is very likely that FDR knew that he alone could choose who would be his vice president, but it had to be done with the utmost of political skill to avoid alienating key party operatives.

June 1944 was a busy month for Roosevelt with the Allied military invasion of Europe in progress. The Democratic National Convention in Chicago was now only weeks away, and FDR had to have been planning his political strategy, an activity at which he was unusually skillful. A 1944 vice-presidential candidate, James Byrnes, wrote:

> His handling of Vice presidential ambitions in 1944 was much more like his crafty, brilliant, management of presidential rivalries four years before. At that time, he had not only encouraged existing candidates to contend with one another, but also had enlarged adroitly the field so that potential opposition would be fragmented and thus more manageable.

---

3. Alfred Steinberg, *The Man from Missouri* (New York: Putnam, 1962), p. 202.

4. Jim Bishop, *FDR's Last Year: April 1944–April 1945* (New York: William Morrow, 1974), p. 59.

If FDR planned to retain Wallace as his running mate in 1944, he would have had to do it by weakening his political competitors by division and deception. The question was how, with his failing health and the deep-seated suspicions of Wallace amongst the Democratic leaders.

CHAPTER 24

POLITICAL MANEUVERING

The Truman vice-presidential nomination in 1944 remains one of the most interesting and controversial in American political history. Studying the events, one cannot fail to be impressed by the many interpretations, varied statements, and confusing facts associated with the Roosevelt-Truman alliance of 1944. Phillips summarized it by claiming:[1]

> The story of how Harry Truman got the Democratic nomination for vice president in 1944 is an almost unbelievable melodrama, set variously in the White House and the smoke-filled rooms of a Chicago hotel and laced through with intrigue, punishment, suspense, and a surprise ending.

By the beginning of July 1944, Roosevelt was ready to make his move toward re-nomination for a fourth term. On Tuesday, July 11, 1944, at 10:20 AM, FDR called a press conference, ostensibly to announce the United States was going to recognize General Charles de Gaulle as the de facto authority in French civil matters. The press corps was not especially surprised at this news since deGaulle had just finished a high-profile, three-day ceremonial visit (July 6, 7, and 8, 1944) with FDR at the White House. FDR, who was coatless, wearing a white shirt, a brown tie, and seersucker trousers, casually read to the reporters a letter—which, he said, he had just sent that morning to Hannegan, the chairman of the Democratic Party. FDR told the reporters they would receive a copy as they left the room. It was a letter stating he would run for a fourth term.

---

1. Cabell Phillips, *The Truman Presidency* (New York: Macmillan, 1966), p. 37.

Dear Mr. Hannegan,

You have written me that in accordance with the records, a majority of the delegates have been directed to vote for my re-nomination for the office of President and I feel that I owe you, in candor, a simple statement of my position.

If the convention should carry this out, and nominate me for the Presidency, I shall accept. If the people elect me, I will serve.

Everyone of our sons serving in this war has officers from whom he takes orders. Such officers have superior officers. The President is the Commander in Chief and he too, has a superior officer—the people of the United States.

I would accept and serve but I would not run in the usual partisan, political sense. But if the people command me to continue in this office and in this war, I have as little right to withdraw as a soldier has from his post in the line.

At the same time I think I have the right to say to you and to the delegates to the convention something that is personal and purely personal.

For myself, I do not want to run. By next spring, I shall have been President and Commander in Chief of the Armed Forces for twelve years—three times elected by the people of this country under the American Constitutional system.

From the personal point of view, I believe that our economic system is on a sounder, more human basis than it was at the time of my first inauguration. It is perhaps necessary to say that I have thought only of the good of the American people. My principal objective, as you know, has been the protection of the rights and privileges and fortunes of what has been so well called the average American citizen.

After many years of public service therefore, my personal thoughts have turned to the day when I can return to civilian life. All that is within me cries to go back on the Hudson River, to avoid public responsibility and to avoid also the publicity which in our democracy follows every step of the Nation's Chief Executive.

Such would be my choice. But we of this generation chance to live in a day and hour when our nation has been attacked and the future existence of our chosen method of government is at stake.

To win this war wholeheartedly, unequivocally and as quickly as we can is our task of the first importance. To win this war in such a way that there is no further world wars in the foreseeable future is our second objective. To provide occupations, and to provide a decent standard of living for our men in the armed forces after the war, and for all Americans, are the final objectives.

Therefore, reluctantly but as a good soldier, I repeat that I will accept and serve in the office if I am ordered by the Commander in Chief of us all—the sovereign people of the United States.

Very sincerely yours, Franklin D. Roosevelt

FDR said in this letter to Hannegan, "If the convention should nominate me for the Presidency, I shall accept. If the people select me, I will serve." This was an inverted paraphrase of General William T. Sherman's refusal of the presidential nomination in 1884; "I will not accept if nominated and will not serve if elected."

Following this announcement, FDR had lunch alone with Wallace even though the two had held a long, private meeting on the previous day (Monday, July 10). Thus, only hours after announcing his intention of running for a fourth term, FDR had another long, private meeting with the vice president, which involved the forthcoming Democratic Convention. It was at this second meeting on July 11 that Wallace and FDR discussed specific political tactics regarding the vice-presidential nomination. At this meeting Wallace showed the president the names of 290 convention delegates who were already committed to him, 589 being necessary for nomination. With an already strong delegate support, Wallace's plan for victory was to encourage favorite-son candidates so as to split the vote, thus assuring there would be no winner on the first ballot.

Wallace also showed the president the results of the latest Gallup poll that was to be released to the public just before the convention. It showed 65% of registered Democrats favored Wallace for vice president, 17% were for Barkley, 5% for Rayburn, 4% for Bird, 3% for Byrnes, with Harry Truman at the bottom of the list with support from only 2% of those polled.

From this discussion Roosevelt was aware of the strong Democratic support that was already committed to Wallace. When their luncheon meeting ended, FDR put his arm around Wallace and said, "I hope it's the same team again, Henry." It seems reasonable to suspect that FDR meant this sincerely given the political and personal closeness between FDR and Wallace.

If FDR had a personal fondness and political closeness with Wallace, why would FDR later allegedly switch his support to Truman, especially if FDR believed he could win a fourth term as president regardless of who ran for vice president? Truman was a man whom FDR probably considered a small-time politician (as did most Americans when Truman became president after FDR's death). Truman had neither social or economic stature, nor formal education; he was a man with only 2% of the Democratic vote as compared to Wallace who not only had 65% of the popular vote, but also was one of FDR's closest friends and staunchest allies in support of his New Deal philosophy. It is hard to believe that FDR had an inclination to have Truman as his running mate, especially since he must have had some awareness that his selection of the vice president might be for the man who could become president of the United States. Jenkins in his book claimed:*

> The hand that Roosevelt played in the approval of the choice (for the vice presidential candidate) was enigmatic at the time, remains puzzling, and now seems unlikely ever to become clear.[2]

Even though Roosevelt planned to assure the convention delegates that he would refrain from all political decision-making at the Democratic Convention, it was not in his character to leave decisions to others. As the Schapsmeiers said,[3] "[I]t would have been a rare thing for the president to throw open the convention and allow it to choose whomever it desired for his running mate."

On the evening following FDR's announcement that he would seek a fourth term as president (July 11, 1944), he hosted a dinner meeting at the White House. The invited guests were the Democratic political bosses: Robert Hannegan; Postmaster General Frank Walker; Edward Pauley, treasurer of the Democratic National Committee; Edward Flynn of New York; Mayor Edward Kelly of Chicago; and George Allen, secretary of the Democratic National Committee. Its purpose was to discuss the various vice-presidential nominees. After dinner, the group retired to the second floor study where they were joined by John Boettiger, Anna Roosevelt's husband.

Various candidates were considered, but Henry Wallace was hardly mentioned. Roosevelt was well aware that everyone in the room disliked Wallace, and all were firmly against his renomination. Individuals who were viable but had a narrow political base were quickly eliminated from contention. These included John Weinart, the ambassador to Great Britain; Cordell Hull; Paul McNutt; and Henry Kaiser, the shipbuilder. Sam Rayburn, the Speaker of the House, was also quickly dismissed; it was concluded that with a recent split among the Texas Democrats, Rayburn wouldn't even be able to control his own state delegation. Senator Alben Barkley of Kentucky was considered but eliminated because of his age being five years older than FDR. (Four years later, in 1948, Barkley became

2. Roy Jenkins, *Truman* (New York: Harper and Row, 1986), p. 56.
3. Edward L. and Frederick H. Schapsmeier, *Prophet in Politics: Henry A. Wallace and the War Years, 1940–1945* (Ames, Iowa: Iowa State University Press, 1950), p. 103.

Truman's vice president). Another reason for Barkley's quick elimination was his short-lived resignation as Senate majority leader, opposing an FDR-supported tax bill debated several months earlier; FDR considered this action disloyal. Barkley was quickly re-elected as the Senate majority leader. Truman, interestingly, openly supported Barkley's stand against FDR's tax issue.

At some time during the meeting, Roosevelt brought up the name of William O. Douglas. FDR had appointed him as an associate justice on the United States Supreme Court in 1939, and Roosevelt is reported to have said that night:

> Douglas has the following of the Liberal Left Wing of the American people, the same kind of people who Wallace had; that he had practical experience in the backwoods of the Northwest as a logger; that he looked and acted on occasion like a boy scout; and would have, in his opinion, appeal at the polls and besides, played an interesting game of poker.

Morgan claimed:[4]

> Pauley was amazed when FDR proposed Supreme Court Justice William O. Douglas. This proposal was met with stony silence and Pauley thought that FDR must have sensed that no one wanted Douglas any more than they wanted Wallace.

Roosevelt had no reason to expect support for Douglas. In fact, Douglas probably never even considered himself a candidate for the vice-presidential nomination; during the Democratic Convention, he was backpacking in Oregon.

Another name raised that night was James Byrnes of South Carolina. FDR had previously taken him from the United States Senate and appointed him to the United States Supreme Court. He was later promoted by FDR to be director of the War Mobilization Board, a position that earned him the title of "Assistant President."

Roosevelt had mentioned to Byrnes during the late spring of 1944 that he thought he would make a very good vice president, a comment Byrnes considered an endorsement from the president. However, the political professionals, including Roosevelt, realized that Byrnes had major political problems that weakened his suitability as a candidate. Being a southerner made him unattractive to the black vote, especially in the large northern cities. Edward Flynn, the political boss of New York, expressed the fear that Byrnes would cost FDR 200,000 votes from New York City alone. Byrnes was also strongly disliked by Labor, who saw him as the man who enforced Roosevelt's strict policies, during the war, on wage and

---

4. Ted Morgan, *FDR: A Biography* (New York: Simon and Schuster, 1985), p. 726.

price control and strike prohibition. Byrnes had left the Catholic Church to become an Episcopalian after marrying a woman of that faith. It was felt that his religious conversion would lose many Catholic votes from the Democratic ticket. Nevertheless, in spite of these drawbacks Byrnes still remained a strong candidate for the Democratic vice-presidential nomination.

Simply through a process of elimination, and after a full discussion of all the candidates, Harry S. Truman emerged as the leading candidate for the vice-presidential nomination. Pauley was strongly for Truman, and Hannegan, who owed his political position directly to the Missouri senator, obviously wanted HST, although there were rumors that it was FDR who asked Flynn to request that Hannegan bring up Truman's name at the meeting to be held in the White House on July 11th since Hannegan was somewhat skeptical about proposing Truman. This scenario makes it appear that it was Roosevelt and not Hannegan who was most enthusiastic regarding Truman's nomination for the vice presidency. It is difficult to accept such a suggestion. In fact it is almost impossible. How could anyone believe that Hannegan was not a strong Truman supporter and that he had never thought of proposing Truman as a vice-presidential candidate? Hannegan had much to gain if HST was the candidate, especially if he suspected that FDR was ill and probably wouldn't survive a fourth term.

As the July 11 dinner meeting in the White House was drawing to an end, there seemed to be complete support for Truman. FDR turned to Hannegan, who was sitting next to him on the divan, put his hand on Hannegan's knee, and said, "Bob, I think you and everyone else wants Truman. Bob, if that's the case, it is Truman."[5]

After the dinner meeting had broken up, Hannegan did the logical thing when he asked FDR to confirm in writing what the president had already expressed verbally; namely, that Truman would be the president's running mate. However, what Hannegan actually received in writing from FDR has continued to remain a mystery over the years. George Allen, secretary of the Democratic National Committee, claimed that when Hannegan returned after visiting FDR in his study after the dinner meeting had just broken up, "He had a note scribbled on an envelope in pencil which simply read, 'Bob, I think Truman is the man. FDR'"[6] (Truman said he was later shown the note by Hannegan, and it was on a scratch pad from FDR's desk.) Such a short, informal note written by FDR, following a late and busy dinner meeting, seems reasonable. It was the simplest statement the president could have written to satisfy Hannegan and the other

5. Shchapsmeiers, *Prophet in Politics*, p. 104.
6. R. H. Ferrell, *The Autobiography of Harry S. Truman* (Boulder: Colorado Associated University Press, 1980), p. 92.

political leaders that FDR was for Truman. However, this note from FDR to Hannegan has never been found. Maybe the reason it has never been found is that the note was of no value to Hannegan since he could not use it as an official FDR endorsement of Truman.[7] A handwritten note on an envelope or scratch pad would not enable Hannegan to convince convention delegates that FDR wanted Truman as his vice president. Hannegan needed a formal letter written on White House stationery.

Another report of this FDR handwritten note that has circulated over the years originated from Frank Walker, the postmaster general, who said that as Hannegan got into the car as they were leaving the White House that night, he told Walker, "I got it," meaning a written note from FDR, which purportedly said:[8]

Dear Bob,

You have written me about Bill Douglas and Harry Truman. I should, of course, be very glad to run with either of them and believe that either of them would be a real strength to the ticket. Always sincerely, Franklin Roosevelt.

If one gives this letter some thought, it makes no sense that FDR would have written it at the end of the July 11th dinner meeting. If the president had already agreed that Truman was the person he and the group wanted for the vice presidency, why would FDR have written a letter which began "Dear Bob, you have written me about Bill Douglas and Harry Truman." Such a letter does not reflect the conclusion of the evening or that FDR had agreed Harry Truman would be his running mate in November.

The story concerning this alleged Douglas-Truman letter has became further embellished, and has led to confusion over the years, by reports that Hannegan and Walker returned the following day to the White House to ask Grace Tully, FDR's personal secretary, to reverse the order of the names at the beginning of the letter that Hannegan had received the previous evening from FDR. Hannegan requested the names be reversed from "Douglas and Truman" to "Truman and Douglas," so it appeared that FDR was more favorable to Truman. I do not believe a Douglas-Truman letter was written by FDR on the evening of July 11 and changed Wednesday, July 12. A letter was typewritten, but not on July 11.

---

7. This is the note Truman searched for years later in his hope to show FDR personally wanted him as his running mate and that he had not become vice president through political intrigue.

8. Frank Freidel, *Franklin D. Roosevelt: A Rendezvous with Destiny* (Boston: Little, Brown, 1990), p. 534.

Grace Tully, FDR's secretary, specifically eliminated the possibility that such a letter was retyped at Hannegan's request on the following day, Wednesday, July 12, and there is no reason for her to have lied or been confused about the date since she acknowledged in detail that a letter was typed on Saturday, July 15, 1944, and there was never any interchanging of the Truman-Douglas names.

Dates, times, and circumstances associated with the vice-presidential nomination during the Democratic Convention in July 1944 are in such disagreement, from so many sources, that it is difficult, if not impossible at times, to put them into true perspective. Some things are clear, however. Throughout the July 11th dinner meeting at the White House, the Democratic bosses were united against Wallace's nomination for the vice presidency. That Roosevelt considered Truman and possibly Douglas to have been viable candidates for the vice-presidential nomination is also verifiable. However, it appears that although Roosevelt mentioned Douglas's name, the president probably never really considered him a strong candidate. Douglas sent the following handwritten letter to FDR on July 27, the week following the Democratic Convention:

Dear Mr. President:

I was way back in the high Wallowa Mountains in Oregon on a pack trip during the convention. So it was only yesterday after my return to my summer place that I learned of your letter to Hannegan saying I would have been acceptable as your running mate. That was a great compliment Mr. President and I want you to know that it touched me deeply. Some of the boys are whooping it up for me much against my will, but I succeeded prior to the convention in subduing that mild uprising. I went away on a pack trip confident that everything was under control. So it was that your letter really touched me. I thank you from my heart for your expression of confidence, Mr. President.

It is difficult to imagine that FDR would have seriously considered Douglas as his vice-presidential running mate without ever discussing the presidential election with him at some time.

Another certainty in the 1944 Democratic Convention was that James Byrnes was a strong candidate for the vice-presidential nomination. Roosevelt respected Byrnes's political wisdom and administrative efficiency, and months before the Democratic Convention, FDR encouraged him to consider himself a strong contender for the vice-presidential position.

Byrnes listed in careful order the events concerning himself and Roosevelt leading to the vice-presidential nomination.[9]

After Harry Hopkins returned from the Tehran conference in December of 1943, he came to my office and told me that during the trip home the President had talked about how well I had managed things during his absence, and had expressed the hope that I could be nominated for Vice President. I did not wish to be considered. I meant it.

Several months later, on June 13, 1944, Hannegan came to Byrnes's office and "tried to talk me into becoming the vice-presidential candidate. I refused."

Byrnes states that several days later FDR told him he wanted him for his running mate, and "I did conclude that he was sincere in wanting me for his running mate and I found myself beginning to think about it seriously." This changed temporarily on Wednesday, July 12, the day following the dinner meeting at the White House, when Frank Walker related to Byrnes the Democratic leaders' reservations about him, which were discussed the previous evening. Byrnes concluded, "My chances for the nomination were not as good as they had been."[10]

Shortly after Byrnes heard these negative comments from Walker, Leo Crowley, director of the Foreign Economic Administration came to Byrnes's office to report a conversation he had just had with FDR. Essentially, Crowley confirmed what Byrnes had just heard from Walker; FDR seemed to have lost enthusiasm for Byrnes as a vice-presidential candidate. Now confused and needing confirmation, Byrnes immediately telephoned the president in the presence of Crowley so there would be confirmation as to what FDR said:

Leo is here in my office and has repeated his conversation with you. I would like to know if you have changed your opinion about my being a candidate.[11]

The president replied:

You are the best qualified man in the whole outfit, and you must not get out of the race. If you stay in, you are sure to win.

Byrnes stated that, as the president made other supportive statements, he repeated them aloud for Crowley to hear.

At 11:30 the next morning, Thursday, July 13, FDR's first meeting of the day was with Byrnes, who once again fully believed he had FDR's support. He states that at this meeting Roosevelt told him:

---

9. James F. Byrnes, *All in One Lifetime* (New York: Harper Brothers, 1958), p 219.
10. Byrnes, *Lifetime*, p. 221.
11. Byrnes, *Lifetime*, p. 222.

He was certain that Wallace could not be nominated but he knew he would insist on running unless the President told him to withdraw. While I differed with Mr. Wallace about many things, in view of his personal loyalty to the President, I did not see how he (FDR) could tell Wallace to withdraw. The President agreed and said that if Wallace did not voluntarily withdraw, he would give him a letter stating that if he were a delegate to the convention he would vote for Wallace but that as President he would not urge his nomination. I said that if he did that, of course, he could not thereafter express his preference for anyone else. He said he would not do so and because he had previously talked to me about being a candidate, he wanted me to know what he was going to do. He also said that in reaching my decision I could rely upon his promise that he would not express a preference for anyone.

FDR's promises and earlier supportive comments convinced Byrnes that the president wanted him as his vice-presidential running mate and that Roosevelt would not show preference for any vice-presidential candidate at the convention, now only a week away.

CHAPTER 25

POLITICAL DECEPTION

Shortly after meeting with Byrnes on Thursday, July 13, FDR had another private, one-hour luncheon with Wallace, at which time FDR agreed to write a letter personally supporting Wallace's nomination for the vice presidency. Both FDR and Wallace knew that the letter must not appear to be dictating to the convention delegates, as FDR had done in 1940. After lunch with Wallace, Roosevelt drafted several letters regarding Wallace before sending the final draft to Senator Samuel D. Jackson of Indiana, who was to be the permanent chairman of the forthcoming Democratic Convention. The convention was to begin on Wednesday, July 19, but Roosevelt dated his final draft five days earlier—Friday, July 14.

My Dear Senator Jackson:

In light of the probability that you will be chosen as permanent chairman of the convention, and because I know that many rumors accompany all conventions, I am wholly willing to give you my own personal thought in regard to the selection of a candidate for vice president. I do this at this time because I expect to be away from Washington for the next few days.

The easiest way of putting it is this: I have been associated with Henry Wallace during the past four years as Vice President, for eight years earlier while he was Secretary of Agriculture, and well before that period. I like him and I respect him, and he is my personal friend. For these reasons I would personally vote for his renomination if I were a delegate to the convention.

At the same time, I do not wish to appear in any way as dictating to the convention. Obviously the convention must do the deciding and it should—and I am sure it will—give great consideration to the pros and cons of its choice.

Very Sincerely Yours,
Franklin D. Roosevelt

This was a strategic message that FDR had to compose which was devoid of any apparent attempt to influence the convention delegates—and yet, a document that would subtly show that he backed Wallace. This is suggestive when one reviews the preliminary drafts of FDR's letter to Senator Jackson. In his first draft of the letter, the president wrote:

Because I have been associated with Vice President Wallace in the past four years, because I like him and because we have always worked together as a team, 1 would personally vote for his renomination if I were a delegate to the convention.

Roosevelt must have been concerned that the statement in the first draft, "we have always worked together as a team," would be interpreted by the delegates as suggesting he and Wallace remain a team. FDR therefore removed this statement from this first draft and, in the second draft, he replaced "always worked together as a team" with "he is my personal friend." Apparently, FDR thought being a personal friend of Wallace would seem less objectionable to delegates than his wish to continue working with Wallace "as a team."

Roosevelt's letter to Jackson, which showed personal support of Wallace, seems to have gone as far as was politically practical at that time. FDR, and probably Wallace, realized that if they made the letter stronger and gave the slightest suggestion that FDR was dictating to the convention delegates, it undoubtedly would have done Wallace more harm than good. Many historians have claimed that the letter Roosevelt sent to Senator Jackson was, at best, only a weak endorsement for Wallace. It is likely that the letter was the strongest that the president could have written in support of Wallace under the political circumstances at that time.

After FDR had private meetings with Byrnes and Wallace on Thursday, July 13, Hannegan met alone that afternoon with the president from 2:15 to 4:30 PM to plan political strategies for the Democratic National Convention only six days away. Up to this time, the president had raised and lowered the vice-presidential hopes of a host of candidates; but he knew the individuals who were politically viable were Wallace, Byrnes, and Truman, the latter having the support of the Democratic political bosses, especially Hannegan. At 10:45 that Thursday night,

FDR left Washington for Hyde Park on the first leg of his train trip to California. From California, he was to leave for Hawaii for a meeting with General Douglas MacArthur and Admiral Chester Nimitz to plan future military operations against the Japanese in the Pacific.

On the evening of Thursday, July 13, Byrnes was once again confident, after his earlier meeting that day with FDR, that he had the president's backing. By the next morning, however, this had changed. Byrnes was again troubled by Hannegan's suggestion that FDR had become less enthusiastic concerning his vice-presidential nomination. During the morning (July 14), according to Byrnes:[1]

> Walker and Hannegan asked me to meet them for lunch at Leo Crowley's apartment. They told Crowley and me that as matters then stood, if any of FDR's friends should question them about the President's position on his running mate, they would have to say he favored Truman or Douglas. Our reply was that this did not square with the President's statement to me on the previous day which I repeated to them in detail.

Hannegan immediately replied, "I don't understand it." "It" was Byrnes's firm belief that he did have the support of FDR.

Given Byrnes's political astuteness, it is very difficult to believe that he would have considered entering the vice-presidential battle without believing he had the security of the president's support. Byrnes stated:[2]

> I had no intention of running unless I was assured that he (Roosevelt) would tell them either he favored me or had no preference and would not interfere with the convention selection. Though I had already had the President's assurance that he would leave the field open, I did not like the way Hannegan was now talking.

Hannegan had so unnerved Byrnes by this time that Byrnes felt compelled to call Roosevelt directly in order to be reassured that he still had the president's support. "After lunch," Byrnes stated, "I asked Crowley to accompany me to my office, telling him that I was going to telephone Mr. Roosevelt at Hyde Park."

Prior to making the call, Byrnes wrote a list of specific questions to ask the president, and then he wrote down the president's answers in shorthand, a skill Byrnes had perfected during his early days as a court stenographer:

---

[1]. *Byrnes, Lifetime,* p. 223.
[2]. *Ibid.*

BYRNES—I understood from you that you would write a letter for Henry Wallace. It was my understanding from your statement to me yesterday [Thursday, July 13] that you would not authorize any person to quote you as saying you preferred any candidate other than Wallace.

THE PRESIDENT—I am not favoring anybody. I told them so. No I am not favoring anyone.

BYRNES—Both Hannegan and Frank Walker stated today (Friday, July 14) that if at the convention they were asked about their views, they would be obliged to say to their friends that from your statements they concluded you did not prefer Wallace but did prefer Truman first and Douglas second, and that either would be preferable to me because they would cost the ticket fewer votes than I would.

THE PRESIDENT—Jimmy, that is all wrong. That is not what I told them. It is what they told me. When we all went over the list, I did not say that I preferred anybody or that anybody would cost me votes, but they all agreed that Truman would cost fewer votes than anybody and probably Douglas second. This was the agreement they reached and I had nothing to do with it. I was asking questions. I did not express myself. Objection to you came from labor people, both Federation and CIO.

BYRNES—I have a letter from Al Whitney asking permission to take charge of my candidacy in the Ohio Delegation. He sent his legal representative and friend, Mr. Miller, to see me this morning. I just wanted to know if Walker and Hannegan would be correct in stating to their friends that you believe I will cost more votes than others.

THE PRESIDENT—They can state their opinion but they cannot state mine. I have not given my opinion to anyone.

BYRNES—If they make the statement, notwithstanding your letter to Wallace, that you have expressed a preference to Truman and Douglas, it would make it very difficult for me.

THE PRESIDENT—*We have to be damn careful of language. They asked if I would object to Truman and Douglas and I said no. That is different from using the word "prefer." That is not expressing a preference because you know I told you I would have no preference.* [Author's emphasis.]

BYRNES—I made the statement to you that should I decide to become a candidate I would resign. I now believe that would be unwise because it would create the impression of a disagreement between us.

THE PRESIDENT—I think that is right.

The conversation concluded with the president expressing the hope that Byrnes would strive for the vice-presidential nomination. FDR ended the call by asking: "Will you go on and run?" and Byrnes replied:

I am still considering it. Before deciding I wanted to know your answers on these questions and whether you had authorized Hannegan and Walker to make the statement that you prefer other candidates.

Roosevelt then said,

After all, Jimmy, you are close to me personally and Henry is close to me. I *hardly know Truman.* [Author's emphasis.] Douglas is a poker partner. He is good in a poker game and tells good stories."

The clear implication of this conversation, as carefully recorded by Byrnes, is that FDR wanted Byrnes to continue to seek the vice-presidential nomination since FDR had no preference for Truman or Douglas over Byrnes. How could he? FDR knew Douglas would have no backing at the convention, and as far as Truman was concerned, the president admitted that he hardly knew him.

After Byrnes had ended his telephone conversation with the president, he called Hannegan to reconfirm, once again, FDR's support of his vice-presidential candidacy. Byrnes read to Hannegan, over the telephone, the transcript he had just recorded of his conversation with FDR, after which Hannegan stated for the second time that day (Friday, July 14), "I don't understand it"—i.e., Byrnes's continued confidence in FDR's support.

FDR had convinced Hannegan at the Tuesday night White House dinner on July 11 that he would join the political leaders in their support of Truman. Even as recent as their two-hour meeting the previous afternoon (Thursday, July 13), Hannegan was certain that FDR would support the Democratic leaders and would not express any new presidential preferences other than the personal support he had expressed for Wallace in his letter to Senator Jackson. Now, less than twenty-four hours later, Hannegan was confused by the president's maneuvering.

The problem confronting Hannegan was that he had known FDR for only a few months and didn't understand how Roosevelt functioned politically. FDR was exercising his mastery of political manipulation; showing support for Truman to Hannegan and the Democratic leaders on the one hand, while extending the same support to Byrnes on the other.

After his telephone conversation with FDR, Byrnes and Leo Crowley left Crowley's White House office and walked down the corridor to see Harry Hopkins, FDR's personal advisor. Byrnes repeated to Hopkins the conversation he had just had with the president:

> Relying on Mr. Roosevelt's statement that he would express no prefer-
> ence and that there would be an open field, I would become a candidate.
> Hopkins repeated that the President was satisfied that if I entered the race
> I would be nominated. I then informed several friends of mine of my deci-
> sion and telephoned Senator Truman in Independence, Missouri.

At last Byrnes was fully confident of Roosevelt's support. Additional assurance of his winning the vice-presidential nomination was delivered over the ticker-tape news wire at this time from Kansas City; Truman had declared he would not be a candidate for the vice-presidential nomination. Pro-Truman support was a reflec-tion of anti-Wallace sentiment, and if Truman was not going to run, Byrnes, as the other leading anti-Wallace contender, could not help but benefit. So Byrnes called Truman at his home in Missouri to ask if the news release was true.

> Truman confirmed the report and added that if I [Byrnes] should be a
> candidate he would support me and help me. I thanked him and asked if
> he would nominate me. This he promptly agreed to do.

Truman gave a different slant to this conversation in his 1955 memoirs; he claimed that Byrnes tricked him in this 1944 call when he asked Truman to nom-inate him. "Byrnes knew that the President had named me as his vice-presidential preference, at the time he called me in Independence and asked me to nominate him at the convention."[3]

It is hard to believe that politically adept James Byrnes would have attempted such clear-cut deception of Truman if he knew Roosevelt wanted Truman as his vice-presidential running mate. It is also inconceivable that Byrnes would have asked Truman to nominate him for vice president if he (Byrnes) believed he was without Roosevelt's support. Byrnes called Truman from Washington and said that "President Roosevelt had decided on him as the new nominee for Vice-President and he asked me if I would nominate him at the convention. I told him

---

3. Harry S. Truman, *Memoirs by Harry S. Truman:Year of Decisions* (New York: Doubleday and Company, Garden City, New York, 1955), p. 192.

that I would be glad to do it if the President wanted him for a running mate."[4]
Discussing the same telephone call, Bishop stated:

> Byrnes must have received the green light from the President and
> Truman must have believed that the green light meant Roosevelt's
> endorsement for the vice presidential nomination.[5]

What Byrnes and Truman actually said will probably never be known, but it
appears that Byrnes was confident that he would win the vice-presidential nomination with Roosevelt's backing. It is also important to keep in mind that at no
time did FDR ever demonstrate any personal wish to have Truman as his running
mate.

FDR was the political glue that held the various factions together within the
Democratic Party, The Democratic political bosses who were strongly anti-
Wallace and pro-Truman were well aware that their power base rested solely on
the shoulders of FDR. No one would be nominated and allowed to run with
FDR without his approval. As Cochran emphasized, "[T]he President, and par-
ticularly a President like Roosevelt, will choose his own running mate."

4. Truman, *Memoirs*, p. 190.
5. Bishop, *FDR's Last Year*, p. 105.

CHAPTER 26

AN HISTORIC MEETING

Collision-course interests, conflicting rumors, and the confusing political actions of the president presaged a monumental struggle for the vice-presidential nomination. Hannegan had a major advantage in the coming contest, however; he and other Democratic leaders would be able to control and manipulate the delegate factions at the convention.

Hannegan, new to FDR's political machinations, feared that Truman was either losing or had already lost the president's support, which he promised at the White House dinner on July 11. What Hannegan hoped to orchestrate was a head-to-head fight between Byrnes and Wallace that he believed could gain victory for Truman. Hannegan feared a three-way fight between Wallace, Truman, and Byrnes, which could split the votes of the latter two and leave Wallace the victor.

Hannegan must have felt that his plan was deteriorating following Byrnes's call to FDR at Hyde Park on Friday, July 14. The situation apparently necessitated a face-to-face meeting with FDR. Even though Hannegan had spent time the previous day with FDR, a telephone conversation apparently would not suffice. Hannegan needed personal reassurance from FDR that he was going to honor his July 11 commitment to Truman, especially since Byrnes, just five days before the Democratic National Convention, continued to believe he had FDR's support for the vice-presidential nomination.

Before leaving Washington on Friday night (July 14), FDR had decided that he would not attend the Democratic Convention in Chicago but would journey in a southwesterly direction slowly across the United States to California from where he would broadcast his acceptance speech over the radio to the convention delegates in Chicago. Hannegan telephoned the president at Hyde Park late on Friday, urging that they have another meeting which required rerouting the president's train to Chicago. Throughout Friday night and into early Saturday morning, FDR's train rumbled through the Northeast.

Hannegan arrived in Chicago by train Saturday morning (July 15) aboard the Capitol Express. He was anxious to avoid answering questions about coming events, and the *New York Times* reported on the following day:

> He left the train through the rear of the station, thus avoiding newspaper reporters who had gathered at the main exit, entered the automobile of Mayor Edward J. Kelly and was driven away.

FDR's train arrived later that day at 12:20 PM in the town of Englewood, Illinois, a small community located just outside Chicago. From there his train was rerouted to the Rock Island Railroad yard in Chicago, which at that time was located at 51st and Westwood Streets. The train arrived at 1:30 PM and Hannegan boarded the train and met alone with FDR.

What FDR and Hannegan said will never be accurately known, but I would like to establish the likely scenario that is not a figment of my imagination but is based on information I received from Joseph Leib and William Hannegan, the son of Robert Hannegan. Neither individual was made aware I knew the other, since I did not wish to influence either party by what the other source had said.

Leib stated that he received his information from Mayor Kelly, who learned of it directly from Hannegan. Kelly accompanied Hannegan to FDR's train but was not in the train compartment with FDR and Hannegan. The information I gained from Hannegan's son was based on personal telephone calls and tape-recorded sessions regarding his father and mother's discussions over the years concerning the FDR-Hannegan meeting in the Chicago train yard in 1944 and the political manipulations carried out that year at the Democratic National Convention.

Joseph Leib claimed he had attended every Democratic National Convention since 1928 and had remained in close personal contact with many political figures. He was in Chicago the weekend before the convention and spent time with Mayor Kelly. On Saturday, July 15, Leib said Kelly told him that Hannegan was to meet secretly with Roosevelt. Kelly and Leib discussed FDR's health with Leib, showing Kelly a medical report (which Leib incorrectly believed was the Lahey Memorandum but was most likely a compilation of FDR's poor health conditions leaked by consulting doctors) predicting FDR would not survive a fourth term. Kelly allegedly told Leib that he and Hannegan had already seen this medical report, which Hannegan said he would discuss with Roosevelt if it became necessary.

Leib told me he had received this medical report of FDR's poor physical condition from a disenchanted member of FDR's staff in the lobby of the Willard Hotel in Washington, sometime in the spring of 1944. I found this information interesting but had no way of confirming it. I called the son of the government official who allegedly passed the report to Leib, but he said his father had died years before and he had no personal knowledge concerning his father's relationship with FDR.

Soon after, however, I received information which gave credibility to Leib's statement that Kelly and Hannegan did have a medical report prior to the Democratic Convention in 1944, showing FDR was in very poor health and was expected to die before the end of his fourth term. Mr. Joseph Molotavsky, a *New York Times* reporter assigned to its Washington bureau, provided the lead to confirm Leib's statements. Molotavsky, in a letter dated March 14, 1986, said he had read in the *New York Times* of my search for information regarding FDR's health and suggested I read a book entitled *Of Spies and Stratagems*, written in 1963 by Professor Stanley P. Lovell.[1]

Lovell was a professor of chemistry at Harvard University at the beginning of the Second World War and had been personally recruited by Harvard President James B. Conant into the Office of Strategic Services (OSS), the United States spy organization later to be renamed the Central Intelligence Agency (CIA). Early in the war, Lovell had been assigned to the European Theater of Operations. When it appeared certain that Germany was facing defeat, he was reassigned in the spring of 1944 to the Pacific war zone. Of great coincidence was that he flew from the East Coast to his embarkation port on the West Coast during the week of the Democratic Convention in Chicago in 1944. Lovell subsequently wrote in his book of this flight:

> As I flew to San Francisco, the Democratic Convention was in full swing. Amid a pandemonium of cheers, Franklin D. Roosevelt was nominated for a fourth term as President. No one seemed to be concerned with the identity of his running-mate, but we in the OSS cared. We had seen a report from the Lahey Clinic in Boston whose doctors, after examining the President, stated that he would not survive another term. One could not share such information. Our mission was entirely military, not civilian, so off I went to the Pacific Theater.

Hoping to speak with Professor Lovell concerning his information about FDR's health, I tracked him from Harvard University to the Raytheon Company in Massachusetts where he had been a former member of their board of scientific advisors. From there the search led to a nursing home in Newton Center, Massachusetts, but on visiting the facility I learned he had died there several months earlier.

---

1. Stanley P. Lovell, *Of Spies and Strategems* (Englewood Cliffs, N.J.: Prentice Hall, 1963), pp. 71–72.

I located Professor Lovell's son, who lived in West Newton, Massachusetts, and he said he never heard his father discuss FDR's health; but he mentioned that his father had a relationship with General William ("Wild Bill") Donovan who had been appointed by Roosevelt to head the OSS during the Second World War, and perhaps the general's associates might have information on the matter. Donovan had remained in close personal touch with FDR throughout the war and in fact saw FDR privately in the White House just days before the 1944 Democratic Convention.

Based on Professor Lovell's written statement that he and other OSS members knew FDR was dying, it seemed feasible that some member of the OSS might still be alive who had knowledge of Donovan's contacts with FDR in 1944; especially important would be any knowledge regarding FDR's health.

Many OSS agents associated with Donovan during World War II had died, but I learned of the OSS Alumni Association that keeps in contact with surviving members of the organization by way of a newsletter and an annual national convention. During World War II there were approximately 25,000 members of the OSS; but at the time of my search, their numbers had dwindled to 10,000.

The then-current president of the OSS Alumni Association was Mr. Max Corso of Middlebury, Connecticut, the editor of the Middlebury town paper. I called him and asked if he could recall anyone who might have known of General Donovan's association with Roosevelt. Unfortunately, he didn't, and he confirmed that most of the people who worked with Donovan during the war had died. Mr. Corso placed an advertisement in the OSS quarterly newsletter, asking any agent to write me if they had information regarding General Donovan and FDR, but I heard nothing further.

On the afternoon of July 15, 1944, FDR's train was standing in the Chicago rail yard, with Hannegan being alone with the president. Leib said Kelly had asked Hannegan if he could accompany him, but Hannegan said he wanted to be alone with the president. Some historians have written that Mayor Kelly and Edward Pauley, Democratic national treasurer were both with Hannegan at his meeting with FDR. Pauley, in fact, wrote a report of the meeting that is in the confidential files at the Harry S. Truman Library in Independence, Missouri: "When the President's train came into the railyards, only Hannegan and myself [Pauley] and the Secret Service went aboard."

In the *Missouri Historical Society Journal* (January 1986) there is a review of the Democratic National Convention of 1944 written by Brenda L. Hester:

> Pauley's account (of the FDR-Hannegan meeting) has caused problems for researchers because he has distorted his involvement by

claiming to have been at meetings which he did not attend (such as the Kelly, Hannegan, Roosevelt conference on the train in Chicago).

Grace Tully, who was on the train at the time, said that Hannegan met privately with FDR for approximately forty-five minutes. Their meeting suggested some degree of contention, since Tully described the meeting as a lengthy palaver (definition of "palaver": "to cajole, to try to persuade in the face of reluctance").

When Hannegan's appointment as chairman of the Democratic National Committee was approved by Roosevelt in January 1944, he had been a minor politician and was little known to FDR. Now, just six months later, Hannegan was about to influence the president's strategy for the upcoming vice-presidential nomination and personally alter history.

Hannegan boarded FDR's train for two reasons. One was to obtain a letter on White House stationery indicating that FDR was supportive of Truman as his running mate. Hannegan's son said that although his father considered the president's letter to Jackson to be weak in his support of Wallace, nevertheless, it had to be neutralized. The second goal of Robert Hannegan on the train that day was to convince FDR that if he would not support Truman, he should at least agree not to support any other candidate for the vice-presidential nomination.

Hannegan knew that the letter the president had written to Senator Jackson, the chairman of the upcoming convention, would be read to the delegates. FDR's letter to Jackson said he would vote for Wallace if he (FDR) were a delegate—but he did not mention how he felt about this in his capacity as the president. If one considers this, the delegates at the convention were all die-hard Democrats who would be expected to vote for a candidate who best represented the United States in general and the Democratic Party in particular. If FDR indicated in his letter how he would vote for the vice-presidential nomination if he were a delegate, one might suspect that as president he also considered Wallace to be the best vice-presidential candidate.

In order to neutralize this impression, Hannegan got FDR to write a letter stating he would be glad to run with either Truman or Douglas:

July 19
Dear Bob:

You have written me about Harry Truman and Bill Douglas. I should, of course, be very glad to run with either of them and believe that either one of them would bring real strength to the ticket.[2]

---

2. Bishop, *FDR's Last Year*, p. 99.

Such a letter, however, failed to show much enthusiasm for Truman. A rumor has persisted to this day that Hannegan asked that FDR's letter be retyped since FDR had originally written that he would be glad to run with Douglas or Truman. Hannegan wanted the sequence of the names reversed so that Truman's name was first, which he felt would have obvious political advantage at the Democratic Convention. One has to question whether there ever was a Douglas-Truman letter and that the story of its existence is just another example of historical imagination that is passed from one historian to the next so that, over time, the story becomes generally accepted.

In the Truman Library in Independence, Missouri, are two copies of the Truman-Douglas letter—one handwritten by FDR, the other typewritten on official White House stationery. No copy of a Douglas-Truman letter has ever surfaced, and Hannegan repeatedly stated to his family and to others that a Douglas-Truman letter never existed.

William Hannegan was told by his parents what happened to the handwritten and typed Truman-Douglas letters that Robert Hannegan took from the train after his FDR meeting. Mrs. Hannegan claimed that when her husband returned from his meeting with the president, he gave her both letters for safekeeping until he would need the typewritten copy the following week at the convention. Because she knew that the Truman-Douglas letters were important, she claimed she carried them in her handbag during the day and placed them under her mattress during the night.

Hannegan allegedly told FDR on the train that there were high-ranking Democrats who were concerned about his health and specifically feared that if Wallace were vice president, and something happened to FDR, it would be a disaster for the United States and especially for the Democratic Party. Hannegan allegedly told FDR that some top-level Democrats felt so strongly about this possibility that they might feel compelled to leak information on FDR's deteriorating health. Such an action would have jeopardized Roosevelt's chances for a fourth term victory since one of the most important question raised during the 1944 election period was whether FDR should run for office because of his health.

At this point in the story, one might ask why FDR would even want to remain as president for an unprecedented fourth term. Roosevelt had been advised in the spring of 1944 that the war with Germany would most likely be over by the following year—and with Japan in the foreseeable future. FDR was already thinking of his cherished priority, the establishment of the United Nations. Robert Hannegan told his son, "FDR wanted to establish the organization and then travel around the world and be the titular head of the organization." But in order to accomplish this and get ratification of the organization through the United

States Senate (something Woodrow Wilson could not accomplish), FDR had to do it using the power of the presidency, which he likely might not have been able to do as an ex-president.

As mentioned earlier, Hannegan went on FDR's train with two main objectives. The first, gaining the Truman-Douglas letter, had been accomplished; but now came the most difficult part of his mission: to commit FDR to silence regarding his interest in Wallace's nomination during the Democratic Convention.

Robert Hannegan went on the train with FDR's poor health report in his pocket, but whether he showed it to FDR is not known. The information in the medical report was critical since it showed FDR probably wouldn't survive a fourth term.

Hannegan knew FDR would not openly support Truman, and he was aware that, any time during the convention, as Hannegan's son said, "All Roosevelt had to do was to say he wanted Wallace and that would have been it." It was crucial that FDR remain silent during the convention. Hannegan told FDR that some leading Democrats knew of his poor health, probably from the same source as had been seen by the OSS. These individuals felt strongly that it might be in the best interest of the country to leak this health report to the media if FDR planned to run with Wallace. FDR wanted a fourth term, and he could not take the chance that what Hannegan had just mentioned might occur.

In order to prevent this veiled threat from becoming reality, FDR agreed to say nothing during the convention in support of any vice-presidential candidate. FDR probably thought that Wallace could win the nomination on his own at the convention since the delegates realized he was personally supporting Wallace. What FDR probably didn't realize was that Hannegan would have the ability to conduct the voting at the convention.

Hannegan's son said this agreement between FDR and his father—for FDR to remain silent during the convention—"changed history on the train on July 15th." The agreement was that "FDR wouldn't contact anyone at the convention and would leave Hannegan alone to let him get his guy in." The "guy" being Truman. Everything had to go through Hannegan, and any conversation between Hannegan and FDR during the convention would be routed through the White House telephone system.

The stage had been set for Hannegan's political manipulation at the convention. Hannegan said throughout the remainder of his life that all he wanted written on his gravestone was that he was the one responsible for preventing Wallace from becoming the president of the United States. A more appropriate gravestone would have stated that Hannegan became instrumental in making Truman the thirty-third president of the United States.

CHAPTER 27

THE ELIMINATION
OF BYRNES

Hannegan left Roosevelt's Pullman car knowing two things stood in Truman's way for the vice-presidential nomination: FDR's letter to Senator Jackson, which would be read at the convention showing personal support for Wallace and Byrnes's continuing belief that he had FDR's backing for the nomination. Hannegan had successfully neutralized the first threat by obtaining a pledge of silence by FDR on any further support towards Wallace. In addition, he now had the Truman-Douglas letter written on White House stationery stating that FDR considered Truman an acceptable running mate. Hannegan's remaining challenge was to eliminate Byrnes as a vice-presidential candidate.

After returning to his hotel room at the Blackstone Hotel, Hannegan called Byrnes in Washington in the presence of Mayor Kelly of Chicago and said, untruthfully, "The President has given us the green-light to support you and he wants you in Chicago."[1] He urged Byrnes to come to Chicago immediately for a meeting that would be in Kelly's apartment the following day. Byrnes arrived the next morning, Sunday, July 16, and was met by the Chicago fire chief, who drove him to Mayor Kelly's apartment. Byrnes had breakfast alone with Kelly and Hannegan, at which time Hannegan quoted FDR as having said, "Well you know Jimmy [Byrnes] has been my choice from the very first. Go ahead and name him."

The three men discussed FDR's letter of personal support of Wallace that had been sent to Senator Jackson, and they concluded that if Wallace received no further support from FDR, it would probably have little influence on the delegates. Both Hannegan and Kelly knew that there would be no further support for either Wallace or Byrnes by the president.

[1.] Byrnes, *Lifetime*, p. 226.

On Sunday evening (July 16th) in an apartment placed at Hannegan's disposal, a dinner meeting was held for Byrnes and other Democratic leaders. It was stressed at the dinner that FDR's letter showing personal support for Wallace was not binding on anyone. The guests were also told that FDR was backing Byrnes for the vice-presidential nomination, which would be announced the following day at 5:00 PM, the same time that Senator Jackson was to give to the press Roosevelt's letter of personal support for Wallace. As the dinner ended that evening, Byrnes was unaware of the Truman-Douglas letter that had been written on FDR's train two days earlier. In his autobiography Byrnes said, "He [Byrnes] could not have become a candidate unless he [Roosevelt] wrote a similar letter regarding me." At the same time, Truman was apparently unaware of Hannegan's and Kelly's deception of Byrnes, and HST continued to work diligently on behalf of Byrnes: "I went to Chicago fully committed to Byrnes and determined to do all I could to see that he won the nomination."[2]

Characteristically, Truman kept his word. During the weekend preceding the convention, he continued to campaign vigorously for Byrnes's vice-presidential nomination. Although Truman strongly denied that he was being considered or that he wished to be nominated for the position, Freidel claimed Truman was already aware of the way Hannegan was moving on his behalf. Truman protested that he did not wish to be the vice-presidential candidate at the same time he sent word to trusted political friends that Hannegan expected him to be nominated and he would need their help in Chicago. Truman told James Forrestal, the secretary of Defense, as early as July 4th that he was being pressed to be the nominee.

An unconfirmed story has persisted since the 1944 Democratic Convention that FDR promised Byrnes his support as long as Byrnes had the backing of Sidney Hillman, the powerful head of the Political Action Committee of the Congress of the Industrial Organizations (CIO). FDR allegedly said that before Byrnes could be nominated for the vice-presidential nomination he had to "Clear it with Sydney."[3]

I have not uncovered information that would substantiate the truth of this "Clear it with Sydney" comment. It was allegedly first reported by Arthur Krock, who said he heard it from a newspaper friend (Catlich) who allegedly heard it from Mayor Kelly of Chicago. What is factual is that FDR saw Hillman alone at the White House at 12:45 PM on Thursday, July 13, for a ten-minute meeting following which Roosevelt lunched alone once again with Vice President Wallace. Hillman had informed FDR and Wallace that he would strongly support Wallace

---

2. Phillips, *Truman Presidency*, p. 39.
3. Byrnes, *Lifetime*, p. 227.

and that his decision represented the majority of the labor organizations in the United States.

In Chicago on Sunday morning (July 16), Truman had breakfast with Hillman, who told him that although he and his union strongly favored Wallace for the vice presidency, Truman would be their choice if Wallace failed to gain the nomination. At this meeting, other labor leaders including Philip Murray, President of the CIO, repeated Hillman's sentiments. Truman was their second choice after Wallace. Truman continued to insist that he was not interested since he was fully supporting Byrnes's vice-presidential nomination. Truman later told Byrnes not to expect support from the labor leaders. Yet Byrnes remained confident that at some time during the convention, FDR would inform the delegates he wanted Byrnes as his vice-presidential running mate, and "everyone knew what FDR wanted, he got."

Byrnes was aware of the importance of Sidney Hillman's backing, and because he still trusted Hannegan, he asked him to seek Hillman's support. Hannegan went to see Hillman sometime that Sunday night (July 16) and on the following day called Byrnes, who recounted:

> The next morning (Monday, July, 17th) I got a call from him (Hannegan) asking me to use the room next to his suite at the Blackstone as an office. Various matters he expected would come up and he would want to consult me. After I went to Hannegan's headquarters at the Blackstone I had a friendly talk with Philip Murray. He said that the CIO membership was overwhelmingly in favor of Wallace and because of this he too had to be for him. However, if the nomination did not go to Wallace, the CIO would still support the President regardless of who the convention named as vice President. When I told Hannegan of this conversation, he was entirely satisfied.

Byrnes knew that the labor leaders were upset when they learned he was confident he had Roosevelt's support, but he was surprised when he learned that the labor leaders had demanded that FDR withdraw his support for Byrnes. Byrnes later wrote, "He (FDR) told the labor leaders and Flynn that in view of their statements he would withdraw his approval of my candidacy and would go along with the desire to nominate Truman." Byrnes had now been abandoned by FDR.

Approximately one hour after FDR had received telephone calls from labor leaders requesting that the president desist in his support for Byrnes, Truman went to Byrnes to confirm that Byrnes had lost FDR's support and that the president was now supporting Truman. Byrnes later wrote:

He [Truman] learned from Hannegan that the President had telephoned asking that he run for vice-president. Mr. Truman felt he should
comply with the President's wishes and therefore must withdraw his promise to support and to nominate me. He [Hannegan] asked if I would run
anyway. I told him I did not think so, but I wanted to think it over that
night.

Throughout that Monday night, July 17th, Byrnes agonized over his vice-
presidential situation but by the following morning had made the decision to
withdraw from the contest. He stated:

On that day, July 18th (Tuesday), I dictated a letter to Senator
Maybank, Chairman of the South Carolina delegation saying that I did
not wish my name presented to the convention. The letter was dated July
19th (which was Wednesday—the beginning of the Democratic National
Convention) and marked for release that day at 10:00 AM because before it
was made public, I wished to tell (Mayor) Ed Kelly of my decision and had
learned that he would not be available on the afternoon of the 18th.

I freely admit that I was disappointed and I felt hurt by President
Roosevelt's actions. Not having wanted to be involved, I was angry with
myself for permitting the President to get me in, but I cherish no animosity toward him nor did I harbor any ill feelings toward Mr. Truman whose
position I fully understood. I assured him of this Monday night when he
called to tell me in view of the President expressing a preference for him
(Truman), he felt he should be a candidate and asked that I release him.

Byrnes's statement confirms that Truman believed as early as Monday night,
July 17th, that he would be candidate for the vice-presidential nomination, and
that he had FDR's support.

Reports have circulated over the years that prior to Byrnes's withdrawal from
the vice-presidential race, he tried to telephone Roosevelt to confirm if it were
true that FDR had switched his support to Truman. FDR supposedly would not
take the call. This story, as with so many other historical vignettes involving
FDR, was apparently not true. Byrnes never mentioned it in his autobiography.
What Byrnes did recollect was:

I believed the President wanted me named and therefore urged my
nomination to be accomplished in order to accomplish his primary purpose. When on Monday night (July 17th) the President switched to
Truman, I think Hannegan was pleased because as head of the Democratic

machine in St. Louis he was friendly to the Pendergast organization of Kansas City.

While Kelly and Hannegan were deceiving Byrnes on the weekend preceding the Democratic Convention, the convention delegates and the press continued to believe that Roosevelt wanted Wallace as his running mate. On Wednesday July 13, the *Chicago Tribune* said, "The President was reported to be loath to drop Wallace."

On the following day, July 14, two additional articles appeared in the *Chicago Tribune*:

> On the matter of the vice-presidential nomination, the Mayor (Kelly) expressed the opinion that the Illinois delegation will go along with any choice the President might indicate.

The *Chicago Tribune* also said: "Await Roosevelt's okay for Wallace."

By Sunday (July 16), the day after the FDR-Hannegan railroad car meeting, the press began to sense a change in the vice-presidential situation. The *Chicago Tribune* reported, "[H]e (FDR) favors the nomination of Wallace, but is not going to insist on it. Hannegan is to reveal the president's position on the vice-presidential nomination at an appropriate time." The *New York Times* on that same Sunday headlined: "Hannegan secrecy on vice presidency mystifies Chicago."

By the time of the opening of the Democratic Convention on Wednesday, July 19, Hannegan and Kelly had eliminated Byrnes and neutralized FDR's preference for Wallace. The political future of the two leading contenders, Wallace and Truman, was now in the hands of Hannegan and Kelly. The drama of the Democratic Convention was about to unfold.

CHAPTER 28

THE PRIME CANDIDATES

After Byrnes had withdrawn as a contender at the Democratic Convention in 1944, the main candidates for the vice-presidential nomination were now Truman and Wallace. Wallace was Roosevelt's friend, shared his political philosophy, and had served him well for four years as vice president and before that as secretary of Agriculture. Truman's reputation, now and in the future, will always remain above reproach, but the question remains—was he, on the basis of reputation and record, the type of individual that FDR would have wanted for his running mate as opposed to Henry Wallace?

TRUMAN

In 1938, Harry S. Truman (HST), then a little-known first-term Senator from Missouri, had publicly declared against FDR's serving a third term. The president was aware that Truman was the protégé of Thomas Pendergast, a corrupt political figure who on May 29, 1939, had entered Leavenworth federal penitentiary to begin serving a fifteen-month sentence for income tax evasion, reduced from three years because of his age and poor health.

Extensive political corruption existed in Kansas City during the 1930s under the control of Thomas Pendergast, the man HST considered his political mentor. Truman had served in World War I with Lieutenant James Pendergast, the nephew of the Missouri political boss, and they remained good friends after the war. Young Pendergast encouraged his uncle to support HST for judge of Jackson County, Missouri, a position which in that state at that time was an administrative appointment and not an elective office. In 1922, HST was elected for a two-year term but was defeated for re-election in 1924. After one term out of office, he was re-elected and held the office until 1934. In May of that year he went to Tom Pendergast and asked for his support in Truman's quest for the Congressional seat in the fourth Missouri district.

Pendergast refused. However, shortly afterward, James P. Aylward, chairman of the Democratic Party in Missouri, and Jim Pendergast met Truman at Sedalia, Missouri, where they asked him to run for the United States Senate with Tom Pendergast's support. Truman said he would rather run for governor but was told that Pendergast would not support him for any office other than that of the United States Senate.

In the Democratic primary election in 1934, HST ran against Jacob L. Milligan and John J. Corcoran for the United States Senate nomination. Wards 1, 2, 3, and 4 in Kansas City were the most politically powerful voting districts in the state and were under the tight control of the Pendergast political machine. During the primary election in these wards, Corcoran got 160 votes, Milligan 557 votes, and Truman, amazingly, received 50,637 votes. HST went on to win easily in November against his Republican opponent. Immediately after the election, strong accusations of fraud were made about the voting precincts of Wards 1, 2, 3, and 4 in Kansas City, which had delivered HST's victory. Maurice Milligan, brother of Jacob L. Milligan, the candidate Truman defeated in the primary, was at that time the U.S. Attorney for the Western District of Missouri. After the election, Milligan uncovered voter fraud that went on to be later recorded in the United States Congressional Record on June 18, 1947:

> Federal agents had gathered evidence of ballot box padding of repeater voters, and of judges refusing to count votes against the machine candidates.

Immediately after the next general election, in 1936, and without telling U.S. Attorney General Homer L. Cummings of his plans, Maurice Milligan contacted Federal Judge Albert L. Reeves to request a federal grand jury be convened to investigate voter fraud in Kansas City.

The local offices of the FBI were instructed to move into action as soon as the voting booths had closed, to impound the ballot boxes and place them under the protection of armed guards. These actions are well recorded in the Congressional Record by United States Representative Lawrence H. Smith of Wisconsin who, on Wednesday, June 18, 1947, described to the House of Representatives the police actions that had taken place immediately following the election in Missouri in 1936.

Within a month of the general election in Missouri in 1936, Milligan had 278 of Pendergast's political workers and election officials indicted; 258 of these people eventually were sent to prison. After several years of legal maneuvering, Milligan had amassed enough evidence by 1939 to convict Thomas Pendergast of income tax evasion. This was undoubtedly a bitter blow to Truman, to see his political mentor convicted and sent to federal prison. It must be stressed, however, that HST was never found to have been involved in any illegal actions during the 1936 campaign or at any time during his lifetime.

Roosevelt was well aware of Pendergast, whom he had disliked since 1932 when Pendergast supported Senator Read of Missouri for the Democratic presidential nomination. Pendergast continued to openly oppose FDR throughout the 1932 election campaign, personally preventing establishment of a Roosevelt for President club in Missouri. The widely known political corruption of Pendergast and his political machine over the years was an embarrassment to FDR and the Democratic Party.

Because of Maurice Milligan's exceptional legal job in destroying the Pendergast political machine in Kansas City, FDR re-nominated him in 1938 as the United States Attorney for the Western District of Missouri. After the Clerk read this nomination to the United States Senate, the first to rise to speak on the floor was Senator Harry Truman. He stood up and said:

> Mr. Milligan is now under consideration for confirmation on a reappointment. I have never thought and I do not now think that Mr. Milligan is qualified for the position of District Attorney for the Western District of Missouri. He is not professionally qualified, nor is he morally qualified.

The United States Congressional Record on February 15, 1938, records that immediately after Truman's comments Senator Stiles Bridges of New Hampshire rose and stated:

> I hesitate to take issue with the distinguished Senator from Missouri as to matters within his own state, but I cannot sit still in this body and see a man who has fought crime, and who has obviously done his duty and who is the personal choice of the President of the United States for this post, and who I assume the President has personally investigated, be the subject of charges of rebuke here without rising to his defense which means defense of clean, honest, decent government.

The debate climaxed with every member of the United States Senate voting in favor of Milligan's reappointment, except one: Senator Harry Truman. HST's fierce loyalty to individuals was consistent with his character and is a personal trait strongly admired today. However, FDR must have been displeased with the Democratic Senator from Missouri giving such strong support to Pendergast, an about-to-be-convicted felon.

Even though it has been well established that HST was scrupulously honest, he was astute enough to know that no one at that time could win political office in Missouri without the support of Pendergast. Lyle W. Dorsett stated in his book *The Pendergast Machine*:[1]

> [O]ne of the wisest decisions that Pendergast ever made was to back Truman for the Senate.
>
> Without the support of the Pendergast machine, Truman would never have been elected, but following HST's appointment to the Senate, Missouri was assured in the era of the New Deal that the state would be provided with thousands of jobs in civil works and in administration.

Gary Wills, on September 1, 1976, in the *Washington Star*, stated from Dorsett's book:

> By promoting Truman to the Senate, he (Pendergast) got money from the WPA to pour his concrete, since Pendergast owned a concrete factory, into a whole series of federal projects including City Hall, the Municipal Auditorium, a court house and a police station.

Wills further added:

> In the Senate, Truman continued his absolute loyalty to Pendergast in the matter of patronage. He refused to help individuals find federal relief employment without first going through the machine.

Just days before delivering his uncomplimentary comments against Milligan on the Senate floor on February 15, 1938, Truman had openly voiced his opposition to Roosevelt's running for a third term. At that time Truman knew that Roosevelt did not want him to serve a second term in the Senate, and HST believed his political career in Washington had reached an impasse. Truman had done nothing during his first term in the Senate that distinguished him in any way, a fact which Truman acknowledged. This was made clear in an article HST wrote after he left office, which was published in the *Washington Post* and *Times Herald* on September 28, 1955, entitled "Roosevelt Opposed Him in 1940." Truman claimed that Roosevelt offered him "a position in the Interstate Commerce Commission rather than running for a second term for the Senate in 1940, but I turned it down".

Joseph Lieb was aware of Truman's opposition to FDR's third term as president and of Truman's embarrassing comments again Milligan's renomination and

---

[1.] Lyle W. Dorsett, *The Pendergast Machine* (New York: Oxford University Press, 1968), p. 112.

the White House's reaction to the affair. Within days following HST's comments about Milligan before the Senate, Lieb wrote and asked Truman directly if he planned to run for a second term for the United States Senate. On February 21, 1938, Truman answered Lieb:

> Replying to your inquiry, I will not be a candidate for re-election to the Senate in view of my speech on the Senate floor on Tuesday and the reaction to it from the White House. This is a personal and confidential letter to you and I request that you do not publish it. Harry S. Truman.

This letter remained confidential for forty years until it was first published in the *Kansas City Times* on Friday, September 15, 1978.

Between 1938 and 1940, Harry Truman changed his mind and decided to seek re-election for a second term in the U.S. Senate. On February 4, 1940, on the front page of the *St. Louis Post-Dispatch* was a story headlined, "Senator Truman Formally Files: Against Third Term." The article stated:

> Senator Harry S. Truman today announced the filing at Jefferson City of his declaration of candidacy for re-election to the United States Senate. He cited his record as a public official and described himself as one who has "worked hard and talked little—and then only when necessary."

With HST's political background and his own admission that he had done little in the Senate during his first term, one can easily understand why FDR most likely did not see him as a political asset in the Senate. The *St. Louis Dispatch* article continued:

> Truman took occasion to declare on principle that he opposed a third presidential term and his colleague, Senator Bennett Champ Clark, was the candidate (HST) favored for the Democratic Convention.

This background of an apparent absence of a relationship between FDR and HST is important to keep in mind when viewing events leading to FDR's acceptance of HST for the Democratic vice-presidential nomination in 1944.

WALLACE

Historians have recorded that prior to the Democratic Convention in the summer of 1944, Roosevelt had come to consider Wallace a political liability and that it was in his best interest to drop Wallace. Much has been written that Roosevelt had decided on Truman as his vice-presidential candidate prior to the

Democratic Convention. I wonder if this is true. It could be argued that, in appearing to draw away from Wallace, Roosevelt was simply living up to his reputation as a master politician with consummate skills of manipulation.

Freidel states:[2]

> He (Roosevelt) played his cards with a gusto and effectiveness that surpassed 1940, less out of indecisiveness that some saw in his strategy than to encourage a number of potential candidates, so many that none would have a clear-cut majority while he would let his own choice be known so late that those opposed to the person selected would not have time to coalesce and thwart him. In the end, this tactic left Roosevelt open to charges that he had been a treacherous aging tyrant lopping off the heads of those who might dare challenge him.

Freidel further stated:

> Through June, Roosevelt purportedly said that Wallace was indispensable because of his knowledge of international affairs—that even if it costs a million votes, he must stay on the ticket. At the same time through conversations he solicited names of other possible candidates encouraged his "the more the merrier" strategy. Roosevelt's duplicity would not have surprised Wallace.

When Roosevelt ran for an unprecedented third term in 1940, he had been able to overcome strong opposition. In fact, he was so politically powerful that convention delegates were informed that if they failed to nominate Wallace for vice president, he (Roosevelt) would not run for the Presidency. Things were different at the 1944 Democratic Convention. While Roosevelt was still the strongest political figure in the United States and was once again expected to be the salvation of the Democratic Party, by 1944 some saw his power and personality verging on being dictatorial. Therefore, it was necessary that he assure the Democratic delegates that they, rather than he or the party bosses, would control the convention.

The Democratic leaders knew that Roosevelt's health was failing and that they were all strongly opposed to Wallace's re-election as vice president. But in spite of the prospect that the country would be run by a left-wing liberal if FDR died during his fourth term as president, the Democratic leaders knew they could not exert their will over FDR, and FDR liked Wallace.

---

2. Freidel, *A Rendezvous with Destiny*, p. 531.

Roosevelt's grip on his party at this time was extraordinary. As Richard J. Walton wrote:[3]

> One perhaps unequaled in our history and the polls made it plain that he (FDR) was the only Democrat that could win ... Henry Wallace was the preeminent figure of the early 1940's after only President Roosevelt himself. He was universally regarded as Roosevelt's heir to the New Deal wing of the Democratic Party.

FDR knew that if Wallace's nomination was to succeed, it had to appear that he was the decided choice of the Democratic Convention delegates. On May 29, 1944, FDR sent Wallace on a two-month fact-finding mission to Siberia and China from which he was to return to Washington just a week prior to the Democratic National Convention. Wallace showed his own lack of concern about being away during this pre-convention period by saying, "Don't worry. I'll be back in plenty of time for the convention." Shcapsmeiers, in their book, said:[4]

> Friends warned the Vice President that his absence prior to the convention would seriously jeopardize his chances for renomination. Secretary of Labor, Francis Perkins, literally begged him not to go, but Wallace detected no guile in the President's request. Having no doubt that his prolonged mission would deprive him of an opportunity to seek delegate strength, he nevertheless felt his political future was in good hands. He trusted FDR.

Many historians have claimed that Wallace's China trip excluded him from the political maneuvering preceding the convention and is proof of FDR's reluctance to have him as his running mate. There could be another interpretation. By sending Wallace abroad, FDR was distancing his vice president from the bitter political infighting that was certain to develop in the weeks preceding the Democratic Convention.

Judge Samuel Rosenman and Interior Secretary Harold Ickes met with Wallace on the day he returned to Washington from the Far East (Sunday, July 9, 1944) and they advised him that FDR felt he would be unable to support his renomination. The story has persisted that FDR sent Rosenman and Ickes to perform this disheartening task because the president would have been too uncomfortable to personally do this to his close friend of so many years. This may be

---

3. Richard J. Walton, *Henry Wallace, Harry Truman and the Cold War* (New York: Viking Press, 1976), pp. 3–4.

4. Schapsmeiers, *Prophet in Politics*, p. 86.

true, but if this were the case and FDR really did not wish to confront Wallace, why did the president spend so much time alone with his vice president during the week following his return from the Far East, the politically crucial week preceding the convention?

Wallace's immediate reaction to Rosenman and Ickes that Sunday upon his return from the Far East was to tell them he wouldn't even discuss his vice-presidential nomination with them, since he and FDR were meeting the next day for a private conference. The president spent that Sunday on a relaxing drive with Mrs. Rutherfurd to Shangrila (Camp David) and returned to Washington at 10:30 PM. Ickes and Rosenman saw the president on the following day (Monday, July 10) from 3:30 to 4:20 PM, at which time they must have discussed their meeting of the previous day with Wallace.

FDR then met alone with Wallace at 4:30; it was their first meeting in seven weeks and it is inconceivable that they did not discuss the Democratic Convention that was to begin the following week.

Wallace had been told previously, as had a host of others, that FDR wanted him to be his vice-presidential running mate. What distinguished Wallace from all other candidates, however, was that he best personified Roosevelt's New Deal philosophy. At a Democratic Jackson Day dinner held on January 22, 1944, Wallace said:

> The New Deal will always live. If it were dead, the Democratic Party would be dead and the New Deal has yet to obtain its full strength. The New Deal is as old as the wants of men. The New Deal is Amos proclaiming the needs of the poor in the land of Israel. The New Deal is New England citizens dumping tea in Boston Harbor. The New Deal is Andrew Jackson marching in the twentieth century. The New Deal is Abraham Lincoln preaching freedom for the oppressed. The New Deal is the new freedom of Woodrow Wilson fighting the cartels as they try to establish national and international fascism. The New Deal is Franklin D. Roosevelt who has never denied the principle of the New Deal and he never will.

Unquestionably, Roosevelt had no greater supporter than Henry Wallace.

CHAPTER 29

THE 1944 DEMOCRATIC NATIONAL CONVENTION

Robert Hannegan called the Democratic Convention to order at 11:30 AM on Wednesday, July 19, in his capacity as Chairman of the Democratic National Committee. Mayor Edward J. Kelly of Chicago welcomed the delegates followed by another welcoming speech delivered by Scott W. Lucas, the United States Senator from Illinois who was the powerful majority leader in the Senate and was a very close friend of FDR. He was aware that FDR was supportive of Wallace's nomination. The smoke-filled convention hall was packed with over eleven hundred delegates and twenty thousand visitors. The temperature was warm and the delegates were unruly. The consensus that morning was that Wallace had the vice-presidential nomination virtually secured, especially since Byrnes had withdrawn from the race and FDR had written a letter that was dated that day that allegedly was non-political but expressed his personal support of Wallace. The *New York Times* on that same Wednesday morning stated, "One of the possibilities is that Mr. Roosevelt will be asked in the final stages to designate his choice and that he would again demand Wallace as he did in 1940."

By the second day, rumors remained rampant as to who would be the vice-presidential nominee. Delegates were confused about their course of action. Hannegan continued to affirm the Truman-Douglas letter as evidence that FDR wanted Truman, but the letter confused both the delegates and the press since the letter was not perceived as an endorsement for anyone, simply a statement that both Truman and Douglas were acceptable to FDR as running mates. A telephone call from FDR to any Democratic state chairman stating a preference for his running mate would have given the delegates direction, but no call came.

On the morning of the second day, July 20, the *New York Times* focused on the Truman-Douglas letter:

Senator Gaffey from Pennsylvania accused Mr. Hannegan of pushing Truman's candidacy. "I doubt very much if Mr. Hannegan quoted all of the letter which the President is supposed to have written. It is time that Mr. Hannegan remembers that he was elected Chairman of the National Committee to serve all the members of our party, to give some of his time to the party and not all of it entirely to the candidate of Hannegan, Kelly, Haag, and Flynn."

From statements like this throughout the press and circulating at the convention, it was clear the delegates sensed what Hannegan was up to; they were resisting pressure to choose Truman who was neither their first choice nor, they suspected, FDR's.

Another story appeared that day in the *Chicago Tribune* regarding the Truman-Douglas letter:

There was a ruckus over the message Hannegan said he had received from the President saying Mr. Roosevelt "would be pleased to have Senator Truman run with him on the party ticket and believes he would add to the ticket." Senator Gaffey intimated his belief that no such message existed and challenged Hannegan to make public its full text. Senator Pepper of Florida seconded the Gaffey challenge.

"I believe the delegates are not going to be controlled or bossed and they are not going to take any word handed out personally as to what they are supposed to do," said Pepper.

If Chairman Hannegan had a letter from the President concerning the Vice-President other than the President's endorsement of Wallace, he should have already read it to the convention or described it to the press.

If Chairman Hannegan has such a letter I as Chairman of the Florida delegation call upon him to produce it and make it public now.

Also let Chairman Hannegan tell the delegates when such a letter was written, circumstances under which it was written and whether he requested the letter or not. Two names were mentioned in the letter as being agreeable to the President. Did Hannegan submit other names to the President also? These are things the delegates want to know and have a right to know."

On the second day of the convention, Senator Jackson read to the delegates the letter he had received from FDR (dated July 19), which stated if he (FDR) were a delegate he would vote for Wallace. This letter confused the delegates since its contents were already well known to them (FDR wrote the letter on July 14).

Further confusing the delegates as to whom FDR wanted as his running mate was Hannegan's showing the Truman-Douglas letter to as many people as he could; however, the letter didn't endorse Truman but merely stated that he would be an acceptable running mate—along with Douglas.

Following the nomination of Roosevelt for president, Senator Jackson said: "The Chair recognizes the Vice President of the United States." Henry A. Wallace rose to give the speech that later was considered the finest he had ever delivered. He began by saying he was speaking[1] "not as the Chairman has indicated, but as Chairman of the Iowa delegation. I am deeply honored to second the nomination for the greatest living American, Franklin Delano Roosevelt." Wallace went on to praise the president "as the greatest liberal in the history of the United States" and proclaimed that "the voice of our New World liberalism must carry on." Wallace further stated:

> The future belongs to those who go down the line unswervingly with the liberal principal of both political democracy and economic democracy regardless of race, color, and religion. The future must bring equal wages for equal work regardless of sex or race. Roosevelt stands for all of this. That is why certain people hate him so. That is also one of the outstanding reasons Roosevelt will be elected for a fourth term.

Wallace's speech was short, emotional, and dramatic; in effect, it was electrifying. At this point Chairman Jackson called for the vote to nominate the president of the United States. At the end of the voting, Jackson said: "The Chair announces the results of the tally: for James A. Farley, one vote, for Senator Byrd, eighty-seven votes, and for Franklin D. Roosevelt, one thousand eighty-six votes." The meeting recessed at 7:05 PM to meet again at 8:30 PM that evening.

Hannegan was alarmed. He kept showing delegates the Truman-Douglas letter but continued to encounter increasing skepticism; the delegates kept questioning why Roosevelt only listed the names of Truman and Douglas in the letter rather than directly stating his preference to the delegates? If FDR really wanted Truman as his running mate, as Hannegan claimed, why wasn't there a spokesman to so state? Delegates were also suspicious of Hannegan's timing; why had he waited so long to show the Truman-Douglas letter? The *New York Times* reported that day (July 20):

> Hannegan had said he had not made the letter public earlier because he considered it necessary to obtain the consent of the sender before releasing

---

1. *The United States News National Political Campaign of 1944 Proceedings of Democratic National Convention Chicago, July 19–21*, p. 29.

a personal letter for publication. He said he had talked today with President Roosevelt by telephone and had received such consent.

The same day, the *Chicago Tribune* raised the issue as to why the Truman-Douglas letter was dated Wednesday, July 19, even though FDR had written it earlier. Hannegan was also asked as to why, as stated in the Truman/Douglas letter, did he write FDR only about Truman and Douglas? And why weren't there other candidates? Under what circumstances was the letter sent? The only question Hannegan addressed concerned the circumstances under which he received the letter. The *New York Times* (July 21) reported a statement made by Hannegan which, as shown previously, was clearly inaccurate: "He [Hannegan] said he had received Mr. Roosevelt's permission to publish the letter which Hannegan said was delivered by messenger."

The evening meeting on the second day of the convention reconvened at 9:00 PM by the chairman, Senator Jackson of Indiana. The temperature in the hall was extremely warm and the humidity was unbearable; the convention had become almost out of control by now with wild demonstrations erupting from the onset, especially in the gallery.

After several introductory speeches, the lights in the auditorium were dimmed and for the first time during the convention, the delegates became quiet. Roosevelt's voice began to resound in an eerie manner throughout the building as he read his acceptance speech from his railroad car at Camp Pendleton near San Diego. FDR's speech was short. He stated his accomplishments during the years that he was president and his goal for the next presidential term. It was simply, "First to win the war, to win quickly, and to win it overpoweringly." He told the delegates that, regretfully, the war effort had to take precedence over his attendance at the Chicago convention. (On the following day, he left California on the heavy cruiser, *U.S.S. Baltimore*, for Hawaii to meet with General Douglas MacArthur and Admiral Chester Nimitz to plan future war strategy against the Japanese in the Pacific.)

Following Roosevelt's acceptance speech, in which he made no mention of a vice-presidential nominee, Wallace supporters went wild when Wallace was nominated for the vice-presidency. People on the convention floor and in the balcony started chanting, "We want Wallace." The organist, who was not supposed to begin his program for another hour, began to play, "Iowa, That's Where the Tall Corn Grows."

Wallace forces gained complete control of the auditorium, and the *Philadelphia Enquirer* on the following day stated that the convention developed into "intermittent pandemonium alternating with utter chaos." The atmosphere was memorable. Margaret Truman, who was at the convention with her father, said that because of the heat, which she said went over 120°, and the humidity, the doors of the convention hall had to be opened, allowing large numbers of people to pour into the auditorium.[2] People soon began to collapse from the heat and the lack of oxygen. The political bosses became powerless and lost all control of the situation.

The delegates were now in a mad frenzy to nominate Wallace—that night. Hannegan and Kelly realized they had to act quickly to salvage their plan to nominate Truman. It was estimated that there were approximately 30,000 people in the auditorium. However, the Chicago city fire laws allowed only 20,000 people to be in attendance in the building at any one time. Hannegan spoke to Mayor Kelly who in turn spoke to Chairman Jackson who then quickly announced:

> Ladies and gentlemen of the convention, we are packing these aisles until it is becoming dangerous. This has been a great day for the party and a great day for the country. Tomorrow will be another day and I recognize delegate David Lawrence from the State of Pennsylvania for the purpose of making a proper motion.

Lawrence did what was necessary—he moved for a recess until 11:30 the next morning. The crowd screamed, "No, no" and "We want Wallace." Chairman Jackson responded by asking those in favor to signify by saying either aye or no. When this question was asked, there was a resounding "no" from the convention floor, and the galleries, yet Jackson said the ayes had it; the meeting recessed at 10:45 PM to reconvene at 11:30 AM Friday, July 21, 1944. The Democratic political bosses had stopped the Wallace steamroller.

Dr. Richard Shapiro gave a vivid eyewitness account of that tumultuous night to me in 1990 at the Michael Reese Hospital in Chicago where he was at that time a senior surgeon and clinical professor of surgery at the University of Illinois.

> I was a freshman in the College of the University of Chicago in the summer of 1944; young, idealistic, politically and intellectually inclined to the liberal left. So when political agents of the CIO-PAC came on campus looking for bodies to attend the Democratic convention, who would oppose an anticipated push to get Henry Wallace, the incumbent Vice President and our liberal darling, off the ticket, I was easily recruited. Four years earlier a well-coached crowd at the Republican convention had, so it seemed, brought about the nomination of Wendell Wilkie against the

---

2. Margaret Truman, *Harry S. Truman* (New York: William Morrow, 1973), p. 178.

wishes of the party pros simply by incessantly and fervently chanting "We want Wilkie," thus creating an atmosphere and a momentum that convinced the delegates that they did too. "We want Wallace" is just as euphonious and probably the pro-Wallace managers had hoped that the magic could be bottled and used again. That's how I came to be sitting in the second balcony at the stadium surrounded by like-minded buddies the night that FDR was nominated for a fourth term.

I remember his acceptance speech. The war was still hot and it seemed only right that the Commander-in-Chief should not leave his post in Washington for a political meeting in Chicago and so we sat quiet and respectful, 20,000 of us in a single space, as the President's words of acceptance came to us from a loud speaker suspended from the ceiling. None of us, except the insiders, knew of FDR's illness and frailty nor of the likelihood that he would die before his fourth term would end. The battle over the retention of Henry Wallace was a relatively simple, principled good guys/bad guys fight, and being against the bad guys—the conservatives—was made even easier because their allies, perhaps even their leaders, were the hated big city political machines, perceived by us pure youths as powerful, arrogant and corrupt.

The uncontested nomination of Roosevelt and his acceptance speech were the first order of business that night and it was still early, around 8:00 PM I believe, when that business was done. When the presiding officer of the convention initiated the call for Vice Presidential nominations, we in the second balcony went into action. Mr. Wallace was nominated and our cheers and chants on his behalf were doubled. I think others may have been nominated that night I don't remember who or by whom. If they were, I am sure we booed and heckled. It seemed clear that we and our candidate were going to make it quickly and easily at that session. It seemed clear not only to us but to Mr. Hannegan as well and he was not at all pleased or cooperative.

He slowed the proceedings. There were awkward long conferences up at the podium while the delegates milled about. After about fifteen minutes the chair entertained a motion for adjournment. We were furious. The odor of the rat was grossly evident and all one could hear were boos, catcalls and nos. But someone was recognized, made the motion and someone else seconded it. The question was asked for the ayes—only more boos and nos. When the nays were asked, the intensity of the response trebled. It was then announced that the motion had carried, that the convention would re-assemble in the morning. We were stunned, angry and aimless. Each time I tell this story I say that if a delegate with charisma, presence, and a bullhorn wanted to, he could have led the delegates out into the Warren Avenue parking lot and nominated Mr. Wallace right there but it didn't happen.

We faithful assembled the next morning still full of fight but the battle was lost. The anti-Wallace factions had coalesced during the night and planned their strategy, essentially one of multiple nominations of favorite sons until the Wallace fervor was dissipated. As part of that plan Edward Kelly, the Mayor of Chicago in 1944, stood to place the name of Scott Lucas, then Senator from Illinois, in nomination. We all booed and heckled our Mayor and he responded marvelously. He ostentatiously thrust his prepared speech aside and stood tall and pushed his jaw out and told us, by God, he was the Mayor of this city and a legitimate delegate to this convention and he had a right to do what he was doing and we were not going to deter him. We actually applauded.

I don't remember who else, besides Mr. Truman, was nominated that morning and my recollection is that it didn't take too many ballots, before his nomination was secured.

In the intervening years when I recounted the story, which I did frequently, we would speculate how much history would have been altered if Mr. Hannegan had counted the votes honestly that penultimate evening. Atom bomb dropped? Cold war avoided? Not clear. By and large history has dealt kindly with Mr. Truman's presidency and history has yet to pronounce whether or not Mr. Hannegan's chicanery served a good purpose.

Thursday night ended with no nomination for vice president. Where was Truman at this point? The story that has persisted over the years is that Truman was a reluctant candidate for the vice-presidential nomination as late as that Thursday evening. Sometime late that day, Truman received a call from Hannegan who asked him to come immediately to his suite on the seventeenth floor of the Blackstone Hotel. There have been varied versions as to what actually happened at this meeting. In Merle Miller's oral biography entitled *Plain Speaking,* Truman said this about his arrival at the Blackstone Hotel:[3]

> The room was crowded, every damn political boss in the country was there, any one of them you would want to name, and half a dozen Governors. They all said "Harry we want you to be vice-president." I said "I am not going to do it."

3. Merle Miller, *Plain Speaking: An Oral Biography of Harry S. Truman* (New York: Putnam, 1974), p. 181.

Well Bob Hannegan had put in a call to Roosevelt who is down at San Diego, they finally got him on the phone and with Roosevelt you did not need a phone, all you had to do is raise the window and you could hear him. I was sitting on one of the twin beds and Bob was on the other in this room and Roosevelt said—(Mr. Truman gave a near perfect imitation of Roosevelt, Harvard accent and all), "Have you got that guy lined up yet on the Vice Presidency?" Hannegan said "no he is the contrariest Goddamn mule from Missouri I ever saw." Well Roosevelt said "you tell him if he wants to break up the Democratic Party in the middle of the war and maybe lose that war, that is up to him—bang." Well I walked around there for about five minutes and you should have seen the faces of those birds. They just worried to beat hell. Finally I said: "all right Bob if that is the way the old man feels, I will do it."

Truman's story of how he arrived at the decision to run for the vice-presidential nomination appears to be based more on imagination than fact. The comment by FDR that Truman's refusal to take the nomination might cause the United States to lose the war is difficult to accept. There are details in the telephone episode that certainly raise questions. Hannegan and Truman were allegedly seated facing each other on twin beds in the hotel suite. If this were the case, and Roosevelt strongly wished Truman to accept the vice-presidential nomination, Hannegan could have easily handed the phone to Truman to hear this request directly from the president. Miller in his book asked Truman, "Did Roosevelt know that you could hear him?" Truman answered,

No, he did not. But hell, he'd been through Chicago a couple or so days before that, and I made my call on him, and he never said a word to me about the situation. [This comment by Truman has been totally unsubstantiated.].

Tom Evans, Truman's longtime friend, was in the room in the Blackstone Hotel at the time of the alleged conversation between Hannegan and the president. According to Evans's version:[4]

Truman himself got on the phone and the President listened for a short time; "well I just think Mr. President that I have done a good job where I am and I am happy and I want to stay there. Yes sir, I know you're the Commander and Chief—yes sir, well if that is what you want, that is what

---

4. Tom Evans's oral presentation is in the Harry S. Truman Library, Independence, Missouri.

I will do. I have always taken orders from the Commander and Chief. I will do it."

Truman's story regarding his decision to run for the vice presidency while sitting on the bed at the Blackstone Hotel was described years after the episode, and his retelling of the events are inconsistent. The longer the time period between an activity and its description, the greater the likelihood of forgetting or distorting details. This is very likely what happened with Truman since after the presidential election, he was asked to write an overview of his political life. This is in the Truman Library in Missouri and consists of a fifty-nine-page statement handwritten by Truman himself. Truman's description of how he decided to accept the vice-presidential nomination is as follows:

> On Thursday night (July 20th) after the convention had adjourned because of a gallery paid demonstration for Wallace, some of the southern Democrats, Hannegan, Walker, and Ed Pauley, told me that I was going to be responsible for a split in the Democratic Party which would result in the election for the New York Governor, Thomas E. Dewey.
>
> Maryland's Governor, the Governor of Oklahoma, Harry Byrnes, the junior Senator from Mississippi and Governor Grays of Alabama along with Tobin and William Green told me they could all take me and save the party. I gave in then and said all right, I will go.

This explanation, which Truman wrote close in time to the event, is probably a more accurate version of what occurred on the night following the Wallace demonstration. In Truman's report, he makes no mention of any phone call from FDR. In a letter to me written from Truman historian William E. Pemberton, he stated, "I believe that call [the bedroom scene between Hannegan and FDR] was one of the many stories, once told, that became too good not to be true."

By the following day, July 21st, Wallace had been stopped and the political bosses were ready. When the convention delegates entered the auditorium late that morning, Mayor Kelly had everything prepared and well organized. Ushers and the Chicago police examined the tickets of people entering the convention hall, and clusters of Wallace supporters were turned away because they did not have "the right kind of tickets."

The convention was called to order at 12:10 PM. The first order of business was the nomination of the party's candidates for the vice president of the United States, followed by seconding speeches. Alabama began the nominations by naming Senator John H. Bankhead as their favorite-son candidate. Arizona, the next state called, yielded to Missouri so that Truman could be quickly placed in nomination. This elicited a significant amount of booing throughout the convention hall, which prompted Chairman Jackson to ask for courtesy from the audience. Senator Jackson had to make this plea since many Wallace supporters were in the gallery still trying to entice support for their candidate, but their momentum of the previous evening had been lost.

The stage was now set for the political fight between Wallace and Truman. The Democratic bosses, especially Hannegan and Kelly, continued to promote a variety of favorite-son candidates, knowing that this would weaken Wallace's chances of winning on the first ballot. Their plan was to push for Truman on the second ballot after the majority of favorite-son candidates would withdraw. Key individuals and delegations could then swing their support towards Truman.

At this point, Senator Bennett Champ Clarke of Missouri, who had been drinking heavily, came to the podium and gave a short and weak nominating speech for Truman. Margaret Truman later said, "Bennett Clarke gave a very brief limp nominating speech and the response of the delegates was tepid."[5]

Nominations for the vice presidency continued. When the time came for Illinois to nominate a candidate, Mayor Kelly offered the name of Illinois's Senator Lucas. Voting for a favorite-son candidate was routine, but Kelly was soundly booed when he put Senator Lucas in contention because everyone knew he was strongly for Truman. The booing may have been somewhat embarrassing to Kelly, but it was especially so for Senator Lucas. The embarrassment was compounded for Lucas when Kelly ended his nominating speech by having a brass band and demonstrators parade around the convention hall carrying signs backing Lucas and acting as if this were a spontaneous display in support of the Senate majority leader from Illinois. Everyone in the auditorium knew it was a phony demonstration. Increased booing finally led to complete disruption of the convention. Mayor Kelly tried to address the audience but failed because of the noise. Eventually he said to the delegates: "I ask the respect of this audience not only as a delegate in this convention, but as chairman of my delegation and as mayor of the city of Chicago."

After the clerk had called each state for its vice-presidential nomination, the time came to vote the first ballot. Of the first southern states called to vote, Georgia cast its entire twenty-six votes for Wallace and Florida cast nine of its eighteen votes for him, indicating that Wallace had strength even in the supposedly conservative southern states. The roll call of states took two-and-a-half hours, and the tabulation after its completion at 7:00 PM showed Wallace had received 429 1/2 votes, Truman 319 1/2, with the remaining thirteen favorite-son

---

5. Margaret Truman, *Harry S. Truman*, p. 179.

candidates amassing a total of 393 1/2 votes. A total of 589 votes was needed to win, so the favorite sons held the balance necessary to gain this majority.

During the afternoon, while the first balloting was taking place, the political bosses were hard at work campaigning in an air-conditioned room marked "H," located beneath the speaker's stand, which could only be reached, dramatically, through "a dark corridor." Hannegan, Kelly, Walker, Hague, and Harry Truman were very busy in room H. Truman spent three hours shaking hands with the various delegates the political bosses brought to meet him.

The delegates had spent long hours in the auditorium before and during the first ballot voting; they were tired and hungry and expected the meeting would break for dinner and recommence later in the evening for voting on the second ballot. However, Hannegan and Kelly weren't going to allow a repeat of the previous evening's disruption by Wallace supporters who had entered the convention hall during the intermission between the afternoon and evening sessions; there would be no intermission.

Voting for the second ballot began almost immediately. Kelly and Hannegan were now running the convention and their plan was to allow the first few small states to vote as they pleased; but when Illinois was called to vote, Kelly would switch Lucas's favorite-son votes to Truman. It was believed that this dramatic announcement would start an emotional tide for Truman, which other states would follow. Truman was aware of the plan and was confident as he sat with the Missouri delegation. Politicians gathered around him as he prepared for the second ballot even before the first ballot began. He was reassured by persons around him that the second ballot would bring victory. Henry Wallace's secretary, Harold R. Young, realized what was going on but was powerless to do anything about it. He remarked that the convention "is in the hands of our enemy."

After the first ten states had voted on the second ballot, with California and Idaho passing, 134 votes had been cast with sixty-five going to Wallace and forty-five and a half to Truman. Kelly was poised for his dramatic move to swing Illinois to Truman, but an extraordinary happening now occurred that was totally unexpected and had the potential to destroy Truman's chances. Kelly lost control of his Illinois delegation. As reported in the *New York Times* on the following day:

> Mayor Kelly found himself unable to deliver the fifty-eight votes of Illinois to Senator Truman at least on the first ballot. To prevent a substantial number of these votes from going to Mr. Wallace he was forced to accept a resolution *binding the delegates to vote for Senator Scott W. Lucas until released by the Senator*. [Author's emphasis.]

In other words, only Senator Lucas, not Mayor Kelly, could decide when Illinois might deliver these votes to another candidate, an agreement that nearly cost Truman the vice-presidential nomination.

The entire auditorium was now awaiting Kelly's announcement that Illinois was switching support to Truman. Kelly was about to grasp the microphone to make this announcement when Senator Lucas told Kelly it was only he, and not Kelly, who could release the delegates. This was based on the resolution on the first ballot that bound the delegates "to vote for Senator Scott W. Lucas until released by the senator."

Lucas had been embarrassed by Kelly's earlier phony demonstration on the convention floor on his behalf, and he wanted to withdraw his name as a favorite-son candidate and release the delegates committed to him. Kelly knew that Lucas, a strong supporter of FDR, was aware that Roosevelt personally wanted Wallace as his running mate, as did the majority of the Illinois delegates. Therefore, Kelly was suddenly faced with the distinct possibility that Truman could lose the vice-presidential nomination.

Kelly acted quickly. He told Lucas that if Wallace and Truman reached a stalemate on the next or succeeding ballots, Lucas could become the dark horse compromise candidate. Therefore, Lucas should stay in the race. The possibility of being a vice-presidential candidate excites most politicians; Lucas accepted Kelly's proposal to remain silent and once again allowed his name to be re-introduced as a candidate for the vice-presidential nomination.

The time was at hand for Illinois to vote; everyone in the auditorium awaited Kelly's announcement of support for Truman. Illinois was called to vote. Kelly took the microphone and again stated, unbelievably, that the state of Illinois voted for Senator Scott Lucas for the vice-presidential nomination. Delegates and spectators went wild. Everyone knew that Kelly strongly supported Truman. They also believed that Kelly had just carried out a monumental political maneuver, but no one knew why. Bishop explained:[6]

> The switch to Truman was supposed to begin with Ed Kelly's big Illinois vote. However, when Chairman Jackson called Illinois, Kelly who had worked hard for Truman, sustained a monumental memory lapse and cast all the votes for Senator Scott Lucas.

When one considers this historically accepted explanation, it is impossible to believe that Kelly could have had "a monumental memory lapse" in front of more than twenty thousand people, all expecting Kelly to vote for Truman. Even if

---

6. Bishop, *FDR's Last Year*, p. 110.

Kelly had had a memory lapse, the unbelieving cries and screams of the delegates in the auditorium would have quickly alerted him to his mistake, which Kelly could have immediately corrected simply saying he meant to say Truman instead of Lucas.

Kelly had temporarily saved the moment for Truman by convincing Lucas to hold the votes of his Illinois delegates. Kelly realized, however, how easily things could change as the voting progressed if Lucas decided at some point to grab the microphone to release his Illinois votes to Wallace. To prevent this, Mayor Kelly did an incredible thing: he called a caucus of the entire Illinois delegation, including Lucas, which he led out of the convention hall and went directly across the street to Touhy's Bar, owned by John Touhy, chairman of Chicago's 27th Ward Committee and the headquarters of this ward.

While the Illinois delegation was deliberating in the bar across from the convention, Kelly kept people running between Touhy's Bar and the convention auditorium to keep him informed as to how the voting was going. Kelly had to be certain that the voting tide had begun to swing towards Truman before he could allow the Illinois delegation, and especially Lucas, to return to the convention hall. A runner came back and said that Alabama's favorite-son candidate, Senator Bankhead, had withdrawn his name and added twenty-two votes for Truman. South Carolina then quickly switched eighteen votes to Truman. The momentum for Wallace was beginning to falter, but there was still opposition. Then Indiana withdrew its support of its favorite-son candidate in order to support Truman, and Maine switched to Truman. Mayor Kelly knew that at this point the tide for Truman was unstoppable. Senator Lucas was no longer a problem.

Kelly rushed the entire Illinois delegation out of Touhy's Bar and raced into the convention hall behind a flying wedge of Chicago policemen. Again, Senator Lucas tried to grab the microphone to release his delegates but Kelly grabbed the microphone first. He said, "Switch the Illinois votes to Truman." Lucas was furious but it was all over.

Joseph Leib told me the story of Kelly, Lucas, and Touhy's Bar. He claimed he remained with the Illinois delegation throughout the voting for the vice-presidential nomination. The episode he described was difficult for me to accept until he showed me a photograph that was published in the July 21 *Chicago Tribune* (the day following the vote). The photograph showed Kelly, Lucas, and Leib all standing together following their race from Touhy's Bar. Kelly is shown at the microphone delivering the Illinois votes to Truman. Lucas is standing directly behind him appearing quite angry at the situation. (Note Leib wearing sunglasses—he said he wanted to be inconspicuous?)

Further confirmation as to what happened in Touhy's Bar was derived from two newspaper sources. On July 22, the *Chicago Tribune* stated:

[TRIBUNE Photo.]

Mayor Kelly (at microphone), turning Illinois' Lucas votes over to Truman at climax of balloting. Behind him is Sen. Lucas, whose name had gone before convention.

CHICAGO TRIBUNE   6-22-1944

Unofficial tallies had given Truman the nomination before Kelly could clutch a microphone and tell of the Illinois decision. The irony of the futile dashing around was that Kelly had been for Truman all of the time.

A week after the *Chicago Tribune*'s mention of the event, *Time* magazine (July 31, 1944) also commented on Kelly's wild race from Touhy's Bar back into the convention hall to get to the microphone:

> At this point Kelly turned to his associates and asked did we make it? He had not, running fast for the Truman bandwagon, Ed Kelly had only managed to get his fingernails on the spare tire.

What *Time* magazine didn't know was why the Illinois delegation left the convention and what transpired thereafter. The magazine claimed that Kelly was "running fast for the Truman bandwagon" but "only managed to get his finger nails on the spare tire." In fact, Kelly appears to be mainly responsible for saving the entire "Truman bandwagon."

When the final tally of the votes was recorded, Truman had received 1031 and Wallace 105. Truman had been sitting with the Missouri delegation, but following the voting, he joined his wife and daughter in their box. Uniformed men surrounded and escorted him to the speaker's platform where he gave a very short (123 words) acceptance speech. The Reverend Harrison Ray Anderson then gave the benediction, and Governor Herbert O'Connor of Maryland adjourned the convention at 8:15 PM.

Knowledge of FDR's poor health, as confirmed in the Lahey Memorandum, was the key that Hannegan and Kelly apparently used to neutralize FDR during the convention, thus allowing Truman to be nominated and eventually become president of the United States. No one could have imagined, on the night that Truman won the vice-presidential nomination, the enormous impact the event would eventually have on the destiny of the world. If Wallace had become president after FDR's death, would the atom bomb have been dropped? Would Wallace, who was a Russophile and spoke Russian, have given Russia our atomic secrets? And most importantly, would Wallace have stood up to communism as prescribed by the Truman Doctrine?

The political machinations of Hannegan and Kelly during the convention in 1944 resulted in geopolitical effects that are present to this day. History has shown that Truman was the right man that night in the summer of 1944.

CHAPTER 30

EPILOGUE

Truman was inaugurated as vice president of the United States on January 20, 1945, with FDR leaving for Yalta several days later to meet with Stalin and Churchill. FDR's poor physical condition at Yalta was obvious as seen in photographs taken of him at the conference. General Marshall and Admiral King both considered Roosevelt to be ill at the meeting. Lord Moran, Churchill's private physician, recorded particularly revealing comments concerning FDR's health at Yalta:

> February 7, 1945: To a doctor's eye the President appears to be a very sick man. He has all the symptoms of hardening of the arteries of the brain in an advanced stage so that I give him only a few months to live, but men shut their eyes and they do not want to see and the Americans here cannot bring themselves to believe that he is finished.

Some of the basic questions FDR addressed to Stalin at Yalta were: 1) how defeated Germany was to be handled following the war; 2) how Russia could help in the final destruction of Japan; and 3) of great significance to Roosevelt, how Russia could help in establishing the United Nations.

Even though FDR may have functioned at a sub-par level at Yalta, he succeeded in gaining many of the things he wanted. MacGregor Burns, the noted historian, felt that FDR did the best that was possible at Yalta:

> Roosevelt was not ill at Yalta or befuddled or weak or unpatriotic. As a result he saw he had reached the limit of his bargaining power. He simply did not hold the cards. He wanted far more from Stalin than Stalin wanted from him.

While FDR was at Yalta, Truman was in Washington sitting in for the president. On the day prior to Roosevelt's trip to his meeting with the Allied leaders, an event occurred that confirmed Truman's well-known trait of fierce loyalty to anyone who had supported him in the past, regardless of the consequences—a characteristic that has made Truman increasingly respected as the years have passed.

Thomas Pendergast died on January 26, 1945. Truman decided, against the strong advice of White House advisors, to attend Pendergast's funeral in spite of the unfavorable publicity the trip was certain to engender. Great effort had been made during the 1944 pre-election period to convince the American public that Truman's ties with Pendergast no longer existed; nevertheless, Truman not only attended the funeral, which had the potential for creating a major, political fall-out, but he also took the controversial step of flying to the funeral in a military plane. This at a time of war when military aircraft use for non-military purposes was being sharply curtailed. Only recently had FDR written a letter to Robert Hannegan, the continuing Democratic national chairman:

January 8, 1945
Dear Bob:

I think there would be tremendous public criticism if you or Ed or the Republicans were given plane priorities when no election is on. We are making such an effort to keep travel down and to eliminate conventions etc, that I think we must live up as closely as possible to the spirit of the regulations.

I even refused to give a priority to my cousin who wanted to go to Utah to see her fiancée who was dying.

I know you will understand, but I say this not only in the public interest, but because I think it would hurt us politically.

When Truman flew to St. Louis on January 29, *United Press* highlighted the story: "Truman Flies on Army Plane to Boss Pendergast Funeral." The newspaper article began, "Vice-president Truman flew here in an army plane today and attended a requiem mass for Thomas J. Pendergast, ex-convict and ex-head of the Pendergast political machine." This story indicates Truman's commitment to loyalty to individuals who had been helpful and faithful to him. However, as will be shown later, Truman's normal response to loyalty was in sharp contrast to his behavior following the early death of Robert Hannegan.

Franklin Delano Roosevelt died two months after returning from Yalta—at age 63, on April 12, 1945—and was succeeded by Truman who had been vice president for only eighty-two days. Two weeks after becoming president, Truman's first cabinet appointment was that of his friend Robert Hannegan to the position of postmaster general of the United States. As the two worked together in a seemingly close relationship over the next two years, a discord developed between them, and Hannegan resigned from Truman's cabinet in 1947.

Hannegan died in St. Louis two years later (1949) at the age of forty-six from hypertension and chronic renal disease that eventually resulted in a fatal heart attack.[1]

[1.] On the night of his death, Hannegan, accompanied by his son, had gone to see a friend. It was raining heavily that evening and on the return home, William noted his father straining to look through the rain-splattered windshield, which was not cleared by the wipers. On the following morning, as young Hannegan left for school, he noted that the sliding doors of his parents' bedroom, which were usually left open, on this particular morning were closed. Several hours later when Hannegan, a sophomore at a parochial school in St. Louis, saw his older sister enter his classroom accompanied by a priest, he said he knew his father had died.

Robert Hannegan suffered severe chest pains sometime between 1:00 and 2:00 AM the night of October 6, 1949. Mrs. Hannegan called the family doctor (Dr. Harry Kline) who immediately came to the house. In spite of Hannegan's stating he was short of breath, with a severe chest pain described "like an icebox pressing on his chest" (a squeezing chest pain is a cardinal symptom of a heart attack), the doctor did not believe the pain was cardiac in origin, and he expected Hannegan would feel better in the morning. Shortly after Dr. Kline returned home, Hannegan's condition markedly worsened, and Mrs. Hannegan again called the doctor and asked that he return quickly. At this point, Hannegan knew he was dying, and during these last few minutes he gave instructions to his wife as to what to do immediately following his death.

By the time Dr. Kline returned, Hannegan had just died or was only minutes away from death. Dr. Kline injected adrenaline through a long needle directly into Hannegan's heart, but it had no effect. Mrs. Hannegan called their parish priest, Reverend Jerry McMann, who came and administered the last rites of the Catholic Church. Before he died, sometime between 3:00 and 4:00 AM on October 6, 1949, Hannegan instructed his wife to remove and destroy certain letters in their safe deposit vault at their bank. After his death, Mrs. Hannegan, Father McMann and Dr. Kline sat with Hannegan's body for approximately five hours until the bank opened at 9:00 AM. Dr. Kline then drove Mrs. Hannegan to the Mercantile Bank in St. Louis where she went to her safe deposit box to carry out her husband's instructions.

Employees in the bank knew Mrs. Hannegan, but no one was yet aware that her husband had died that morning. When it was announced the next day that Hannegan had died early on the previous day, people at the bank questioned why Mrs. Hannegan had visited her safe deposit box while her husband was in the throes of death or had just died.

The Internal Revenue Service (IRS) was alerted, and the event was fully investigated. Mrs. Hannegan proved to the IRS that she had removed not money from the safe deposit box but only "personal correspondence" that her husband wished to be kept private.

As Hannegan lay dying, he believed his safe deposit box would, upon news of his death, be immediately sealed; he feared that the individuals who would later open it would see what he considered confidential information. As told by his wife and son, Hannegan felt a sense of responsibility for protecting the identity of the people in the White House and for safeguarding the anonymity of previous sources of information. What personal correspondence was removed by Mrs. Hannegan remains unknown.

The friction between Truman and Hannegan, leading to Hannegan's resignation in 1947, to some extent was from Hannegan's insistence that he played the major role in securing Truman's nomination for vice president in 1944. Truman was convinced that he had become vice president because Roosevelt personally wanted him as his running mate, and Hannegan's assertions to the contrary were disquieting. Truman's actions following Hannegan's death bore this out.

Truman attended Pendergast's funeral in 1945 at great political risk, and it was expected that he would likewise demonstrate his loyalty to Hannegan after his death. That did not happen. The funeral was delayed for four days to accommodate those who had to travel from great distances. Four thousand people attended the requiem mass celebrated by Reverend Joseph E. Ritter, Archbishop of St. Louis, on October 10, 1949, with many cabinet members, as well as other national, state, and city political figures attending. Newspapers throughout the country proclaimed the importance of Hannegan because "he steered Truman into the White House." Yet President Truman never went to the funeral, and his absence was greatly upsetting to many, who wondered why.

I contacted the Truman library in Independence, Missouri, and requested Truman's official schedule for October 10, 1949, to learn if there might have been mitigating circumstances that precluded his presence at the funeral in St. Louis. It showed only routine appointments, several being with individuals seen merely as a courtesy to Truman's friends and political associates.

The continuing suggestion by Hannegan, from 1945 to 1947, that he was responsible for Truman's being president must have caused Truman increasing annoyance because he truly believed his achievement had been gained through merit and not from Hannegan's political pressure or manipulation at the 1944 Democratic Convention. Truman believed he would never escape from his earlier Pendergast associations, but what he especially wanted to avoid was having his presidential career darkened by any suggestion that FDR had been forced to take him as his vice-presidential running mate in 1944.

Few people today realize just how vicious were the attacks Truman suffered concerning his political association with Pendergast. Two months prior to the presidential election in 1944, Paul Weigman, a national columnist, wrote a five-part series of articles from Kansas City (September 18, 1944) for national distribution. The purpose of the articles was to convince the American people just how corrupt Truman was. The fifth article in the series was headlined, "Truman Fought Prosecutor Who Jailed 50 Election Crooks." The article began:

> When the Federal District Court here started to blow the lid off the corrupt Pendergast machine in 1938, the heat of the explosion reached all the way to Washington, D.C., where Harry S. Truman was sitting in

the Senate by the grace of votes counted for him by the Pendergast organization.

The article was explicit in charging that Truman was a crook and it detailed his efforts to block the re-appointment of Maurice Milligan, the U.S. attorney responsible for sending Pendergast and dozens of his followers to jail:

> Milligan's term as Prosecutor had expired and the Justice Department wanted him reappointed. Senator Truman rushed from Washington to Kansas City to confer with the boss, Thomas J. Pendergast on January 31, 1938. The conference which lasted nearly an hour was not held in the Senator's office in the Federal building, but in the boss's office at 1908 Main Street, where Pendergast held court each morning with his subjects. No stenographic report was taken on the conversation, but when it was over Truman announced that he would oppose Milligan's appointment.

The *Kansas City Star* on February 16th, said: "In the primary election of 1934 when Truman was nominated, they expressed doubt that Truman would be in the Senate if that primary had been honestly conducted."

The article further stated: "The people of Kansas City knew that in all the history of rotten elections in this city, Senator Truman never once has done anything to help clean them up."

Although Truman had been deeply involved over the years with Pendergast and his associates, it should be stressed that in spite of extensive searching by Milligan and others into Truman's relationship with Pendergast, no one has been able to show that Truman ever carried out a dishonest act. Truman may have felt that the invective directed against him by the newspapers and his political opponents was the punishment exacted for political success in a state that was run by a corrupt political machine whose support was necessary if one wanted to be politically successful.

Truman's present and increasing popularity makes it difficult to envision the low esteem in which Truman was held in his early years in Washington. He had earned little respect from his colleagues during his first term in the Senate, and he himself stated that all he did during this term in office was remain silent. After assuming the presidency in 1945, following FDR's death and being elected in 1948 in a stunning political upset, Truman knew his place in history would be carefully studied over the years. Any suggestion that deception had been the vehicle that carried him into the presidency must have caused him great concern, especially since his relationship with Pendergast seemed permanent. Truman venerated the office of the president of the United States, and he felt any hint of deception as to how he achieved the honor of becoming president would cast a shadow on the presidential office itself.

Truman's conviction that he was Roosevelt's choice as vice-presidential running mate most likely was based on two pieces of evidence. One of these was the typewritten Truman-Douglas letter, which did not say FDR wanted Truman but merely said HST would be acceptable, along with Douglas, as a running mate. Truman knew that Douglas had minimal national support and no political infrastructure at the Democratic Convention in 1944, and he probably believed that FDR had inserted Douglas's name in the letter merely to avoid appearing dictatorial in his choice of running mate.

The other piece of evidence, which to Truman was convincing, was the handwritten note Hannegan had retrieved after the dinner meeting with Democratic leaders in the White House on July 11, 1944, the note written on an envelope and saying, "Bob, it's Truman—FDR."

Truman always claimed that he had personally seen the short note. FDR's comment on the envelope was enough to convince Truman that the president wanted him as his vice president. It therefore became crucial to Truman to find this envelope to prove for the historical record that he was truly Roosevelt's choice.

Following Hannegan's death in 1949, Truman began a concerted effort to find the short note written by FDR, showing the president wanted him as running mate, the note proving that Truman was not the vice-presidential nominee in 1944 through deception. Unaware of Hannegan's dealings with FDR on the train in Chicago, Truman most likely believed FDR favored him because of his good works as chairman of the Truman Committee during the Second World War.

In an attempt to confirm that he had FDR's personal support at the Democratic Convention in 1944, Truman began to seek information within days of Hannegan's death from people who had been present at the Chicago convention and might have been aware of political manipulations that were unknown to HST. Pauley, treasurer of the Democratic National Convention, responded first with a long memorandum that was inaccurate and self-serving, as seen in his description of how Hannegan procured the Truman-Douglas letter on FDR's train:

> Hannegan told FDR that Byrnes and others were still refusing to get out of the race and said we must have a letter we can use if necessary. The President said sure and taking an envelope and jotted down a note in longhand. He said he would have Grace Tulley his private secretary type it up on White House stationary. The train was ready to pull out and by the time the President gave this letter to Hannegan with the train starting we had no time to read it and we jumped off the platform with the train

already in motion. Then I asked Bob what does the letter say? He pulled it from his pocket and looked at it. He actually turned white as he explained, "My God its got Douglas on it."

Pauley's comments were worthless to Truman, and he then asked Judge Rosenman to contact Mrs. Hannegan for her recollection of the 1944 Democratic Convention. Rosenman wrote to Mrs. Hannegan on December 15, 1944, and she promptly responded; Rosenman thanked her for her letter on January 3, 1950:

> I certainly appreciate your thoughtful letter. It solves a great many of the questions which were in my mind and shows pretty completely that Bob's account was correct and not Miss Tulley's.

Even though six years had passed since the convention, Truman asked his secretary, Matthew J. Connelly, to think back on the meeting, and Connelly responded on January 24, 1950:

> You will recall that about one week before the Democratic National convention in 1944 I was sitting at your desk when you received a telephone call from Mr. James F. Byrnes. Of course I only heard your part of the conversation, but I recall that Mr. Byrnes asked you to support him for the Vice-presidency. I recall that you told him you would be happy to do that and after completing the phone call, you discussed Byrnes's request with me.
> I recall you also informed me that you were going to Chicago to further the nomination of Mr. Byrnes as you were not personally interested in seeking the nomination and as a matter of fact, if the nomination were offered to you, you would be forced to decline.
> I recall, at the time, that you mentioned that you had at some time previous made a speech in San Francisco in which you endorsed the nomination for Vice-president of Speaker Sam Rayburn, but due to a local situation in Texas, Rayburn had taken himself out of the race.
> I thought it would be interesting for you to have my recollections as above outlined.

Although Connelly's letter was also of no help to Truman, within days Truman instructed him to send Pauley's memorandum to the key figures of the pre-Cconvention drama (Jonathan Daniels, Judge Samuel Rosenman, and probably others) in order to try to rekindle their memories of how he (HST) had been nominated for vice president. A brief explanation by Connelly was included with Pauley's memorandum and sent on January 27, 1950:

> The President asked me to furnish you with the attached. It was prepared by Pauley and is substantially his recollections of the events preceding the convention in Chicago in 1944.

Mrs. Hannegan was the first to come up with useful material for Truman by responding to Rosenman's request; she sent him photostatic copies of two letters that Rosenman showed to Truman, who promptly wrote Mrs. Hannegan on January 24, 1950:

> Sam Rosenman was in to see me yesterday and we discussed the two documents which you have in your safety deposit vault. I'll appreciate it very much if you will send me a couple of copies of each for the record. There has been a great deal of misinformation out about these two documents.
>
> *Of course I did not find out about their existence until the Wednesday before the nomination of the Vice-president of the Democratic convention in 1944 when Bob brought both of them over to my room at the Steven's Hotel and showed them to me.* [Author's emphasis.] It was Thursday afternoon the day before the nomination for Vice-President were to come up, before I finally concluded to let Bob go ahead with his program and that was only after I had heard him in a conversation with President Roosevelt over the telephone to San Diego.
>
> I hope you will continue to guard these two documents closely and if you ever decided to dispose of them that you will make a decision so they can go in the files of the President.
>
> I hope everything is going well with you and that all your family are in good health and getting along all right.
>
> Sincerely yours,
> Harry Truman

The photostatic copies of the two letters Mrs. Hannegan sent to Rosenman were the handwritten and typed Truman-Douglas letters that Hannegan had received from FDR on his train. Unfortunately, these letters were not helpful to Truman. What he was searching for was the personal handwritten July 11 statement by Roosevelt on the back of an envelope that simply said, "Bob, its Truman—FDR." Truman so indicated in his handwriting at the bottom of the typed letter that he sent to Mrs. Hannegan: "I thought Bob showed me another memo written at the White House which mentioned only me."

When Mrs. Hannegan on February 13, 1950, sent Truman the copies of the documents she had already sent Rosenman, Truman thanked her and again requested:

> I would appreciate it most highly if you would keep looking through Bob's private papers and try to find the memorandum which he showed me in Chicago and which Frank Walker is very sure is in existence somewhere. I imagine he had that reply in his private papers.
>
> There will be a great number of misstatements of facts on this subject and I am trying to get the facts all together so that nothing can be said that will reflect on Bob, the President, or me.

Truman never found the note he was looking for; the note by FDR that had only his name on it: "Bob, its Truman—FDR."

Although Truman never found evidence to prove he was Roosevelt's choice as his running-mate in 1944, his place in history has become so secure after leaving the presidency that critical comments concerning his political connections to individuals like Pendergast have little significance.

Hannegan and Kelly were instrumental in gaining the vice-presidential nomination for Truman, and Hannegan achieved what he wished history would remember him for—preventing Wallace from becoming the president of the United States. But he accomplished something far more important: he made it possible for Truman to become the thirty-third president of the United States.

The full impact of Franklin Delano Roosevelt's health on world history can only be hypothesized. However, the Lahey Memorandum is direct evidence that in 1944 FDR and McIntire fully understood the consequence of the party's choice of a vice-presidential candidate. In 1982, I believed, as did historians, doctors, librarians, Roosevelt family members, and others, that the Lahey Memorandum belonged in the Roosevelt archive. Attempts to acquire the memorandum for that purpose, however, provoked an unexpected and vituperative resistance. An excessive effort was made by a team of notable Boston lawyers not only to withhold the historically significant document from Mrs. Strand, but also to destroy it upon her death. It was incomprehensible.

When I contacted Edward Hanify by telephone in 1982 to request his assistance in Mrs. Strand's efforts to recover her document from her former law firm, I believed he would have some recall of the case he had tried in court some twenty years earlier and would agree to help. He immediately became quite agitated and told me I had no right to get involved in this case and that I should "let sleeping dogs lie."

Hanify's initial belligerence continued as he fought in the Massachusetts lower courts to keep the document from Mrs. Strand. His vigorous argument against the return of the Lahey Memorandum to Mrs. Strand was built almost solely upon the Hanify-Willcox letter, which Mrs. Strand maintained she had never seen. As Dr. Lahey's former business manager, she alone was solely responsible for the handling of the Lahey Memorandum, and she surely would not have signed off on the Hannify-Willcox letter had she seen it. When the Hanify-Willcox letter was introduced in court, neither her signature nor her initials were present on it. Furthermore, the stipulations in the submitted letter were contrary to her written instructions that surfaced, *only after Mrs. Strand's trial was concluded in 1985;* these instructions contained arrangements as to how the Lahey Memorandum was to be preserved if it were not published prior to Mrs. Strand's death. The document was *not* to be destroyed.

Mr. Hanify was unquestionably an excellent lawyer and formidable opponent, and without doubt his prominent public role and connections contributed to his considerable prestige. His longtime close association with President Kennedy, and his positions of trustee, secretary, and director of the John F. Kennedy Library Foundation in Boston, added to his authority. I respected his service and achievements but cannot help but question his motivation for attempting to conceal Dr. Lahey's memorandum.

Mr. Hanify died on December 31, 2000. I find it difficult to raise unfavorable comments concerning a highly respected individual who, because of his death, cannot respond to unpleasant suppositions, but it becomes necessary to do this in order to explain my theory regarding Hanify's attempt to suppress the Lahey Memorandum.

In 1944, Hanify was a junior naval officer and lawyer in Washington representing Admiral Husband E. Kimmel during his court martial for dereliction of duty at Pearl Harbor. It was a momentous case and well publicized. Hanify may have become acquainted with Admiral Ross McIntire, FDR's personal physician, while attending the numerous naval functions in Washington during that period. Hanify surely would have been aware of McIntire's continued public assertions of the president's good health, both before and after the president's death.

Mrs. Strand's lawsuit against the Lahey Clinic began in 1958, and Hanify was the attorney for the clinic. Settlement, which was reached in 1962, required identification and transference of a mass of documents concerning Mrs. Strand and the clinic, and Hanify would have learned of the existence of the Lahey Memorandum when it was classified as Mrs. Strand's personal property. Mrs.

Strand was represented by Harold Willcox, to whom she had entrusted the memorandum and a few other personal papers.

Admiral McIntire had continuously lied about the president's health, even after his death, and it is logical to believe that McIntire was responsible for the disappearance of FDR's medical records. However, Dr. Lahey, who had examined the president in 1944 at Admiral McIntire's request and had advised the admiral of FDR's deteriorating health, later wrote an account of the examination and discussion for his own records. By whatever means, McIntire probably heard of the Lahey Memorandum's existence through rumor or a well-meaning colleague. He would have found it extremely unnerving that an impartial report of the president's imperiled health, written by an internationally acclaimed doctor, was lying in a safe in a Boston law firm. Public disclosure of the document would prove disastrous to McIntire's reputation and had the potential to affect President Roosevelt's stature as well, if the public learned that the president had withheld information regarding his failing health when he went to Yalta.

If McIntire contacted Hanify and convinced him that the Lahey Memorandum had to be suppressed in the national interest, it would have fallen to Hanify to gain the complete cooperation of Willcox, whose firm held Mrs. Strand's papers. In 1962, Mrs. Strand gave Willcox written instructions as to how she wanted the Lahey Memorandum handled after her death. The Hanify-Willcox letter was a complete fabrication, with the authors being Hanify and Willcox.

When Hanify, after a year and a half of assiduously fighting in the courts to prevent the Lahey Memorandum's return to Mrs. Strand, suggested before the Massachusetts Supreme Court that there might not be a Lahey Memorandum, we all were stunned. Perhaps he was laying preliminary groundwork to explain the memorandum's non-existence if the court were to rule in favor of Mrs. Strand. When Herrick Smith was ordered to return Mrs. Strand's papers to her, her first comment on viewing the Lahey Memorandum was, "What's this? This isn't the original." If Willcox did remove the original Lahey Memorandum, which he might have done against his better judgment, or with the best of intentions, one can only speculate how such an act might subsequently have affected him.

Willcox left the law firm of Herrick and Smith sometime after the Lahey-Strand case and in 1974 started his own law firm in Boston. During the following year he was committed, on April 21, 1975, to the Georgia Regional Mental Institution in Savannah, where tragically, four days after admission, he committed suicide by cutting a major artery in one of his ankles, leading to massive hemorrhage and death within minutes.

FDR dealt with certain important issues in a questionable manner, decisions which future historians may view with increasing criticism. The probability of this is sad for those who still retain a feeling of personal closeness to President Roosevelt. Most Americans loved FDR during his lifetime. He conveyed to the people that his main goal was to help the ordinary citizen. Everyone was aware of FDR's pedigree of wealth and position, but he always had a way of creating a personal intimacy—a feeling that he and you were on the same level, that you were friends. This personal relationship carried over to the war effort. Americans were confident that, with FDR as our commander in chief, America could not fail to be victorious in World War II. Both in peace and in war, FDR was a magnificent leader, and America will always be grateful for his leadership.

This story began in 1963 after my hearing Dr. Pack lecture on "The Impact of Illness on World History." The journey of discovery regarding Franklin Delano Roosevelt's health revealed how great an impact an American president's medical condition can have on the well-being of the country and the world, and how powerful politicians can step into a void created by an ailing world leader in order to chart their own favorable political goals. Since history has a way of repeating itself, it is important that we remember these concerns.

BIBLIOGRAPHY

Allen, Robert S., and William V. Shannon. *The Truman Merry-Go-Round*. New York: Vanguard, 1950.

Asbell, Bernard. *When FDR Died*. New York: Holt, Rinehart &Winston, 1961.

———. *The FDR Memoirs*. New York: Doubleday, 1973.

Bishop, Jim. *FDR's Last Year: April 1944–April 1945*. New York: William Morrow, 1974.

Brownell, Will, and Richard N. Billings. *So Close to Greatness: A Biography of William C. Bullitt*. New York: Macmillan, 1988.

Bruenn, H. J. . "Clinical Notes on the Illness and Death of President Franklin D. Roosevelt." *Annals of Internal Medicine* 72 (1970): 579–591.

Burns, James MacGregor. *Roosevelt: The Soldier of Freedom*. New York: Harcourt Brace Jovanovich, 1970.

Byrnes, James. *Speaking Frankly*. New York: Harper, 1947.

———. *All in One Lifetime*. New York: Harper, 1958.

Catledge, Turner. *My Life and Times*. New York: Harper and Row, 1971.

Collier, P., and D. Horowitz. *The Roosevelts: An American Saga*. New York: Simon and Schuster, 1994.

Cook, Blanch Wiesen. *Eleanor Roosevelt*, vol. 2, *1884–1933*. New York: Penguin, 1992.

Damore, Leo. *Senatorial Privilege: The Chappaquiddick Cover-Up*. Washington, D.C.: Regnery Gateway, 1988.

Daniels, Jonathon. *The Man of Independence*. New York: Lippincott, 1950.

———. *The End of Innocence*. Philadelphia: Lippincott, 1954.

———. *White House Witness: 1942–1945*. New York: Doubleday, 1975.

Dallek, Robert. *Franklin D. Roosevelt and American Foreign Policy 1932–1945*. Oxford: Oxford University Press, 1981.

Divine, Robert A. *Foreign Policy and Presidential Election: 1940–1948*. New York: New Viewpoints, 1974.

Dorsett, Lyle W. *The Pendergast Machine*. New York: Oxford University Press, 1968.

Dunbar, Andrew. *The Truman Scandals: The Politics of Morality*. Columbia: University of Missouri, 1984.

Farley, James A. *Behind the Ballots: The Personal History of a Politician*. New York: Harcourt Brace, 1938.

————. *Jim Farley Story: The Roosevelt Years*. New York: McGraw-Hill, 1948.

Ferrell, R. H. *The Autobiography of Harry S. Truman*. Boulder: Colorado Associated University Press, 1980.

————. *Dear Bess: The Letters of Harry to Bess Truman 1910–1959*. New York: W. W. Norton, 1983.

————. *FDR's Quiet Confidant: The Autobiography of Frank C. Walker*. Niwot, Colo.: University of Colorado, 1997.

————. *The Dying President: Franklin D. Roosevelt 1944–1945*. Columbia: University of Missouri Press, 1998.

Flynn, John T. *The Roosevelt Myth*. New York: Devine-Adair Company, 1961.

————. *You're the Boss*. New York: Viking, 1947.

Freidel, Frank. *Franklin D. Roosevelt: A Rendezvous with Destiny*. Boston: Little, Brown, 1990.

Gallagher, Hugh G. *FDR's Splendid Deception*. Arlington, Va.: Vandamere Press, 1994.

Geddes, D. P. *Franklin Delano Roosevelt: A Memorial*. New York: Pitman Publishing, 1945.

Gies, J. *Franklin D. Roosevelt: A Portrait of a President*. New York: Doubleday, 1971.

Goldberg, Richard T. *The Making of Franklin D. Roosevelt*. Cambridge, Mass.: ABT Books, 1981.

Goldsmith, H. S. "Unanswered Mysteries in the Death of Franklin D. Roosevelt." *Surgery, Gynecology and Obstetrics* 149 (1979): 899–908.

Goodman, Doris Kearns. *No Ordinary Time*. New York: Simon & Schuster, 1994.

Graham, Otis L., Jr., and Meghan R. Wander. *Franklin D. Roosevelt: His Life and Times*. New York: DaCapo Press, 1985.

Gunther, John. *Roosevelt in Retrospects: A Profile in History*. New York: Harper, 1950.

Hassett, William D. *Off the Record with FDR 1942–1945.* New Brunswick, N.J.: Rutgers University Press, 1958.

Jenkins, Roy. *Truman.* New York: Harper & Row, 1986.

Lash, Joseph P. *Eleanor and Franklin.* New York: W. W. Norton, 1971.

———. *Eleanor and Franklin: The Story of Their Relationship.* New York: W. W. Norton, 1971.

———. *Eleanor: The Years Alone.* New York: W. W. Norton, 1972.

Levy, William T., and Cynthia E. Russett. *The Extraordinary Mrs. Roosevelt.* New York: John Wiley & Sons, 1999.

Looker, E. *Liberty Magazine.* July 25, 1931.

Lovell, Stanley P. *Of Spies and Strategems.* Englewood Cliffs, N.J.: Prentice Hall, 1963.

MacMahon, Edward B., and Leonard Curry. *Medical Cover-Ups in the White House.* Washington, D.C.: Farragut Publishing, 1987.

McCullogh, David. *Truman.* New York: Simon & Schuster, 1992.

McIntire, Ross T. *White House Physician.* New York: Putnam, 1946.

Miller, Merle. *Plain Speaking: An Oral Biography of Harry S. Truman.* New York: Putnam, 1974.

Moran, Lord. *Churchill: Taken from the Diaries of Lord Moran: The Struggle for Survival 1940–1965: Taken from the Diaries of Lord Moran.* Boston: Houghton Mifflin, 1966.

Morgan, Ted. *FDR: A Biography.* New York: Simon and Schuster, 1985.

Miller, Nathan. *FDR: An Intimate Portrait.* New York: Doubleday, 1983.

Murphy, Robert. *Diplomat Among Warriors.* New York: Doubleday, 1964.

Parks, Lillian R., and Francis S. Leighton. *The Roosevelts: A Family in Turmoil.* Englewood Cliffs, N.J.: Prentice Hall, 1981.

Perkins, Francis. *The Roosevelt I Knew.* New York: The Viking Press, 1946.

Phillips, Cabell. *The 1940s: Decade of Triumph and Trouble.* New York: Macmillan, 1975.

———. *The Truman Presidency.* New York: Macmillan, 1966.

Reilly, Michael F. *Reilly of the White House.* New York: Simon and Schuster, 1947.

Rigdon, William M. *White House Sailor.* New York: Doubleday, 1962.

Roosevelt, Elliott. *As I Saw It.* New York: Duell, Sloan & Pierce, 1946.

Robinson, Edgar Eugene. *The Roosevelt Leadership 1937–1945.* Philadelphia: Lippincott, 1955.

Roosevelt, Eleanor. *The Autobiography of Eleanor Roosevelt.* New York: DaCapo Press, 1992.

Roosevelt, James, and Sidney Shalett. *Affectionately, FDR.* New York: Harcourt Brace, 1959.

Roosevelt, James, and Bill Libby. *My Parents: A Differing View.* Chicago: Playboy, 1976.

Rosenman, Samuel I. *Working with Roosevelt.* New York: Harper, 1972.

Schapsmeier, E. L., and F. H. Schapsmeier. *Prophet in Politics: Henry A. Wallace and the War Years, 1940–1945.* Ames: Iowa State University Press, 1950.

Sherwood, Robert E. *Roosevelt and Hopkins: An Intimate History.* New York: Harper & Brothers, 1948.

Schmidt, K. M. *Henry A. Wallace: Quixotic Crusade, 1948.* Syracuse, N.Y.: Syracuse University Press, 1960.

Smith, A. M. *Thank You, Mr. President: A White House Notebook.* New York: Harper, 1946.

Steinberg, Alfred. *Mrs. Roosevelt: The Life of Eleanor Roosevelt.* New York: Putnam, 1958.

———. *The Man From Missouri.* New York: Putnam, 1962.

Stone, I. E. *The War Years 1939–1945: A Nonconformist History of Our Times.* Boston: Little, Brown, 1988.

Toland, J. *Infamy.* New York: Doubleday, 1982.

Truman, Harry S. *Memoirs by Harry S. Truman: Year of Decisions.* New York: Doubleday, 1955.

———. *Memoirs by Harry S. Truman: Years of Trial and Hope.* New York: Doubleday, 1956.

Truman, Margaret. *Harry S. Truman.* New York: William Morrow, 1973.

Tully, G. *Franklin Delano Roosevelt, My Boss.* Chicago: People's Book Club, 1949.

Underhill, Robert. *The Truman Persuasions.* Ames: Iowa State University Press, 1981.

Veronica, L., and D. Bain. *Veronica.* London: W. H. Allen, 1969.

Walton, Richard J. *Henry Wallace, Harry Truman and Cold War.* New York: Viking Press, 1976.

Ward, Geoffrey C. *Before the Triumph: Young Franklin Roosevelt.* New York: Harper & Row, 1985.

————. *Closest Companion: The Unknown Story of the Intimate Friendship between Franklin Roosevelt and Margaret Suckley.* Boston: Houghton Mifflin, 1995.

White, G., and X. Maze. *Henry A. Wallace: His Search for a New World Order.* Chapel Hill: University of North Carolina Press, 1995.

LIST OF SOURCES

1. George T. Pack, M.D., chief, Gastric and Mixed Tumor Services, Memorial Sloan-Kettering Cancer Center, New York, N.Y.
2. Mrs. George T. Pack
3. Arthur M. Tiernan, assistant district attorney, Suffolk County, Massachusetts
4. Irving M. Ariel, M.D., attending surgeon, Memorial Sloan-Kettering Cancer Center, New York, N.Y.
5. Andrew A. Kiely, M.D., attending surgeon, Long Beach Hospital, Long Beach, California
6. Joseph T. Horgan, rear admiral, USN, chief, Bethesda Naval Medical Center, Bethesda, Maryland
7. William Emerson, director emeritus, Franklin D. Roosevelt Library, Hyde Park, N.Y.
8. Vernon Newton, director, Franklin D. Roosevelt Library, Hyde Park, N.Y.
9. Howard G. Bruenn, M.D., emeritus clinical professor of medicine, Columbia Medical School, New York, N.Y.
10. Chester Dalrymple, vice president, First National Bank of Boston
11. Linda M. Strand, business manager, Lahey Clinic, Boston, Massachusetts
12. Blanche Wallace, private operating nurse for Dr. Lahey, Lahey Clinic
13. Louise Poe, private secretary to Frank H. Lahey, Lahey Clinic
14. James Roosevelt, Jr., son of FDR, California businessman
15. James Roosevelt III, grandson of FDR, Boston lawyer (Herrick, Smith)
16. James Farley, Jr., New York, N.Y.
17. Thomas Throckmorton, M.D., Mayo Clinic, Rochester, Minnesota
18. George B. Webster, M.D., chief, Plastic Surgery, Bethesda Naval Medical Center, Bethesda, Maryland
19. Kenneth Warren, M.D., chief of Surgery, Lahey Clinic
20. Les Whitten, Washington journalist
21. Madeline Wilkinson, informant

22. Loyal Davis, M.D., editor, *Surgery, Gynecology & Obstetrics*, professor of neurosurgery, Northwestern University

23. Herbert Brownell, attorney general of the U.S., Dewey campaign manager

24. Edward Martin, brother of Representative Joseph Martin of Massachusetts

25. Jan Gilbert, informant

26. John Fine, night agent, Pullman Company, South Street Station, Boston

27. Mark Gorham, baggage handler, South Street Station, Boston

28. George Slattery, station master, South Street Station, Boston

29. William W. Jeckell, informant

30. William V. McDermott, M.D., professor of surgery, Harvard Medical School, chief of Surgery, Deaconess Hospital, Boston

31. John Brooks, city editor, *Boston Record-American*

32. Theresa McGovern, M.D., informant

33. Hugh L'Etang, M.D., medical historian and author

34. David Boyd, M.D., chief, Thoracic and Cardiovascular Surgery, Lahey Clinic

35. Mrs. Thomas Alm, informant

36. Edward C. Holland, editor, *Boston Record-American*

37. William Remine, M.D., attending surgeon, Mayo Clinic, Rochester, Minnesota

38. George McClure, M.D., surgical resident, Lahey Clinic

39. Rutledge Howard, M.D., surgical resident, Peter Bent Brigham Hospital, Boston

40. Harry Ungerleider, M.D., insurance company physician

41. Samuel Day, M.D., Florida surgeon

42. William V. Roth, U.S. senator, Delaware

43. Jane Roth, U.S. district judge

44. Jan Stearns, informant

45. William Webster, director, FBI

45. David C. Flanders, chief, Freedom of Information Section, FBI

46. Dorothy Jacobson, archivist, U.S. Secret Service

47. Jack French, special agent, FBI

48. W. Scott Cameron, informant

49. Robert Snow, assistant director, U.S. Secret Service

50. James Halsted, M.D, medical historian, FDR's son-in-law

51. Robert T. Wilsons, chief, U.S. Record Center, Maitland, Maryland

52. Robert Goldwyn, M.D., professor of surgery, Harvard Medical School, and chief of Plastic Surgery, Beth Israel Hospital, Boston

53. E. Killman Sterling, attorney, Washington, D.C. (son of William C. Sterling, M.D.)
54. Madame Elizabeth Shoumatoff, artist
55. Peter Desmeules, attorney, Hanover, New Hampshire
56. Gerald Bricker, D.O., informant
57. John W. Norcross, M.D., Lahey Clinic
58. Marguerita Allerdice, Grosse Pointe, Michigan (daughter of William C. Sterling, M.D.)
59. Robert W. Pritchard, M.D., informant
60. W. Scott McDougal, M.D., professor of urology, Harvard Medical School, and chief of Urology, Massachusetts General Hospital, Boston
61. Dwight J. Dalbey, special agent, FBI
62. Andrew M. Dinsmore, special agent, FBI
63. Richard B. Gipson, M.D., informant
64. Dabney Jarman, M.D., urologist, Washington, D.C.
65. W. Bradford Patterson, M.D., professor of surgery, Harvard Medical School
66. Robert Tedrick, M.D., Ohio surgeon
67. Branon Lesesne, Georgia mortician (FDR embalmer)
68. William Duff, special agent, FBI
69. Michael Austin, attorney, Herrick, Smith, Boston
70. Samuel Binkley, M.D., informant
71. Mildred Miller, *Cincinnati Enquirer*
72. Lawrence Altman, M.D., medical writer, *New York Times*
73. Joseph Reber, informant
74. Robert H. Ferrell, medical historian, author
75. Alger Hiss, attorney, New York, N.Y., informant
76. Robert E. Ferrand, M.D., informant
77. Pamela Harriman, wife of W. Averell Harriman
78. Herbert D. Adams, chief of Surgery, Lahey Clinic
79. Robert Shapiro, M.D., Chicago surgeon
80. Caroline Cox, informant
81. George Marshman, Georgia mortician
82. Yorke Jacobson, M.D., informant
83. Nicholas Shoumatoff, nephew of the artist

84. Fred Stewart, M.D., chief of Pathology, Memorial Sloan-Kettering Cancer Center, New York, N.Y.
85. Richard P. Melick, attorney, Melick & Porter, Boston
86. Robert Powers, attorney, Melick & Porter, Boston
87. Thomas Porter, attorney, Melick & Porter, Boston
88. George E. Wakeman, Jr., attorney, Melick & Porter, Boston
89. Margaret Sullivan, informant
90. Edward B. Hanify, attorney, Ropes & Gray, Boston
91. Roscoe Trimmier, attorney, Ropes & Gray, Boston
92. Judge J. J. Lynch, equity court, Boston
93. Theodore S. Bober, informant
94. Joseph Leib, journalist
95. George Stubbs, M.D., informant
96. Richard K. Willard, assistant attorney general
97. Joseph Pratt, M.D., informant
98. Robert E. Hannegan, son of Democratic Party chairman in 1944
99. C. J. Hennessey, chief justice, Massachusetts Supreme Court
100. E. Harris Pierce, M.D., informant
101. Richard M. Gelb, attorney, Gelb & Heidlage
102. Guy Robbins, M.D., surgeon, Memorial Sloan-Kettering Cancer Center
103. Richard Garten, headmaster, Gulfstream School, Florida
104. Jane Nettleton, informant
105. J. Bryant Fritz, court stenographer
106. Jeremiah J. Sullivan, Massachusetts Superior Court judge
107. John E. Powers, clerk, Massachusetts Court of Appeals
108. Richard Gibson, informant
109. William F. Weld, U.S. attorney, governor of Massachusetts
110. Mark Johnston, attorney, Civil Division, Department of Justice
111. Charles C. Cabot, Jr., attorney, Herrick, Smith
112. Leonard Schaitman, appellate staff, Department of Justice
113. Andrew R. Linscott, Massachusetts Superior Court judge (Strand versus Lahey Clinic)
114. Robert Hopkins, Informant
115. Arthur M. Schlesinger Jr., Historian

Index

Tehran conference, 193
Thompson, J., 182, 183
Throckmorton, T., 49–50
Tiernan, A., 20, 134
Tillman, E. S., 99
Tolland, J., 136
Treaty of Versailles, 17
trial
    appealing the decision, 155. *See also* appeal
    closed session, 149
    closing arguments, 149–152
    fees, 156
    opening statements, 146–147
    ruling, 152
    Willcox-Hanify letter, 146–147
    witnesses, 147–149
Trimmier, R., Jr., 136, 139, 146, 153
Truman, H., 190
    attacks on, 252–253
    beliefs of, 252
    and Byrnes, 212
    characteristics of, 199–200
    confirming FDR's support, 254–257
    decision to run, 241–242
    and the Democratic National Convention,
        240–241. *See also* Democratic National
        Convention (1944)
    and Hannegan, 193–194, 252
    inauguration of, 249
    and Leib, 185–186
    loyalty of, 250
    and Pendergast, 250, 252–253
    as president, 250, 253–254
    reputation of, 193
    support for, 202
    as a U.S. senator, 193
    and the vice presidency, 173, 194,
        212–213, 226–230
Truman, M., 237–238, 243
Truman Committee, 185–186, 193
Tully, G., 33–34, 195, 203–204, 218

tumors, 61
    feature of, 41
    possibility of, 88
    references to, 172
    speculation about, 172

Ungerleider, H., 70–71
United Nations, 43
United States Supreme Court, 180

Van Devanter, W., 180
Veidenheimer, M. C., 24
vice presidency
    candidates for, 194, 200–206, 207–213,
        226–233, 257
    Democratic National Convention. *See*
        Democratic National Convention (1944)
    Gallup poll, 199
    Garner, 178
    importance of, 172–173
    nominations for, 214
    Truman, 173, 185–186, 194
    votes for, 243–248
    Wallace, 199

Wakeman, G. E., Jr., 146
Walker, F., 193, 203, 205
Wallace, B., 24–25
Wallace, H., 199
    characteristics of, 192
    choice of, 193, 194
    re-nomination of, 192
    speech of, 236
    and the vice presidential candidate, 200,
        207, 230–233
Ward, G. C., 54
Warm Springs Hotel, 101–102
Warren, K., 73–74
Webster, G., 50–53
Webster, W., 75
weight, 39

978-0-595-39942-0
0-595-39942-8